Dr. Carolyn Dean's

Natural Prescriptions
for Common Ailments

Carolyn Dean, M.D., N.D.

KEATS PUBLISHING

The purpose of this book is to educate. It is sold with the understanding that the publisher and author shall have neither liability nor responsibility for any injury caused or alleged to be caused directly or indirectly by the information contained in this book. While every effort has been made to ensure its accuracy, the book's contents should not be construed as medical advice. Each person's health needs are unique. To obtain recommendations appropriate to your particular situation, please consult a qualified health care provider.

Library of Congress Cataloging-in-Publication Data

Dean, Carolyn.
    [Natural prescription for common ailments]
    Dr. Carolyn Dean's natural prescription for common ailments / Carolyn Dean.
      p. cm.
    Includes bibliographical references and index.
    ISBN 0-658-01216-9
    1. Naturopathy. 2. Dietary supplements. I. Title: Doctor Carolyn Dean's natural prescription for common ailments. II. Title: Natural prescription for common ailments. III. Title.

RZ440 .D433 2001
615.5'35—dc21

00-054457

Published by Keats Publishing
4255 West Touhy Avenue, Lincolnwood, Illinois 60712, U.S.A.

Design by Mary Ballachino/Merrimac Design

Printed in the United States of America
International Standard Book Number: 0-658-01216-9
00 01 02 03 04 DOH 18 17 16 15 14 13 12 11 10 9 8 7 6 5 4 3 2 1

TO BOB

With whom all things are possible

Contents

Introduction
------- ✎✐✎ -------
When You Can't Reach the Doctor

atural Prescriptions for Common Ailments offers commonsense health information that I have compiled and utilized over the past twenty years in my practice and research; guidelines on taking responsibility for your body; and nontoxic, noninvasive options and choices. This book and its treatment protocols may be used until you need drugs or surgery or while you are awaiting the results of diagnostic tests. In the interim, between discovering symptoms and clarifying a specific diagnosis, definitive medical treatment is usually withheld. This period of time can be utilized by investigating and incorporating natural remedies suited to your symptoms. Most diseases have multiple causes and are treatable only by combining various modalities, as you will learn in this book. We are living in a world of options and choices in all levels of society, including medicine. We no longer have to ascribe to the allopathic notion that one symptom evokes one diagnosis for which there is one drug.

Remember, conventional medicine and natural medicine are not mutually exclusive. It is no longer either/or; it is both/and. Yes, you can have your cake and eat it too. Taking advantage of all the benefits of highly sophisticated medical technology to diagnose disease and then using natural medicine until you need surgery or stronger medication gives you the best of both worlds. Sometimes natural remedies solve the problem entirely. Sometimes they can speed healing and alleviate the side effects of more conventional and invasive therapies.

A wide variety of conditions are discussed with treatment suggestions; at the end of the book a list of homeopathic and herbal remedies are described. Many remedies described in part 1 are also discussed in part 4 with additional information to aid in prescribing. If you study the remedies, you will know which one is suitable to use for treatment when a condition arises.

This manual is not meant to take the place of good, sound medical advice and necessary treatment. If you have any questions at all, be sure to consult with your medical doctor before employing any of its suggestions. In short, use your common sense and do not take any chances with your health.

The Supplement Controversy

In the first edition of this book, I recommended average dosages for the various supplements mentioned. I'm not at all sure, however, what we get when we purchase a bottle of supplements anymore. We tend to look for bargains when we shop for supplements, and seem to think that the higher the dosage and the cheaper the price, the better the supplement. That just isn't so; organic, food-based supplements are available, and they are effective at much lower dosages than the synthetic variety.

The whole notion of supplementing the diet with vitamins and minerals has gone through various twists and turns. Decades ago, we became aware that farmlands were being stripped of nutrients. Fruits and vegetables lose even more nutrients because they are picked early and shipped long distances. Rachel Carson, who wrote *Silent Spring* almost forty years ago, made us aware of chemical poisoning in our environment by herbicides and pesticides used in farming. Nutrition-minded doctors recommended supplements to counteract the loss of nutrients and to detoxify the body. Only a few true activist groups demanded that farms focus more on organic practices than on factory-farming. Unfortunately, even more chemicals have been used on our foods in the last forty years. In fact, genetically engineered foods are being designed, not to provide more nutrients, but to withstand even more chemicals!

Thankfully, a courageous group of farmers have stuck with organic farming and its popularity is spreading. I personally belong to a rapidly growing community-supported agriculture (CSA) movement. In the area where I live, every spring a group of about 150 families buys a share in an organic farm. Every week for twenty-four weeks, fresh organic produce is delivered to a local church. It is a win-win situation for both the farmers and the members.

The supplement market itself has spun totally out of control. With the popularity of alternative medicine sweeping North America, more and more companies are manufacturing health products, and pharmaceutical companies have also gotten into the supplement industry in a big way. Because of fierce competition, the demand for cheaper and cheaper products is driving the industry; there is no longer a focus on the nutritional value of the supplements. This translates into almost *no* natural, organic supplements on the market. They are mostly synthetic derivatives made from coal tar. Technically, they might have a molecular structure that resembles the natural supplement, but they are, at best, only its mirror image. The body does not recognize mirror images; they are treated as foreign chemicals. When they try to jam their way into the body's receptors to act as cofactors in metabolic processes, they often destroy those receptors. This explains the baffling results from some recent vitamin research showing that vitamins are not effective against disease and, in fact, seem to be causing disease—synthetic derivatives of coal tar are toxic to the living body.

Let's look at calcium supplements. There are many products on the market, but calcium lactate is the most readily absorbed form of calcium. Other forms may require up to a dozen metabolic steps to make them recognizable to the body for absorption. Calcium lactate requires only one step. This means that supplements claiming to contain 500 or 1,000 milligrams, if only 10 to 30 percent absorbed, will only give you 50 to 150 milligrams or 100 to 300 milligrams of available calcium. This is yet another incredibly frustrating hurdle for the health product consumer.

What Supplements Are Safe to Use?

What companies are producing safe and effective natural supplements? What are the criteria for choosing supplements? It starts with the right supplement manufacturer. Here are the requirements: companies should own or have access to their own organic farmlands that maintain a nutrient-rich topsoil; should use minimal processing (no heat, no pressure, no chemicals) to extract supplements directly from organic plant and animal sources; should use ecologically sound, recyclable packaging; and should maintain moderate pricing.

It appears that Standard Process and a growing number of other ethically driven companies meet these requirements. Standard Process, founded by Dr. Royal Lee (a true genius) in 1929, sets the standard for natural supplementation. Standard Process allows only health practitioners to prescribe its products so that they are used optimally. (See the Resources section in the back of this book.)

At a certain point, I just gave up on nutritional supplements. Alternative practitioners were prescribing higher and higher doses of supplements. If patients weren't responding, they turned to intramuscular and intravenous injections of vitamins and minerals; it seemed like allopathic medicine all over again with supplements instead of drugs. I turned to homeopathy, along with an organic diet and a minimal supplementation protocol from natural sources, as a much less expensive way of treating disease.

In the original edition of this book, I mentioned specific dosages of vitamins and minerals for various conditions. Not only is every individual different, however, requiring differing amounts of nutrients, but the supplement's source is crucial. In this edition, I therefore remove the dosages, except for conditions requiring megadoses of supplements as medications. I advise you to obtain supplements from guaranteed natural sources produced by reputable companies. You have a right to know what you are ingesting. If you like a particular brand of supplements, call up the president and find out if the company's supplements meet the standards above. Remember, we as consumers can determine what we get by demanding what we want. If we settle for less, we get rock bottom.

Dosages of natural supplements are considerably lower than those from synthetic sources because the nutrients are extracted from the plant or animal source and made into a tablet or capsule. The benefits are much higher, though, because you are getting living nutrients and not synthetic, "virtual" substances.

As you read this new edition, especially the cancer section, you will realize that my focus on the use of natural products arises from a concern that we are living in a toxic chemical soup that we are forced to swim in and drink from every day of our lives. Part of the process of keeping your body healthy and pure may involve looking around at your micro (body) and macro (world) environment and limiting the use of chemicals in your body, your home, your community, your country, and your planet.

Supplement Warnings

Fat-soluble vitamins A and D can be toxic if taken in high doses for a long period of time. When taking cod liver oil, be sure and check the label. Don't take more than 10,000 International Units of A or 400 International Units of D per day. Excess vitamin A can cause headaches and skin irritation. Excess vitamin D can allow too much calcium absorption.

Vitamin C is best taken in the C-complex form to include bioflavonoids. Ascorbic acid is akin to orange juice and the bioflavonoids are the white rind and pulp; they work best together. For short-term therapy, ascorbic acid may be helpful, but avoid high doses over the long term.

The State of Herbal Medicine

I have been involved with herbal research for the past several years, working on formulas to treat various layers of infection in the body. When it came time to find a manufacturer for these products, I was stunned to learn that most herbs are purified by irradiating them, microwaving them, or gassing them with ethylene oxide. Companies that balk at the lethal effect of these methods do produce herbal tinctures. In alcohol tinctures, however, only the alcohol-soluble component is extracted, leaving out other components of the whole plant and concentrating the pesticides and chemicals used on nonorganic herbs.

The tincturing process fits into an attempt to reach a standardization of the most active ingredient of an herbal healing plant. Such standardization is really just allopathic-herbal medicine. When a plant contains hundreds and hundreds of active ingredients, how on earth do we know which is the most active one? Years are spent researching "the most active ingredient," only to find when more studies are done that it is not the correct one. I advise herb companies to use a whole-plant extract. If they must conform to the prevailing trend of standardization, they should assay the tincture up to the standardized level of the current "active ingredient." Using the whole plant balances any potentially negative side effects of using only one active ingredient.

In choosing herbs, look for organic sources and ask what type of cleaning process is used.

How to Use This Book

Natural Prescriptions for Common Ailments gives you accessible, commonsense alternatives to drugs that you can use for common health complaints. Part 1, Ailments and Remedies, gives herbal, homeopathic, nutritional, commonsense advice for 123 ailments listed alphabetically.

You can turn to the problem that is most important to you, but don't hesitate to read the entire book; then you will be prepared if you or someone in your family develops a particular problem. Please read the section on supplementation on page xiv first; I do recommend certain vitamins and minerals for particular conditions and I explain why I usually don't include dosages.

Part 2 is called Advice and Information on such topics as antibiotics, first aid, naturopathic medicine, pregnancy, surgery, and traveling advice. Part 3 covers Diet and Detoxification, but I also share some simple recipes for bean sprouts and beet kvaas as well as talk about soy, sugar and aspartame, and water purification. Part 4, Homeopathic and Herbal Remedies, consists of a valuable description of twenty-eight homeopathic and three herbal remedies that I find particularly useful in treating the ailments in this book. (Please note: The 12C potency that I recommend for most acute conditions can usually be interchanged with 6C or 30C potency.)

The appendix is a quick reference guide to remedies with a list of symptoms and matching homeopathic remedies. A helpful resource list, references, and index follow. Because I feel so strongly about the beneficial qualities of homeopathic remedies (inexpensive, effective, no side effects) I have asked Boiron, a leader in homeopathy, to make their homeopathic home remedies kit available to readers. Please see the description of this kit at the end of this book.

Note the address of my personal Web site www.drcdean.com, which will keep you informed about my activities to promote natural healing and taking responsibility for our personal health and the health of the planet.

PART ONE

Ailments and Remedies

Acne
(See **Skin Conditions,** page 143)

Acne Rosacea
(See **Skin Conditions,** page 143)

Addictions

The treatment of addictions encompasses diet, remedies, and behavioral and psychological counseling.

Alcohol

Alcohol addiction can be treated with homeopathic Sulphuric acid 12C 4 drops every few hours. This remedy is completely safe and has absolutely none of the properties of regular sulphuric acid in this extremely dilute form. It acts like Antabuse, a prescription drug that causes a feeling of nausea and illness when you drink while taking it.

A rare remedy called Quarkus alba can reduce the desire for alcohol. Nux vomica can curb desire as well as treat a hangover. The dosage is

12C 4 drops every hour for a hangover; use it three to four times a day to prevent alcohol cravings.

High doses of vitamin C will help metabolize alcohol as well as sugar; don't use this just so you can drink more, however. High doses means 2 to 8 grams throughout the day; cut back if you develop diarrhea.

Alcoholism is a psychological and physical addiction and must be treated in a holistic manner. An excellent diet of grains, vegetables, fish, chicken, and fruit, avoiding refined foods and sugar, coffee, and tea, can prevent alcohol cravings. Some people feel that low blood sugar can trigger addiction to sugar or alcohol. Investigate this condition by reading books on low blood sugar and the section in this book on hypoglycemia on page 102. Food allergies, according to nutritionists, can be synonymous with addiction. Read the section on allergies on page 6 for more information.

Allopathic vitamin therapy for alcoholism consists of the already mentioned high doses of vitamin C; high doses of niacinamide (B$_3$), 500 milligrams anywhere from two to eight times a day; B$_6$, 100 milligrams three times a day; and B complex, 50 milligrams two or three times a day. Zinc is also important; take 50 milligrams per day for a month and then reduce to 25 milligrams per day. In addition, take a multiple vitamin and mineral supplement from natural sources. (Schizophrenia is beyond the scope of this book. However, the above protocol is similar to one developed by Dr. Abram Hoffer for the treatment of schizophrenia. Read his book *Vitamin B-3 and Schizophrenia* for more information.)

Dr. K. Iwata in Japan was one of the first researchers to investigate *Candida* overgrowth. He diagnosed "drunk" disease in people who had not consumed any alcohol but appeared to be intoxicated. This is caused by excess *Candida albicans* (yeast) in the intestines, which creates a fermentation process and produces alcohol after sugar ingestion. Some people who consume even a small amount of alcohol can stimulate excessive yeast growth in the intestines with sugar and feel drunk.

When alcoholics get sober, they often use sugar as a crutch. Blood tests before and after a large amount of sugar can show a rise in blood-alcohol levels. By continuing your addiction to sugar, you are producing alcohol and still suffering its effects. Study candidiasis and treat it as well as the alcoholism. Read the sections on sugar addiction on page 4 and candidiasis on page 40.

There are alcohol and drug detox clinics that employ ear acupuncture, Chinese herbs, and intravenous vitamin and mineral therapy in their protocols. These modalities are extremely useful for balancing neurochemistry and treating deficiencies caused by alcohol.

Coffee

My first advice is to switch to black tea and take Chamomilla 12C, a homeopathic remedy for withdrawal symptoms of irritability, sensitivity, and headaches. The dosage is 4 drops orally three or four times a day; don't exceed six days in duration. Then stop black tea; Chamomilla can be continued another few days. Then switch to herbal teas or a grain coffee substitute, available in health food stores.

Smoking

The main point to be made about smoking is to avoid it. However, for this addiction, the remedies are:

Caladium, Nicotine, and Tabac, all homeopathics in the 12C potency, taken 4 drops three to six times a day.

The herbal tinctures lobelia or Avena sativa, 5 to 10 drops in 4 ounces of water three times a day.

A remedy called Calc. phos. can be used in the 12C potency for residual bronchitis that may remain after giving up cigarettes.

Fenugreek seed tea, 1 teaspoon per cup of boiling water steeped for seven minutes, can help loosen the mucus that accompanies cigarette withdrawal.

The first month or so after quitting is often a difficult time because the small hair cells that line the bronchial tracts begin to grow again after being paralyzed and start creating and clearing a lot of mucus. Although uncomfortable, this is a good sign.

Ear acupuncture can help curb the craving for nicotine. There are four points in the ear that can be used to balance the body by easing irritability and clearing the lungs of the buildup of waste material. These can be administered by a doctor trained in ear acupuncture.

Other basic advice is to maintain a good diet, avoiding red meat, sugar, coffee, and refined foods, and taking a good multiple vitamin and mineral as well as zinc. Zinc will help bring back your taste buds so that you can enjoy food more fully. Try to avoid substituting one addiction for another. Most people who give up smoking begin eating sweets and gaining weight. Try to get to the bottom of the reason for your addiction and avoid being dependent on any substance.

Sugar

Dr. Abram Hoffer, along with Linus Pauling, coined the term *orthomolecular medicine* over thirty years ago. For decades, Dr. Hoffer has successfully treated schizophrenia with diet, vitamins, and minerals. He has recently gone on record as saying, "Refined sugar and all refined foods such as polished rice, white flour, and the like are nothing less than legalized poisons," and that "sugar is an addiction far stronger than what we see with heroin. It is the basic addictive substance from which all other addictions flow."

This is why it's so hard to stop eating sugar. For long-term health, though, you must curb your sugar intake. Dr. Hoffer, along with many other notable doctors, says that it takes roughly fifteen to twenty years of steady consumption of refined sugar and junk food before an individual develops a chronic illness such as diabetes. As long as sugar consumption stays below 35 pounds per person annually and constitutes less than 20 percent of daily caloric intake, a population remains reasonably healthy. Once the average consumption of refined sugar rises to 70 pounds per person annually, chronic disease becomes a measurable problem for an entire population. It is estimated that in North America about 35 percent of our daily calories are derived from refined sugar, and our annual intake is a whopping 140 pounds per person!

When you eat too much sugar or carbohydrate, you put a lot of strain on your pancreas, which produces insulin. You may already know that insulin keeps your blood sugar levels under control. Insulin also works as a protective mechanism that allows our bodies to store food in times of starvation. A high-carbohydrate diet (sugar, fruit, bread, grains, beans, root vegetables) triggers the release of lots of insulin to deal with the high sugar levels. The body thinks this is a signal to store most of those calories as fat, to increase the production of cholesterol, and to conserve water for the famine that historically comes after the feast. This reaction is a basic survival mechanism and is etched in our genes.

The only way to keep insulin from surging and storing calories as fat is by eating a diet that *does not* trigger insulin release with every meal. It is not just excess fat in the diet that makes fat but any sugar, fruit, or carbohydrate. In fact, a high-protein, moderate-fat, low-carbohydrate diet keeps insulin levels low. As the baby boomers age, I see more strict vegetarians battling weight gain and having to add protein to their diets to lose weight and for various other health complaints. Read the section on sugar and aspartame on page 185 for more information.

A balanced diet should include protein, complex carbohydrates (beans, grains, nuts, and seeds), and fruits and vegetables, and should eliminate refined sugar and flour. Read the section on diets on page 181 to individualize your own diet. Also, read the section on allergies on page 6, because you can become allergic and addicted to things you eat all the time.

Agoraphobia

This condition produces anxiety on leaving the home, due to a morbid dread of open or public places. Symptoms can extend to many anxiety-provoking situations. A person in an extremely stressful situation who begins to panic may forever after link that type of stress with a feeling of dread. On a physical level, if blood sugar drops suddenly while you are under stress, the adrenal reaction produced to restore the blood sugar level can cause a fight-or-flight reaction, which feels like a panic attack. Thereafter, you will unknowingly link this hypoglycemic reaction with the stress and the panic attack, and it is likely to recur under similar stressful conditions.

Treating agoraphobia is multifaceted. For information on how to avoid low blood sugar, read the section on hypoglycemia on page 102. Avoid caffeine, sugar, and alcohol. Vitamin supplementation can help, especially the B vitamins. B_{12} injections from your doctor can be beneficial. A nonyeast B source is best to avoid possible yeast allergy or stimulating the growth of *Candida* in the body.

The best psychologic treatment is support and behavior modification. To modify your behavior:

1. Face the fear.
2. Hum or sing. This activates the right side of the brain and deactivates the left side of the brain, which is worrying and escalating the fear.
3. Celebrate each small victory against your fears. These small steps add up.

4. Try to move; don't lie down or give in to the fear.

5. Don't let fear of fear control your life.

The homeopathic remedies for agoraphobia are Aconite, Kali arsenicum, and Arsenicum. These can be taken in the 12C potency, 4 drops as needed.

Allergies

Allergies are a widespread problem. Conventional medicine considers inhaled allergens as the main form of allergic reaction. For example, there's hay fever, with its symptoms of itchy, runny eyes, runny nose, and cough in specific seasons, predominantly spring and fall. Spring allergies are usually to grasses and pollens. The best treatment is prevention. In the very early spring or late winter (February or March), begin taking homeopathic grasses and pollens. The dosage is 12C, 4 drops two or three times a day. If these remedies are taken one month before the onset of the season, usually symptoms will be diminished. Similarly, to avoid ragweed allergies that occur in mid-August, take homeopathic ragweed, also called Ambrosia 12C and Mold 12C, two or three times per day in late July. These remedies can be continued during the season if you are still experiencing some symptoms.

Vitamin supplementation should include vitamin C and bioflavonoids such as rutin and quercitin; these are natural antihistamines. Dessicated adrenal tablets help support the adrenal glands, which produce natural cortisones that fight allergy symptoms. Evening primrose oil supports the immune system; vitamin E and selenium are antioxidants; magnesium is a natural tranquilizer; and pancreatic enzymes and hydrochloric acid can be taken with each meal to prevent incomplete food digestion, which can potentiate food allergies.

Herbs useful for treating inhaled allergies from inhaled irritants include astringents (yarrow and myrrh), antimucus herbs (fenugreek, sage, and barberry in place of goldenseal, which is becoming extinct), and immune-boosting herbs (echinacea and astragalus root).

During allergy season, it is also helpful to cut back on mucus-producing foods such as sugar, dairy, and wheat. By doing so, you cut down the irritation in your mouth and nasal membranes and are therefore less susceptible to inhaled pollens and other irritants. Ridding the body of excess mucus and toxins will help to reduce your body's total burden.

You may find that you react to things in your environment all year round. First, investigate the household products and pesticide sprays used in and around your home and try to eliminate as many toxic chemicals as you can. There are many nontoxic products available; for example, borax is an all-purpose cleaner available in most grocery stores.

For indoor allergens such as dust, mites, and mold, you must keep the air dry and clean with air conditioners, air cleaners, and dehumidifiers. Make sure mold doesn't grow in these appliances; mold spores can cause considerable symptoms in susceptible people. Mold in bathrooms and basements can be cleaned away with bleach or trapped with zeolite/clay powder. Dust mites, nasty-looking, microscopic insects that feed off flakes of our shed skin, are the most common inhaled allergens. Prevent problems by vacuuming your mattress, covering it with plastic, washing your pillows and bedclothes frequently, and removing carpeting from your bedroom floor.

Sometimes after a bad cold with nasal congestion, you can develop hay fever or dust allergies because your mucous membranes become very sensitive. If this happens, have someone else clean your home thoroughly, or use a cotton mask, because cleaning and dusting itself can lead to a sneezing attack. Pets can also be a problem, with their hair, fur, dander, skin oils, and secretions. They should at the very least be isolated from your sleeping space.

Different substances in your work environment can produce "sick building syndrome." This is a real condition that began to manifest when we tried to make our office buildings airtight and heat controlled. The fumes from hundreds of chemicals, including paint, copy machine chemicals, formaldehyde, plastics, and pesticides, became too much for a segment of the population and produced a considerable amount of disability. The dramatic increase in children's asthma in recent years could be a result of chemical exposure in school. One of our greatest tasks in the twenty-first century is to demand safer, cleaner, and more efficient standards from both industry and government to clean up our environment.

Allergy shots have not, in my experience, been very helpful for most people. I commonly hear people say, "Well, I've been on allergy shots for several years now, and I think they're helping." If they don't help within a few months, they probably never will. My advice is to purify the body first before adding even more things to the mix.

The predominant food allergies recognized by allopathic allergists are to eggs, peanuts, nuts, fish, shellfish, and strawberries, which create an immediate IgE reaction of hives, asthma, or severe swelling of the throat and face because they trigger a release of histamine. These instant reactions are easy to spot, and most people identify these foods early in life. Also on this list are bisulphites, MSG, aspartame (NutraSweet), food colorings, and food additives, which number in the thousands.

MSG is used as a flavor enhancer, which means it can stimulate taste buds and trick the brain into thinking that a meal of sawdust is gourmet cuisine. Animal studies indicate that it causes brain damage, however; it also triggers headaches and asthma in susceptible people. Bisulphites keep salads looking green and fresh but also trigger asthma. Medical doctors have now declared aspartame to be more of a toxin or a direct poison than an allergen. It causes headaches, seizures, anxiety, depression, and fluid retention. Read the section on sugar and aspartame on page 185 to learn more about the ninety-two side effects of ingesting aspartame.

Other food allergies are being mediated by the IgG immunoglobulins and display delayed reactions in the form of antigen-antibody complexes that travel in the bloodstream and can settle anywhere in the body, producing a myriad of symptoms from headaches to diarrhea. The identification of these allergies is very difficult; however, there are blood tests available through various laboratories on referral by your naturopath or medical doctor.

If you don't have access to blood testing, you must create a detailed list of the foods in your diet. First eliminate all processed, dyed, and synthetic foods. Using a process of elimination and challenge, work through each food group. For example, avoid sugar for two weeks, then challenge your body with sugar several times in a forty-eight-hour period and observe your reactions. Do the same with all dairy, then all wheat products. This is time consuming but can provide very useful information.

Warning: Do not challenge foods to which you already know you have serious reactions.

If you constantly crave a particular food, it may mean you are addicted to it and allergic at the same time. In fact, you may unconsciously learn to eat it every day to prevent withdrawal symptoms. For example, if you are addicted/allergic to caffeine, you will probably experience headaches when you eliminate it. You may have been having vague head symptoms all along; you'll feel much better without coffee at all.

Allergies can cause many diverse reactions: fatigue, heart palpitations, racing heart, runny nose, headaches, sweats, abdominal pain, irritable bowel, bladder irritation, skin reactions, dizziness, memory impairment, and brain fog. You can even experience anxiety and depression purely as a result of the foods you ingest (or things you inhale).

One of the oldest ways to detect a food allergy is to use Dr. Coco's pulse test. Take your pulse before and after eating a meal of one particular food; if your pulse increases by more than ten beats, you may be allergic to that food.

The underlying cause of allergies may be a toxic body with an impaired immune system due to bad diet, stress, and chronic infections leading to candidiasis and allergies. Read the sections on candidiasis on page 40, detoxification on page 178, diets on page 181, stress on page 149, infections on page 107, and antibiotics on page 155 to learn how to deal with these conditions without resorting to antibiotics. A major requirement in treating the above conditions is a probiotic such as lactobacillus acidophilus to support the normal intestinal flora. A probiotic is obtained from biodynamic yogurt grown with live culture or live preparations of acidophilus available from the health store.

Alzheimer's Disease

Alzheimer's disease, a cause of senile dementia, is becoming epidemic in our aging population. The symptoms can mimic other conditions and include fatigue, depression, disorientation, memory impairment, paranoia, and aggressive behavior. Alzheimer's disease is often misdiagnosed. Half the people diagnosed with it may, in fact, not have this condition but suffer from a brain toxicity due to a lifelong accumulation of toxins, chemicals, poisons, and nutrient deficiency. While allopathic medicine tries to find the "one cause" for Alzheimer's and the "one drug" that will cure it, in alternative medicine we practice detoxification and supplementation to effectively treat this condition.

Other possible causes of Alzheimer-like symptoms include thyroid deficiency, vitamin B_{12} deficiency (pernicious anemia), ministrokes,

Parkinson's disease, allergies, candidiasis, polypharmacy, drug reactions, environmental allergies, and nutritional imbalances. Read the sections in this book covering these conditions.

Prevention takes into consideration the theory that aluminum might be one of the underlying causes. Avoid all aluminum pots and pans and aluminum foil, antiperspirants, and antacids. Prevention must go much further; avoid as many chemicals, toxins, and poisons as possible; avoid (and remove) mercury dental fillings; avoid gas heating and cooking; use water filters and air filters; eat organic foods; and protest the overuse of chemicals in our environment. Aspartame, found in over 9,000 diet products, is neurotoxic and causes headaches and seizures, among its ninety-two side effects. Organophosphate pesticides found in your own garage or shed are associated with Parkinson's disease and brain syndromes.

Vitamin and mineral deficiencies have been implicated in Alzheimer's. An organic diet and supplements are the best ways to ensure a balanced nutrient load. Many of the supplements on the market today are themselves synthesized from coal tar and inappropriate for an already toxic body.

An excellent herbal medicine that increases blood flow to the brain and improves memory is ginkgo biloba. Gotu kola is another important herb that improves cerebral function; it is used widely in Asia as an antiaging remedy.

Chelation therapy, oral or intravenous, is an expedient way of dealing with symptomatic Alzheimer's. Chelation therapy is most commonly used for atherosclerosis as an alternative to bypass surgery; it removes mercury, aluminum, and other heavy metals from the body and increases brain circulation. Check the Resources section for information on ACAM, an organization that trains doctors in chelation.

Chinese medicine provides a comprehensive treatment program for conditions such as Alzheimer's by combining herbal formulas that both detoxify and nutritionally support the body, along with acupuncture that treats energy blocks.

Amenorrhea

This is a delay or absence of the menstrual period. Primary amenorrhea is diagnosed when the period does not occur at the usual age in young women. If the period has not begun by age fifteen or sixteen, investigations are advised. If you are under 100 pounds or are an extremely active athlete, however, this may account for the lack of menstruation. Menarche begins at a weight and not an age. At around 100 pounds, there is usually enough fat in the body to be processed by the liver into the necessary hormones to create the menses. The age for menarche is getting earlier and earlier, and happens sooner in overweight girls.

If cycling has been established and the period stops for several months, this is called secondary amenorrhea. Some specialists don't regard it as a problem unless the period is absent for one year. It can be the result of severe stress, either emotional or physical (including another disease process), weight loss (going below 100 pounds), overwork, anemia, grief, or disappointment. Clinical investigation includes tests for pregnancy and anemia.

Natural treatment with homeopathic remedies includes:

Calc. Carb.	12C, 4 drops three times a day, for overwork and exhaustion.
Ferrum met.	12C, 4 drops three times a day, for anemia and resulting weakness. An oral iron supplement should also be taken.
Ignatia	12C, 4 drops three times a day, for grief, fear of failure, or disappointments causing the amenorrhea.
Rhus tox.	12C, 4 drops three times a day, for suppression of periods in an overactive athlete.
Sepia	12C, 4 drops three times a day, for amenorrhea due to the birth control pill, miscarriage, or abortion.

These remedies should be used for a maximum period of two to three months. For further prescriptions, consult a homeopathic physician.

Anemia

Low levels of hemoglobin have to be thoroughly investigated to determine blood loss, blood destruction, or lack of blood production. The nutritional causes of anemia can be low iron, low copper, or low B_{12} and folic acid. These can be determined by blood tests. The treatment for nutritional causes of anemia is supplementation. The best supplement is a synergistic combination of all the nutrients that are used in the production of hemoglobin, including B complex, folic acid, iron, copper, vitamin C, and additional B_6. As for diet, red meat, prune juice, legumes, collards, spinach, and blackstrap molasses are good sources of iron.

During pregnancy, the excess strain on a mother's blood supply lowers blood levels from the normal 12 to 16 grams of hemoglobin by 1 or 2 grams. The supplements most required during pregnancy for hemoglobin are iron and folic acid. The best source is a food-based iron, not the ferrous form of iron. The ferrous form is given in 300-milligram doses, but only 7 percent of it is absorbed; it often causes constipation and dark stools. Food-based iron is more readily absorbed, up to 100 percent; therefore, less is required and there is no constipation.

Folic acid must be taken during pregnancy for hemoglobin and to prevent birth defects. This is only available in adequate amounts by prescription; 5 milligrams one or two times a day is necessary throughout the pregnancy. Remember, the more natural the supplement, the better it is for the body. The body is not able to use synthetic forms of supplements. Herbs such as kelp, watercress, and nettles are very rich in blood-building nutrients. All dark green leafy vegetables are also excellent sources of iron. Homeopathic Ferrum phos. and Ferrum met., best in the cell salt 6X form, help the body's absorption and utilization of iron.

Angina Pectoris

This is a condition in which the blood vessels of the heart either go into spasm or are blocked, causing crushing chest pain on exertion. The pain can be directly over the heart and go down the left arm or up into the left jaw. Such symptoms should be thoroughly investigated by a medical doctor. Treatment includes a variety of medications to increase blood circulation in the heart muscle, increase the width of blood vessels, and decrease blood pressure, or bypass surgery, which replaces the arteries of the heart.

There is also an array of natural treatments that are being investigated and show promise in treating heart disease. Dr. Dean Ornish made medical history with his strict vegetarian diet, exercise, and stress reduction protocol, which was successful in reversing heart disease. This program seemed to confirm that high cholesterol is the culprit in heart disease. If you read the section on diets on page 181, however, you will learn that it may be the A blood types that do best on Ornish's diet, whereas O types can become very deficient in essential fatty acids. When it comes to diets for heart disease, one size *does not* fit all. Read more about the cholesterol controversy in the atherosclerosis section on page 19.

Following the right diet for your blood type will also help you lose weight. Excess weight puts a strain on the heart, because all the extra miles of capillaries that feed the extra fat tissue have to be pumped by an overworked heart.

Exercise also helps with weight loss and provides natural stress release. Walking is probably the best form of exercise. If an angina attack comes on while walking, just stop and rest. As endurance builds and circulation improves, health will return.

Smoking, of course, is out. It dramatically decreases oxygen levels throughout the body and the heart has to work furiously to try to keep the body oxygenated.

Supplementation focuses on supplying oxygen to the heart muscle. Coenzyme Q10 is the master nutrient in this regard. It is necessary for the production of adenosine triphosphate (ATP), which is the energy source in each cell of the body. Vitamin C and vitamin E are antioxidants; magnesium is the original calcium-channel blocker and treats heart spasms and palpitations; B complex calms the nervous system; and a natural multiple vitamin and mineral combination makes sure you have all the necessary trace minerals for body processes.

Hawthorne berry is an herbal tonic that is useful for supporting and strengthening the heart; take 5 to 10 drops in 4 ounces of water three times a day. Spigelia in herbal tincture form can be used for severe chest pain in an emergency but should not be used in place of prescribed medication. Check with your doctor to see whether you can use herbal tinctures as well as medication. Please don't take chances with a life-threatening condition by using only natural remedies in the beginning. As your health improves, you may be able to wean off medication with the help of your doctor. Avena sativa tincture can help treat palpitations. Take 5 to 10 drops three or four times a day. Remember, the most common cause of heart palpitations is drinking coffee—stop it.

Chelation therapy is being used with great success for angina and atherosclerosis. Apparently more than half a million patients have been treated over the past forty years by over a thousand doctors. It is an intravenous therapy using a chelating agent called EDTA that chelates or "claws" out heavy metals. In hardening of the arteries, EDTA presumably pulls out calcium from the plaque that is lining artery walls. Circulation is restored to normal with better memory and eyesight, elimination of chest pain and leg cramps, and improved oxygenation to the whole body. For some people, chelation therapy is nothing short of a miracle. Check the Resources section for the number of ACAM, the medical organization that rigorously trains and tests doctors in the practice of chelation therapy.

Anorexia

This condition is very complex and requires treatment on both the physical and psychological levels. One very important nutrient for anorexia is zinc; some people with zinc deficiency have poor wound healing, white spots on the nails, increased susceptibility to infections, and lack of sense of taste and smell. If you are anorexic, this could mean that food has no taste and begins to seem revolting or disgusting, and is therefore avoided. In bulimia, you may eat more and more food in order to get some sense of taste, eat stronger or sweeter food, or binge on foods just to be satisfied. The treatment can start with zinc (50 milligrams chelated, daily for at least a month). A good multiple vitamin and mineral with copper should be added so that the copper in the body will not be suppressed by the high zinc intake. There are several homeopathic remedies considered useful for anorexia; these should be administered by a qualified homeopathic physician. It is also important to do a thorough medical workup and make an appointment with an eating disorder clinic to investigate and treat all aspects of this condition.

Anxiety

Valium and Prozac are the top-selling drugs in America. What is causing this drug epidemic? One cause may be the amount of diet sodas and foods that we consume. Aspartame (NutraSweet) is a neurotoxin; the phenylalanine in aspartame lowers the brain's seizure threshold and depletes serotonin. Low levels of serotonin trigger panic attacks, anxiety, and mood changes. If you have anxieties, eliminate aspartame from your diet for at least sixty days. Read the section on sugar and aspartame on page 185 for more information.

Emotional freedom technique (EFT) is a recent development in personal psychotherapeutics. I've checked this out and it seems to really work. It is based on tapping thirteen Chinese acupuncture points. The founder, Gary Craig, claims that it is over 80 percent clinically effective for trauma, abuse, stress, anxiety, fears, phobias, depression, grief, addictive cravings, children's issues, and hundreds of physical symptoms including headaches, body pains, and breathing difficulties. Craig says, "EFT often works where nothing else will. It is usually rapid, long lasting, and gentle. It involves no drugs or equipment. And it is easily learned by anyone and can be self-applied." The EFT Web site is www.emofree.com.

Other recommendations for anxiety are found in the agoraphobia section on page 5. One aspect of anxiety that is becoming more recognized is the effect of electricity on our nervous systems. It is said that electricity extends our nervous systems onto our skin, which may make sensitive people more aware or susceptible to the stresses of our society. For more on this, study the works of Marshall McLuhan.

Arthritis

This is a very complex and multifaceted disease. Arthritis means inflammation of the joints. A diagnosis of arthritis is made by x-rays, blood tests, and clinical examinations. If the x-rays and blood tests are essentially normal but you continue to experience joint swelling, stiffness, and pain, other causes must be investigated. Some people have joint symptoms due to food allergies, candidiasis, or postviral infections such as Epstein-Barr or chronic mononucleosis. The arthritic symptoms are caused by antigens from foods and antibodies that join together in the blood and create antigen-antibody complexes that can then deposit in any area of the body, frequently the joints, which may then appear to be arthritic.

First, you should avoid artificial sweeteners. Next, try eliminating the most allergenic foods such as wheat, dairy, corn, and sugar and determine if there is an improvement. Then eliminate yeast-growing foods such as sugar, yeast, breads, moldy foods, cheeses, and excess fruits and see if this improves the joints. A common cause of small-joint arthritis is allergy to the deadly nightshade family of potato, tomato, green pepper, tobacco, eggplant, and paprika. These should be avoided for at least two months to determine possible allergy.

Reaching optimum weight is also very important, because any excess weight on an inflamed joint creates more pain.

Menopausal women often have arthritic symptoms. I wonder if the absence of the monthly period, which serves to rid the body of toxins, means that instead the toxins are building up in the joints. If you are going through menopause, go on a detoxification program. (Read the section on detoxification on page 178 for more information.) Treatment for arthritis includes a good healthy diet, including whole grains, vegetables, nuts, seeds, fruit, fish, and chicken.

Simple advice for relief from the pain of arthritis includes:

- ✒ Castor oil compresses or rubs. This oil has been proven to increase lymphatic blood flow to clear away toxins and inflammatory by-products.
- ✒ Gentle stretches and exercise; tai chi and yoga are especially helpful. Hydrotherapy in a heated pool can do wonders. Do easy exercise in the pool or swim. Massage therapy really helps circulation and clears away inflammatory by-products.
- ✒ Simple meditation, prayer, or affirmations help to calm and remove stress. The Silva method is a nonsectarian meditation-affirmation technique that has an excellent worldwide reputation.
- ✒ Be careful with heating pads and ice. Use heat only on stiff joints and for only a short time. Use ice if a joint is hot and inflamed. Be sure to check with your doctor for special instructions on your case.
- ✒ Supplements can treat arthritis in several ways: they can alleviate symptoms caused by vitamin deficiencies, build cartilage, treat pain and inflammation, and help you avoid the potentially life-threatening side effects of anti-inflammatory medications.

Glucosamine sulphate, made from the shells of shrimp and crab, actually rebuilds cartilage, prevents its breakdown, and supports its shock-absorbing capacity. Most studies show that the effective dosage is 1,500 milligrams per day in divided doses. It may not work for everybody, but it enjoys a high rate of success and is worth investigating. Chondroitin sulphate, which is found in cartilage, has also been touted as a cure for joint pain; however, in the oral form it is apparently not soluble and not absorbed by the body. More research is needed to show if it really works and to determine ways to aid its absorption.

For pain and inflammation use vitamin C, 1 gram three times a day, along with bromelain and/or pancreatic enzymes, two tablets three times a day. Bromelain is an enzyme found in pineapple. Enzymes in conjunction with vitamin C act as anti-inflammatories that have proven to be as effective as most anti-inflammatory medications. Evening primrose oil, flaxseed oil, and fish oils improve joint mobility and decrease inflammation. The B-complex vitamins are helpful in supporting the immune system, nervous system, and circulatory system.

There are many herbal approaches to the treatment of arthritis. A minister, a longtime friend of the family, swears by devil's claw since he heard me recommend it during a TV interview. I chuckle to think of him advocating it to parishioners, but it does work for many at a dosage of 100 milligrams several times a day.

Homeopathic remedies for arthritis are based on symptoms: for pain worse after rest use Rhus tox. 12C; for pain worse with motion use Bryonia 12C. The dosage for either remedy is 4 drops three times a day. Try it for two weeks; if it hasn't worked by that time it is not the right remedy. A chronic condition requires the skills of a homeopath to take a detailed case history and prescribe an individualized remedy. Read the sections on allergies, detoxification, candidiasis, chronic fatigue, and digestion to understand your condition and pick up more health tips.

For more in-depth information, an excellent reference book on arthritis is *Arthritis: Alternative Medicine Definitive Guide,* edited by Burton Goldberg.

Asthma

This is a condition of bronchial tube spasm that results in shortness of breath and wheezing and can be life threatening. Asthma is recognized more and more as both a stress and allergic reaction. You can use medication and also natural methods to give more relief and to gradually decrease medications.

For stress, one very important recommendation is to participate regularly in relaxing exercise such as yoga, swimming, or tai chi. Going even further into the mind-body connection is Kathryn Shafer, Ph.D.

Her book, *Asthma Free in 21 Days,* utilizes visualization and the power of imagination to "take the weight" of asthma off your chest. She helps you understand the connection your lack of breath can have to a suffocating relationship or not being able to speak your mind. It's a wonderful, inspiring, and powerful book.

Some people have allergies to any number of inhaled or ingested substances that can trigger asthma attacks. Such substances include chemicals in our air, water, and food. The incidence of asthma is rising in children, probably because schools are bombarded by oil-based paints, pesticides, and toxic cleaning products. Food additives such as MSG cause symptoms in many people. I know when I've eaten MSG, because the sides of my head at my temples tighten up. A similar tightening effect occurs in the lungs of asthmatics. Aspartame (NutraSweet) can cause shortness of breath, among its ninety-two side effects.

Read the section on allergies on page 6 to learn how to eliminate foods that may be causing problems. Some doctors feel that asthmatics do not digest their food because of a deficiency of hydrochloric acid in the stomach. Read the section on digestive disorders on page 63 for more information.

If you get asthma at night, be sure you have a dust-free and animal-free bedroom. Remove the carpets, cover your mattress with plastic, and wash pillows and bedcovers frequently. And keep vacuuming!

Avoid smoke-filled environments, incense, cigarettes, or wood-burning fires. Use air conditioners, air cleaners, and water purifiers.

Useful vitamins include vitamin C with bioflavonoids as a natural antihistamine and support for the adrenal glands, and B complex for the stress on the nervous system and on the adrenal glands caused by asthma.

Homeopathic remedies for asthma include Arsenicum 12C, especially for night asthma with panic attacks, 4 drops every few minutes. If the episode does not subside quickly, seek medical assistance. There are many homeopathic remedies for asthma, which include Aconite and Nux vomica. You can read about these remedies in part 4. Study them to see if they fit your case.

Herbal remedies such as Brigham tea have natural ephedra, which is a bronchial relaxant, but use no more than 1 to 2 cups a day. Acupuncture is also very helpful for asthma, especially ear acupuncture, which can relax the lung point and diminish symptoms.

In an acute attack, take in lots of fluids so that the lungs don't get dry and turn the mucus into hard plugs that further block the breathing. Use fenugreek tea to liquefy mucus, and inhale steam or use a humidifier. You may not realize how much moisture can be lost during a fever or an asthma attack. If you aren't urinating out as much as you are taking in, you are getting dehydrated.

Atherosclerosis

Atherosclerosis, or hardening of the arteries, is thought to be caused by elevated cholesterol. Cholesterol is an essential building block for hormones; it protects all the nerves in the body with a special layer of fat; and it helps to produce bile, which is necessary for digestion. Cholesterol also acts as an antioxidant that sponges up excess free radicals that cause damage in the body. The more free radicals, the higher the cholesterol as it tries to contain them. One avenue of treatment might be to get rid of free radicals, rather than the cholesterol.

In fact, if too little cholesterol is eaten in the diet, the liver will manufacture its own to complete its necessary tasks. The only cholesterol that is bad is rancid cholesterol. The early cholesterol studies used eggs, because they are high in cholesterol, but it appears that they used rancid egg powder, giving both eggs and cholesterol a very bad rap. Huge advertising campaigns developed around egg-free, cholesterol-free products and drove the food industry down a very unhealthy path that we have only recently begun to understand. We now know that margarine, with its trans-fatty acids, is causing heart disease. It is the processing of fats and oils that creates unnatural products that damage the heart.

Another theory about atherosclerosis is that arteries can be injured by an infection which allows LDL (bad) cholesterol to bind with calcium, causing hardening of the arteries and leading to angina, stroke, heart attack, and impaired circulation to the extremities. Read the section on angina on page 12 for more information.

Low-fat and low-cholesterol diets have been the rage for heart disease, and in a certain percentage of the population, they can be helpful. Everyone is different, however. Read the sections on diets on page 181, diabetes on page 58, and obesity on page 128 to learn about the best diet for your body and how to prevent weight gain and blood sugar problems, all of which can affect your heart and circulation.

Homocysteine is the latest buzzword surrounding heart disease. Homocysteine is an amino acid which requires vitamins B_6, B_{12}, and folic acid to be broken down into methionine. If it is not broken down, homocysteine builds up and interacts with LDL cholesterol to damage artery walls and build up plaque. If you are on a poor diet without enough of these B vitamins, you may suffer from heart disease.

The best diet for atherosclerosis is suited to your blood type. Read the section on diets on page 181 to see how you can individualize yours; it's not the same for everyone. Although a very strict low-fat, high-carbohydrate diet may help eliminate plaque in your arteries, it can also lead to essential fatty acid deficiency in the long run. Similarly, a high-protein, low-carbohydrate diet can help you lose a lot of weight initially but can lead to strain on the kidneys.

The supplements for atherosclerosis include vitamin C, which helps heal artery damage; vitamin E, which acts as a blood thinner; bioflavonoids as part of the vitamin C complex, which also help heal arteries; and calcium and magnesium, which help lower blood pressure. It is interesting that the newest heart medicines are calcium-channel blockers; the best calcium-channel blocker is magnesium. Lecithin capsules balance the cholesterol and bile in the liver. Trace minerals are also important in a good natural multivitamin and mineral supplement, since all vitamins and minerals act as cofactors in the metabolic processes of the body.

In Japan, coenzyme Q10 is widely used for heart disease because it is essential for the production of adenosine triphosphate (ATP), the body's ultimate energy source. This energy is produced in cellular mitochondria, and the heart has the body's highest concentration of mitochondria. Therefore, coenzyme Q10 is most appropriate for the heart.

Organic natural oils should replace margarine and processed oils. Flaxseed oil (in a lightproof bottle) can be used on salads and cereal. This polyunsaturated oil contains essential fatty acids obtainable only from diet. The best oils for cooking are olive oil and coconut oil. These oils are monosaturated and won't become denatured or rancid on heating. Recent studies actually show that people who use olive oil have half the rate of heart disease than those who don't. Even though it is a fat, it actually causes the undesirable cholesterol to fall, and maintains the good cholesterol. In choosing between butter and highly processed polyunsaturated margarines, butter is actually healthier. Manufactured margarines cause more harmful oxidative effects than even completely saturated butter. Read the 1999 edition of Sally Fallon's book, *Nourishing Traditions*, for a real education on fats and oils.

One important aspect of cholesterol metabolism is that cholesterol can be reabsorbed back into the system instead of being eliminated through the intestines. This means detoxification and cleansing are very important to pull as much old cholesterol out by this route as possible. If there is an overabundance of abnormal bacteria in your colon, cholesterol will be reabsorbed. Therefore, a high-fiber diet, bulking agents such as psyllium, and detoxifying with aloe vera gel are all important. See the section on detoxification on page 178.

Exercise is also extremely important; begin with slow short walks and gradually increase intensity to allow the blood vessels to multiply to improve the circulation in all parts of the body.

Athlete's Foot

Athlete's foot is a very common condition caused by a fungus that lives on the skin and toenails. Its growth is encouraged by warm, dark, and damp areas. People in tropical climates are more prone to this infection, but sweaty footgear is a common cause in North America. In the acute stage, the skin may blister and crack and discharge clear liquid. Most often it is chronic irritation and itchiness, however. In the acute stage, keep the area dry and uncovered; for inflammation, soak the foot in a solution of 1 tablespoon of white zeolite clay or green clay, 1 tablespoon of salt, or 1 tablespoon of baking soda in a quart of water. Taheebo tea can also be used to soak the feet. This tea is made from the bark of a tree that grows in Brazil on which fungi or mold won't grow. A solution of a tablespoon of this bark boiled for an hour in a quart of water can be used over and over again. Simply reheat before reusing. After soaking, which lessens the inflammation, pain, and itching, apply antifungal cream or lotion.

There are many over-the-counter medications that can be used two or three times a day but must be continued for at least four weeks. Preparations available in health food stores include tea tree oil and garlic oil, which are powerful antifungals. Fungus grows best in oxygen-deprived areas; by using vitamin E, a powerful oxygenator, you can discourage fungal growth. Zeolite powder, used for removing the odor from footwear, helps to trap fungus spores, to dry athlete's foot blisters, and to keep the foot dry inside the shoes. After soaking your feet, scrub them to remove any dead skin that can harbor the fungus, and dry them well—perhaps even with a hair dryer. Then powder with zeolite or clay powder, put on fresh cotton socks, and put another ½ teaspoon of powder directly inside your shoes. Change your socks several times a day if your feet perspire heavily, and change your shoes once or twice a day, because they hold the moisture and the fungus. The worst types of shoes and boots are rubber and plastic, which hold sweat and moisture inside.

People often ask me why they get athlete's foot while their next-door lockermate has never been bothered. Some people are just more susceptible; if you are, prevention also requires that you cover your feet in areas where others go barefoot, such as gyms, spas, and swimming pools. Your susceptibility may be due to an overgrowth of yeast on your mucous membranes and skin, which makes you more susceptible to fungal growths. Yeast mainly grows in the gastrointestinal tract, but when it overgrows, it can cause oral thrush in the mouth, and vaginitis in women, and it can be undetectable on the skin but create an environment in which other fungi can grow. Treatment of this condition includes avoiding sugar, yeast breads, dairy, and alcohol for a period of time to starve the yeast in the gastrointestinal tract. See the section on candidiasis on page 40, which fully explains this condition.

Back Pain

This can be a very frightening condition and can mean anything from a muscle spasm to an actual prolapsed or slipped disc. This occurs when the pad between the vertebrae is forced out from between the vertebrae and the bones crush or press the nerves that come off the spinal cord. The diagnosis definitely must be clarified by a doctor and an MRI. If the advice is bed rest, muscle relaxants, and painkillers, you can also use ice alternating with heat.

The following homeopathic remedies can be useful for an acute attack and are nontoxic: Arnica 12C for pain, shock, and swelling, 4 drops every half to one hour while pain is severe. If the pain is more like stiffness, Rhus tox. 12C can be used in the same amounts. If there is definite nerve tingling and irritation, Hypericum 12C can be used.

The best treatment for pain in the acute injury period is ice. Never use heat on an acute inflammation. If the pain is chronic, use ice and heat (ten minutes of one, rest ten minutes, and ten minutes of the other). You can use castor oil packs for both acute and chronic pain. Take an old hand towel and rub in 4 to 5 tablespoons of castor oil.

Cover the affected area but protect your bedclothes with plastic. You may use a heating pad on low to help the action, but it works just fine at room temperature too. Leave on at least one hour or overnight. Castor oil has been proven to reduce inflammation. Warm to moderately hot Epsom salts baths will help chronic back pain.

The nutrients for easing back pain include vitamin C, 1 gram three times a day, along with bromelain and/or pancreatic enzymes, two tablets three times a day as a natural anti-inflammatory, and calcium and magnesium.

Gentle and structured exercises are vital for healing back pain. They should focus on strengthening the abdominal muscles, and that means sit-ups done with your knees bent and the lower back flat on the floor. Massage therapy can also help to stretch and relax tense muscles that feed into a chronically painful back. If you are overweight, the excess strain of that weight can aggravate the back, so a weight-loss program is indicated.

Several recent studies have proven that the optimum care for acute and chronic back pain is by a good chiropractor who recognizes that misalignment of any part of the body can contribute to back pain. The best chiropractors work on muscles as well as bones, prescribe a series of exercises, and encourage you to learn how to take care of your own body rather than creating a dependency on them. The emergency exercise for acute back pain is a yoga position called "the cobra." Lie on your stomach with your arms lying at your sides, and very slowly lift your head and upper shoulders. This position seems to align the spine and can help alleviate back pain.

If the muscles in your neck and back are tight and painful when you roll your neck or when you try to touch your toes, you need stretching exercises. Yoga is probably the key. Several sessions a week will help you stretch out those tense muscles so that they won't go into spasm. You will also develop good posture and improved breathing habits.

Acupuncture is another excellent modality for back pain. Make sure you get a good referral to a practitioner who has had experience and success in treating back pain.

Don't forget the mind-body connection. In order to truly appreciate how the mind is involved with creating pain, read *Mind over Back Pain: A Radically New Approach to the Diagnosis and Treatment of Back Pain*, by Dr. John Sarno. Dr. Sarno will help you understand how stress and tension can create pain and how you limit your physical activity due to fear of pain, causing you to get even more out of shape and unable to heal.

Homeopathy for Musculoskeletal Healing by Asa Hershoff, D.C., N.D., is the best resource for homeopathic remedies for the musculoskeletal system; if you have trouble finding a remedy, it is best to consult a homeopath for specific advice suited to your case.

Prevention, of course, is the best treatment. Learn how to lift by bending your knees and keeping your back straight. Don't twist your back to move an object; move your whole body.

A firm mattress that doesn't sag is very important, as is your sleeping position. Sleep on your back with support under your knees and under your head and neck. Or sleep on your side with support under your neck and head and another pillow between your knees. There are many styles of neck pillows available now. These have a rounded center that conforms to the shape of the neck, holding it in proper alignment during sleep. Chiropractors say that a person with a bad lower back can have a corresponding problem in the neck and vice versa. Therefore, pay attention to the neck as well as the back.

Bad Breath

As with so many other conditions, bad breath may be just a symptom of a body out of balance. Most people think that bad breath comes from eating food that is highly spiced or very strong. These foods include the obvious ones such as garlic, onion, spicy and heavy meats and cheeses, fish, coffee, and alcohol. But bad breath is mostly due to bacteria in the mouth that feed off the food we eat, and they are especially attracted to sugar. Plaque forms on the teeth and the bacteria attach to the plaque. Brushing the teeth and rinsing the mouth after eating are important ways of dealing with bad breath. Flossing is also very important. Local treatment, such as breath mints and mouthwashes, are only short-term solutions. Cloves after a meal are very useful as a natural breath mint. I use them for their antibacterial action in order to keep my mouth healthy and also prevent catching bacteria from my patients. Just gently chew and suck them, but don't swallow them. The real solution, however, is to look at your diet to see what you are eating on a regular basis that is causing bad breath. The most likely thing is sugar, which feeds bacteria and allows them, in the dark, moist recesses of the mouth, to create gases that can cause bad breath.

Let us consider the function of the tongue. In animals, especially dogs, it eliminates moisture, much as our skin eliminates perspiration.

Perspiration or sweat is not just pure water; it contains salt and by-products of chemical processes in the body, in which waste is excreted by the kidneys, through the intestines and through the skin. The tongue serves the same function, so the body in trying to eliminate waste uses the tongue. It is conceivable that waste products find their way to the tongue and coat it, contributing to bad breath. The more waste products and the more toxic the waste products from the body, the more the tongue is coated, and the breath has a foul odor. People who have a very clean diet—by which I mean plenty of fresh vegetables, fruits, nuts, seeds, grains, fish, and chicken—rarely have bad breath. People who eat sugar, dairy products, coffee, alcohol, and meat tend to have more bad breath.

Most people do not chew their food properly. If you chew properly, you can digest up to one-third of your carbohydrates right in your mouth. Meat is a protein, however, and it requires hydrochloric acid in the stomach for digestion. Meat takes up to seven hours to digest in the intestines, because it takes that long for enough hydrochloric acid to be built up and to break down the protein molecules. During the seven-hour period, more and more food is eaten and combined with the digesting protein. This leads to gas and fermentation in the stomach, which, besides causing belching and flatulence, can bring the odors into the mouth and create bad breath. Similarly, when sugar is eaten and there are other foods in the stomach, they can ferment and create alcohol in the stomach and intestines. This can be easily measured in the bloodstream after the intake of sugar or even fruit. Read the sections on digestive disorders on page 63, candidiasis on page 40, and diets on page 181 for more information on this topic.

Bed-Wetting

At a certain age, children are expected to sleep through the night without wetting the bed. This can be anywhere from age two to seven. The cause of bed-wetting is often psychological stress, especially if there is another child born around the time when the older child has been dry at night for several months. Bed-wetting can be an attention-getting device on an unconscious psychological level. Other stresses in the home can result in bed-wetting. Sleepovers often produce bed-wetting because of excitement and stress. In my practice, I also make a point of looking for food allergies that can contribute to irritation or relaxation of the bladder neck muscles, which allows the urine to leak during the night. Urination can come during the very deep sleep phase when there is not enough arousal to wake a child up and allow him to go to the bathroom. The foods that seem to cause the most problems are milk, orange juice, peanut butter, and sugar, but almost any food can conceivably be a problem. Drinking before bed can fill the bladder. Limiting food and liquid intake after supper is appropriate. Also, getting the child up to urinate when the adults are going to bed helps to keep the bladder empty. See the section on allergies on page 6 for more information on this topic.

Bites

Let's first discuss the infamous West Nile virus, which is a mosquito-borne flulike illness. It is an extremely mild condition that has produced massive hysterical spraying of carcinogenic pesticides on the northeast coast of America; it is even milder in children than in adults. Children, however, are the ones who suffer most from pesticide sprays. West Nile has a mortality rate of less than 1 in 1 million infected people, and mainly affects immune-suppressed or elderly people. Compare this to the 1 in 12,000 mortality rate for seasonal influenza and you, like me, will scratch your head and wonder what on earth all the fuss is about. It will also make you take action to try and stop the insanity of pesticide spraying.

Mosquitoes seem to dislike the odor produced from the ingestion of B vitamins, especially thiamine (B_1), so in mosquito season, you can take extra dosages of the B complex, including B_1. Most commercial mosquito sprays are strong chemical compounds that might affect one adversely when absorbed, but there is a natural one: a citrus lotion called citronella. This insect repellent seems to have no side effects when absorbed. There are anecdotal reports that citronella may not be safe for pets, so check with your veterinarian for a natural pet bug repellent. Health food stores are carrying more natural insect repellents that you can try out. They are sure to be safer than commercial pesticides, which I call "humanicides" because they are deadly to all life forms, not just insects.

A moistened aspirin on the cleaned bite area can relieve the pain and stop the inflammation. Homeopathic remedies for bites and stings include Apis and Ledum. If someone has a bee-sting allergy, Apis can be used every few minutes. An Anakit (bee-sting kit) should also be handy. This contains adrenalin and a needle, and should be used, especially if the sting is around the face or throat. Ledum is a good remedy for spider bites, or even cat and dog bites. These bites can produce an infection; the area should be cleaned well and should be examined by a doctor, who may advise an antibiotic cream, a tetanus booster, and possibly antibiotics by mouth. Sometimes soaking the wound in an herbal antibiotic, such as echinacea, and poulticing with a clay pack, comfrey, or even a bread poultice, can prevent infection from occurring. An infection will produce a red line from the wound toward the nearest lymph node as the body tries to clear the infection; this indicates to doctors that an antibiotic should be used. If you use an antibiotic, be sure to take acidophilus bacteria along with it to prevent an overgrowth of *Candida*.

Bladder Infections

Anyone suffering from chronic or frequent bladder infection should read *You Don't Have to Live with Cystitis*, by Dr. Larrian Gillespie. There are sections on how to deal with acute and chronic infection; information on the allergic causes of bladder symptoms; and advice on all aspects of bladder and kidney disease. The most common cause of bladder infections in women is postcoital infection. During intercourse, the urethra can be trapped and irritated. This causes the urethra to swell. If there is bacteria near the urethra, which can migrate from the bowel area, the inflammation and swelling provide an ideal environment for bacteria to grow. Check Dr. Gillespie's book for specific details. In general, to avoid bladder infections after intercourse, be sure to avoid excessive jamming action with the penis. Wash before and after intercourse with a neutral pH soap, and urinate before and after intercourse to wash bacteria out of the urethra. Taking a homeopathic remedy called Staphysagria 12C, 4 drops one to two times after intercourse, may prevent infection in susceptible people.

Inserting a nonsterile diaphragm can also result in bacteria overgrowth. The diaphragm as it rests inside the vagina above the pubic bone cuts off the urethra, irritating it and inhibiting bladder emptying. If the bacteria are not flushed out after intercourse they can overgrow.

Tampons may also cause some of the same problems as diaphragms and lead to bladder infections.

If bladder symptoms such as frequent urination, burning, and pressure begin, it is important to submit a urine sample to your doctor so that she may have it tested for bacterial overgrowth. While waiting for results, natural treatments include ½ to ¼ teaspoon of baking soda in one glass of water every thirty minutes. This can help make the urine less acidic and therefore less burning. (Warning: don't use baking soda [sodium bicarbonate] if you are being treated for a heart condition.) Avoid caffeinated tea and coffee and take parsley or chamomile tea in large quantities. Lots of water is the key to flushing out bacteria. Homeopathic remedies such as Cantharis or Causticum in the 12C potency taken every hour can be helpful. For postcoital irritation, Staphysagria 6 or 30C can be taken every hour. Do not take chamomile tea with homeopathic remedies, as it can neutralize their action.

Another cause of burning urination is aspartame (NutraSweet). Read the section on sugar and aspartame on page 185 to learn what to avoid.

In young girls, bladder infections can be the result of taking bubble baths; avoid them.

Simple commonsense advice to prevent bladder infections includes avoiding tight jeans, wearing loose cotton underwear, and avoiding scented tampons, pads, or even colored toilet paper. After a bowel movement, wipe from front to back to avoid pulling bowel bacteria into the vagina/urethra area.

Studies show that pure cranberry juice or even cranberry tablets help bladder infections. If you must take an antibiotic, ask your doctor for a urinary antiseptic such as nitrofurantion or nalidixic acid, which have their own side effects but do not affect the intestinal bacteria and cause candidiasis. If you have to use an antibiotic, be sure and take yogurt or acidophilus tablets as well. Read the sections on candidiasis on page 40 and antibiotics on page 155.

Boils

Boils are usually caused by a staphylococcal infection. They can produce a lot of pain and are a considerable nuisance. The medical treatment is strong antibiotics. Until antibiotics are necessary, several natural remedies can be used. Boils usually occur in people who have a zinc deficiency; zinc is important for wound healing. Zinc is found in sunflower seeds, pumpkin seeds, and oysters.

Another possible cause of boils is an overload of toxins in the system. This stresses the liver, kidneys, and colon, and the toxins are released through the skin. People who have boils should avoid constipation and read the section on detoxification on page 178. Boils can be treated with poultices to try to bring the boil to a head and discharge the contents. Clay is available in health food stores and can be mixed with water and applied to a boil. Poultices of bread moistened with water can be applied to the area; even a hot water compress may bring a boil to a head. If fresh or dry comfrey is available, pulverize or chop 1 tablespoonful, steep in ½ cup boiling water for fifteen minutes, strain, wrap in gauze, and apply to the boil, covering with plastic wrap. Leave on a maximum of twelve hours per day.

Homeopathic treatments are with oral doses of:

Hepar sulph. 12C, which is used to bring boils to a head. Calc. sulph. 12C for recurring crops of boils. Silicia 12C for boils that are slow to heal. Sulphur 12C for burning and itching boils. All remedies are taken 4 drops three times a day.

Herbal tincture of echinacea can be used for a person who is toxic and produces boils, 10 to 15 drops three times a day in water. This can be taken orally or used to soak a boil. Other boil soaks are Hypericum tincture and Calendula tincture.

Bronchitis

Bronchitis often begins with a simple cold that develops into a chronic cough. Therefore, the best treatment for bronchitis is to ensure that a cold is not prolonged. See the section on colds and flus on page 48. Colds are most often due to a virus, so antibiotics will not help.

For bronchitis itself, avoid mucus-forming foods such as dairy and wheat. Lots of fluids are important, as are mucus-thinning herbs such as fenugreek. Use steam or a humidifier to help liquefy the mucus. Dehydration is quite common with bronchitis. If your urine output does not equal your water input you may be dehydrated, which can elevate your fever and solidify the mucus.

Bronchial herb tea available in health food stores (labeled Bronchial Tea) might include herbs such as mullein and lobelia, which are useful for this condition. There are many homeopathic remedies for bronchitis. Bryonia 12C, 4 drops every few hours, is one of the best. A full list of remedies allows you to identify the best remedy for a particular cough. Study part 4 of this book.

Smoking (or smokers) should be avoided—cigarette smoke is the most common reason people get bronchitis. If the cough persists, especially in certain environments, allergies should be considered. An allergy to animal dander, dust, mold, or medications can be the underlying pathology of a prolonged cough. Another modality useful for treating bronchitis is acupuncture. Properly trained acupuncturists can perform pulse diagnosis and determine if there is an energy imbalance contributing to your bronchitis. Treatment may include an individualized acupuncture protocol and herbal formulas.

Bruising

Bruising usually occurs after an injury, after bumping into a piece of furniture, or even after running or exercising, which can break small capillaries through gravity and impact. For bruises caused by injury, the most important treatment is Arnica 12C by mouth and Arnica cream on the bruise, as long as there is no broken skin. Arnica is a mountain plant and is an amazing treatment for any injury, from a black eye to a stubbed toe. The more serious the injury, the more frequently the Arnica is taken, anywhere from every fifteen minutes to every two hours. Ice is also useful for the first twenty-four or thirty-six hours to stop the inflammation and keep inflammatory cells from leaching out into the surrounding area and triggering off more inflammation. Ice packs can be applied every fifteen to twenty minutes. After thirty-six hours, heat can be used to clear the dead blood cells from the area by increasing circulation.

Frequent bruising may be due to medication such as aspirin, or other drugs such as antidepressants and asthma drugs, which can inhibit platelet aggregation, thereby slowing clotting and leading to even larger bruises. Alcoholics tend to bruise easily because of liver impairment. Others who bruise easily may have a vitamin C deficiency; it may not be just vitamin C but the bioflavonoids—part of the vitamin C complex—that are important. Bioflavonoids are useful for varicose veins, hemorrhoids, stroke prevention, heavy menstrual bleeding, and bruising. Vitamin C along with bioflavonoids several times a day will help strengthen blood vessels. Vitamin B_{12} and folic acid are two vitamins responsible for the size of the red blood cells. If these vitamins are deficient, the cell size expands, the membrane weakens, and there is bleeding and bruising. A doctor should perform blood tests to determine if there is a rare B_{12} deficiency condition called pernicious anemia. If there is not, and B_{12} or folic acid is indicated, take supplements.

Burning Feet

This unusual condition is often very difficult to diagnose. Your doctor must rule out impaired circulation, hardening of the arteries, B_{12} deficiency, or diabetes. Medically, these conditions can be ruled out only when they are in the full-blown state. The syndrome may be caused by a mild form of any one of these conditions, however. Therefore, read the sections on atherosclerosis on page 19 and diabetes on page 58 and be sure to increase the amounts of vitamin B_{12} in your diet or take supplements. Some doctors may be willing to try B_{12} injections to treat this condition. Vitamin E and calcium and magnesium may be needed. B complex for proper nerve nutrition might be useful. Adequate exercise is very important and certainly detoxification can help. (See the section on detoxification on page 178.) Some people improve by taking Epsom salts baths or footbaths. In some cases, diluted cider vinegar as a footbath is helpful. Chinese water therapy uses cold water footbaths just prior to bedtime for this particular condition. Each individual will have to explore a variety of these natural methods to determine the one that suits him best.

Burning Mouth

This condition can be due to sensitivity to a chemical food additive, food allergies, or vitamin and mineral deficiencies. The most basic advice is to avoid all products that contain food additives, especially aspartame (NutraSweet), to see if they are causing your problem. The wood alcohol in aspartame can cause burning. Read the section on sugar and aspartame on page 185 to find out more. Read the section on allergies on page 6 to determine common allergens you might be ingesting that could be causing your problem. Vitamin and mineral deficiencies that can make the mouth more sensitive include magnesium, B_{12}, folic acid, iron, and zinc. Mineral deficiencies can be assessed by ordering a hair analysis through your doctor or naturopath.

Burns

The immediate treatment for burns is cold water on the burn and oral ingestion of homeopathic Cantharis 12C every few minutes. Cantharis should be in everyone's first aid kit. You must never break a burn blister because this can allow infection to set in. The burn blister protects the underlying skin while it heals. Aloe vera gel or the cut leaf from an aloe vera plant can be placed on burns. Vitamin E oil is also good for the local treatment of burns and scars after the blister has healed. Calendula lotion or Hypericum lotion can also be applied. Homeopathic first aid kits are available using the remedies outlined in part 4 and in the section on first aid on page 168. See Resources under "Homeopathy" for more information.

Bursitis

This is a painful condition of the bursa (a small sack of lubricating fluid that is found cushioning every joint in the body), usually of the shoulder, but there can be bursitis of any bursa in any joint. With the shoulder, it is often caused by overuse, injury, or lying on the shoulder in a painful position for a long period of time, such as overnight. The condition is best treated with natural anti-inflammatories (before going to medication). These are vitamin C and pancreatic enzymes: 1 gram of vitamin C three times a day and two pancreatic enzyme tablets three times a day. Also useful are castor oil packs to decrease the inflammation. Put several tablespoons on an old cloth or towel and wrap it over the area. Use ice during the day and castor oil at night.

Rest is important at first. Then begin gentle exercise. The best exercise is performed by leaning your chest over the end of an ironing board with the painful arm hanging; swing it gently back and forth for a few minutes several times a day. Physiotherapy can be beneficial using ultrasound or interferential or diathermy treatment.

Acupuncture or laser-acupuncture can also alleviate the condition and a good chiropractor can also help. The longer bursitis is ignored, the greater chance there is of it becoming chronic.

Calluses and Corns

A callus is a buildup of tough skin in an area subjected to extra pressure and extra work. Calluses on the hands may be from using a hammer all day; calluses on the feet may be from ill-fitting shoes. If the pressure gets very severe, a corn may develop. A corn is merely a callus with a hard core. To prevent calluses and corns, wear proper footgear that does not put pressure on the heels or toes. Some people must wear insoles or custom-made orthotics, which are insoles specially made by podiatrists or chiropractors to keep the foot in the proper position within the shoe.

To treat calluses, soak the feet in various solutions. Epsom salts in warm water relieves inflammation from a corn pressing on a bursa. To remove a callus, cut a leaf from an aloe vera plant that is the same size as the corn or callus, slice the leaf down the center so that the interior gel can be placed against the callus, and then cover with several Band-Aids. Wear this to bed, and in the morning you can rub off the callus or corn with a dry facecloth or a pumice stone. If the calluses are around the heel, you may have thick, cracked skin. An excellent soak is half-and-half vinegar and castor oil. This can be kept in an old pot and reheated as needed. It's a very messy solution, but it works wonders—after soaking, preferably near a tub, wash off the material and use a pumice stone to smooth away the dead skin. Podiatrists advise people with pressure areas between the toes to put toe pads made of foam or lamb's wool between the toes. The best way, as mentioned above, to avoid corns and calluses is to choose proper footwear.

Cancer

In the first edition of this book, published over ten years ago, I did not cover the subject of cancer in any detail except to emphasize that diet, lifestyle, and environmental factors were involved. Since then, the incidence of cancer has risen from 1 in 6 to 1 in 2 people being diagnosed with cancer in their lifetime. It is a terrifying statistic and a horrendous disease that most people try to ignore. After all, if the "war on cancer" has failed so miserably, what can an individual do about this disease? We cannot stay in denial, however; we must arm ourselves with knowledge about the real causes of cancer so that we can fight the causes as well as the disease.

The known causes of cancer include chemical exposures, smoking and secondhand smoke, radiation, malnutrition, and excessive stress. The World Health Organization (WHO) stated thirty years ago that 89 percent of all cancer is caused by pesticides, radiation, and other toxic chemicals in our environment. Diet and smoking have become cancer scapegoats, however, while the chemical industry continues to pollute our air, water, and food.

Two things recently propelled me to become more active against the use of chemicals: the indiscriminate spraying of carcinogenic malathion and pyrethroid pesticides on millions of people in the northeastern United States in a hysterical reaction to a mild flulike virus called West Nile (see the section on bites on page 26), and finding Rachel Carson's biography in my local library. In 1962, Rachel Carson woke up a sleeping world with *Silent Spring,* a world in denial about the effects of chemicals on our environment and our health. We are still in denial. I won't spend time philosophizing about the so-called scientific struggle to "tame" nature, aerial spraying of people instead of using proper pest management for mosquitoes, the war against disease, the failing drug-oriented approach to health care, and the multibillion-dollar drug and chemical industry's propaganda that chemicals are good—but I will give you some basic information.

First, let's understand what actually happens to chemicals when they enter our bodies. Any toxin introduced into the body by eating, touching, or breathing activates the liver's detoxifying enzymes. If the liver is already busy trying to detoxify prescription medications or a synthetic-food diet, any extra chemical insult can overwhelm the enzyme system and the chemical can be directly toxic to the body. Liver enzymes readily break down water-soluble toxins, but not those that bind to fat cells (for example, pesticides). In metabolizing these man-made toxins, liver enzymes become a double-edged sword by making toxins out of some of the chemicals not previously so toxic (for example, benzene and malathion). These metabolic toxins created by our own enzymes then go on to bind with cellular DNA, where they cause mutations and cancers. Once this process has begun, all other bodily defenses, such as tumor suppressor genes, are also turned off because the toxin is now attached to a body protein and recognized as safe! The inevitable mutations in DNA are not hunted down and destroyed by immune surveillance and are incorporated into new DNA/RNA base-pairs. Cancer cells proliferate, create their own blood supply, thrive on hormones and sugar, and finally kill the host.

We have become so detached from our bodies and in so much denial that we have lost our common sense about staying healthy. Think of the aluminum in antiperspirants that men and women put on lymphatic-rich armpits. In women who shave, the microscopic nicks in the skin enhance absorption of this toxic material into the vulnerable area of the lymphatic system around sensitive breasts. Or what about the talc with which we powder ourselves and our babies that is readily absorbed and plays a role in pelvic adhesions, endometriosis, and cancer? It used to be that men were more often exposed to oil-based paints, lawn chemicals, and garden herbicides, but women have waded into that territory too. Men and women suffer the same chemical assault with colognes and perfumes. Cancers of the sex organs (breast, prostate, uterus, testes) are on the rise, because many of these chemicals are hormone disruptors.

Cancer Facts

1. Children are more sensitive to chemicals than adults. Cancer is the leading cause of death, after accidents, in children.
2. The greatest increase is in hormone-dependent cancers of the breast, prostate, and testicles because of chemical hormone disruptors.
3. Cancer care costs $5 billion annually in North America.
4. We have lost the war on cancer. Since President Nixon declared a war on cancer, treatments have been limited to drugs, surgery, and radiation; the survival rate has become no better and the incidence of cancer is now 1 in 2.
5. Dr. Samuel Epstein of the University of Illinois (active in banning DDT) says, "We have so much information on cancer prevention which we are not using. I wouldn't give a damn if we didn't do any more research for the next fifty years. The worldwide cancer epidemic is primarily the responsibility of the cancer establishment, comprised of the American and

Canadian Cancer Societies and the National Institutes of Health of both Canada and the United States. On their boards sit people who are directly connected to the very industries that are known to produce carcinogens" (pesticides, drugs, and industrial xenobiotics).

6. Dr. Epstein warns that all of us now carry more than 500 different compounds in our cells, none of which existed before 1920, and that "there is no safe dose for any of them."

7. Devra Lee Davis, internationally renowned toxicologist and epidemiologist of the World Resources Institute in Washington, D.C., speaks about the need to adopt the Precautionary Principle. This would require industry to prove that a new substance causes no harm. Currently, North American law requires that citizens have to prove a substance is dangerous before it can be banned or restricted.

8. Sandra Steingraber, U.S. presidential advisor on cancer prevention and author of the best-selling book, *Living Downstream,* reminds us that cancer has "become a human rights issue" that can only be tackled with "old-fashioned political organization." That is why "scientists are now going directly to the public" in order to expose "the deception at the heart of the chemical industry; namely, that these pesticides are necessary."

Cancer Myths

1. Fat is not the cause of cancer, but cancer-causing chemicals accumulate in fat cells. Obese people store a lot of chemicals in their fat cells. Follow a detoxification protocol (see the section on detoxification on page 178) and an optimal diet (see the section on diets on page 181).

2. The argument that the amounts of endocrine disrupters, or chemicals that mimic hormones, are too small to cause harm in the body is completely invalid, because hormones themselves work in infinitesimal doses. Endocrine disrupters and synthetic hormones, according to neuroscientist Candace Pert, Ph.D., rape the hormonal receptor sites because they have the same chemical structure, but they are mirror images and don't fit the intricate three-dimensional mechanism of the receptor sites.

3. Early detection is not the answer. Rosalie Bertell, Ph.D., an internationally respected radiation expert, testifies that having regular mammograms causes cumulative radiation damage, especially in premenopausal women.
4. Dr. Susan Love says cancer is not genetic: "We have perfectly good genes, and then something comes along to screw them up." Cornell University ecologist Sandra Steingraber states, "A cancer cell is made, not born."

What You Can Do

Activism
1. Boycott chemicals and demand alternatives.
2. Return chemicals to the manufacturer complaining about their negative effects on the environment.
3. Purchase products containing chemicals, then return them to the store manager, complain about the contents, and ask that alternatives be sold instead.
4. Start a pesticide awareness group. Demand full disclosure of all chemical ingredients (including inert ones) being sold today; approach your local golf course manager and discuss alternative ways of maintenance; go to your city council and get members to explore alternatives to chlorine in public swimming pools and to put a stop to the use of chlorine and fluoride in the water supply.

Things to Avoid
1. Avoid chemicals: perfumes, antiperspirants, deodorizers, hair dyes, dry cleaning, fabric softeners, smoking, mercury amalgams, cosmetics, fluoridated and chlorinated water, pesticides, herbicides, fungicides, bug killers, fertilizers, cleaning products.
2. Avoid surgery: breast implants, cosmetic surgery.
3. Avoid the electric environment: electromagnetic fields (EMFs), especially with children. Use appropriate protection on your computer screen and microwave oven; avoid living near hydro towers.
4. Avoid foods: salt-cured, smoked, and nitrate-cured foods, artificial sweeteners (especially aspartame), hormone- and antibiotic-treated meat and bovine growth hormone (BGH)

dairy, heating or storing foods in plastic containers, food additives, margarine, hydrogenated vegetable oils.

5. Avoid medications: antibiotics (except in emergencies), prescription drugs (except in emergencies and if there is no natural substitute), drugs given to prevent an illness (for example, Tamoxifen).

What You Can Do for Yourself and Your Family

1. Read this book and others for information on alternative health options, including diet and supplements. See Resources for further books or Internet reading.

2. If you are exposed to chemicals at work or at home, wear a heavy-duty charcoal-filtered mask and protective clothing.

3. Wash all your fruits and vegetables in VegiWash to remove the majority of pesticide surface residues. Use grapefruit seed extract to soak vegetables and fruits to eliminate parasitic contamination. See the section on parasites on page 133 for more information.

4. Purchase certified organic milk, meat, and food products in health food stores and demand that your local grocery store carry them. See Resources for contact information for community-supported agriculture.

5. Use natural sugar substitutes, such as stevia, unpasteurized honey, maple syrup, and brown rice syrup, but don't overdo them.

6. Invest in nonpolluters. Learn about ethical mutual funds and similar investment opportunities.

The details of specific cancer treatments are beyond the scope of this book, but I will briefly describe several herbal formulas and treatment protocols that you should research now in preparation for the possibility of cancer arising in your family.

1. Essiac tea (burdock root, sheep sorrel, turkey rhubarb root, slippery elm bark), Hoxsey Formula (cleansing herbs plus kelp or iodine), and La Pacho tea (antifungal herb) have detoxifying and immune-boosting properties and can be used preventively.

2. 714-X, a substance invented by Gaston Naessens, is injected into the right groin lymphatic chain. It shows a positive effect on the immune system and is used for degenerative diseases such as cancer, lupus, fibromyalgia, and chronic fatigue syndrome. A recent scientific report concluded that "714-X is thought to elevate the immune response and to play some role in killing tumor cells." 714-X is sold in fifty-five countries and has been administered by more than 1,500 physicians around the world. It has been legally available to Canadians since January 1990, under the provisions of Health Canada's Special Access program and more than 15,000 requests have been submitted by Canadian doctors for their patients.

3. Dr. Stanislaw Burzynski's antineoplaston peptide therapy is helpful. Antineoplastons are nontoxic substances shown to be a promising therapy for difficult-to-treat brain cancers, low- and intermediate-grade non-Hodgkin's lymphoma, and many common types of solid tumors. Antineoplastons consist of small peptides, components of protein, and peptide metabolites given by mouth or intravenously. They work by entering the cell and altering specific functions of the genes: some activate the tumor suppressor genes that prevent cancer, while others turn off the oncogenes that force the cancer cell to divide uncontrollably. Burzynski first isolated these natural compounds from blood and urine in the early 1970s. He feels that they are part of the body's natural defense mechanism. He now synthesizes them in his own FDA-approved, 47,000-square-foot pharmaceutical company, which he personally designed and had built.

4. Insulin hypoglycemia is a medically induced condition that lowers the blood sugar in order to starve and kill cancer cells. It is described on www.alternativemedicine.com and in back issues of *Alternative Medicine Digest*. Call 1-800-333-4325 for more information.

5. Hyperthermia involves heating the body to a temperature between 107 and 111°F for one to three hours after a week of detoxification. Heat increases the metabolic rate of the body, makes the body more acidic, and kills rapidly growing cancer cells by depriving them of oxygen. Read more about

this therapy in *Alternative Medicine Digest,* Issue #37, page 42, September 2000. Call 1-800-333-4325 for back issues.

6. Dr. Nicholas Gonzalez's metabolic protocol consists of enzymes taken between meals, dozens of supplements, coffee enemas, and cleansing fasts. Recent positive results on a clinical trial of end-stage pancreatic cancer led to a larger trial with Columbia University Hospital.

7. Gershon Diet Therapy consists of thirteen glasses per day of organic vegetable and fruit juices on average, plus raw calf's liver juice and iodine.

I wish to thank writer and activist Helke Ferrie of Ontario, Canada, for sharing her cancer files with me.

Candidiasis

This condition has been renamed candidiasis-related syndrome, because it is a complex of different causes, symptoms, and treatments. The yeast *Candida albicans* normally lives in the lower gastrointestinal tract and vagina and on the skin. Women seem to be more susceptible to candidiasis because they have three times the mucous membrane surface of men, and female hormones favor the growth of yeast. Under the influence of antibiotics, the birth control pill, cortisone, estrogen therapy, stress, alcohol, and a highly refined bread-and-sugar diet, *Candida* evolves from a budding yeast to a mycelial form, which invades mucous membranes. The yeast then grow into the mucous membrane tissue, and their metabolic by-products, of which there are at least seventy-nine, are absorbed into the bloodstream, adversely affecting the whole body. Among the toxic products are alcohols and aldehydes. Read the section on alcohol addiction on page 1 to find out about "drunk" disease caused by *Candida*.

Symptoms range from headaches, head congestion, brain fog, depression, and anxiety to throat and chronic cold symptoms, swollen glands, coated tongue, gastric upset, gas and bloating, constipation or diarrhea, vaginitis, arthritis, cystitis, muscle and joint aches, and numbness and tingling of the extremities. The symptoms are so widespread it is difficult for an individual or her doctor to even comprehend that it could be due to one organism.

It is important to read the classic books on candidiasis: *The Yeast Syndrome* by Dr. John P. Trowbridge, *The Yeast Connection* by Dr. William Crook, and *The Missing Diagnosis* by Dr. Orian Truss. It is only through reading and understanding the syndrome that you can relate it to your specific case.

This condition is best diagnosed by a blood test for *Candida* antibodies. With these scientific tests, doctors are able to diagnose and treat each person individually. Especially in the United States, most complementary medicine doctors and naturopaths are familiar with nutritional assessment laboratories that use these tests. See Resources for more information.

Step-by-Step Treatment for Candidiasis

Step One: Begin a very strict anti-*Candida* diet. For the first few weeks avoid sugar, yeast breads, fruit, fermented foods, and gluten grains (rye, oats, wheat, and barley). What's left, you ask? Truckloads of vegetables, millet, rice, amaranth, kamut, fish, and antibiotic-free, hormone-free chicken and beef.

Most people with candidiasis report that they begin to feel much better by the second or third week of the diet. During the first week, you might feel some aggravation of symptoms as the yeast that are dying off flood the system with their toxic by-products, causing even more symptoms than before. After several weeks on a strict diet, reintroduce foods, one by one, to get an indication of whether you should, in fact, be consuming that food. Problems can represent either a food allergy or perhaps a yeast-promoting food. Often they go hand in hand; irritation by yeast to the lining of the gastrointestinal tract can cause incompletely digested foods to be absorbed through the injured intestinal wall. Food allergy blood tests may help determine specific allergies if simple food avoidance and challenge are too cumbersome.

Step Two: Add acidophilus bacteria to your diet. Acidophilus is a good bacteria that helps build up the normal flora in the bowel as the yeast are killed off and leave vacancies in the intestines and vagina.

Step Three: Add foods: garlic, onions, coconut milk, and coconut oil.

Step Four: Use antifungal herb teas such as hops and Pau d'Arco, also called Lapacho or Taheebo.

Step Five: Cellulase is an enzyme that breaks down plant walls, and Dr. Lita Lee in her book on plant enzymes claims it will break down *Candida*.

Step Six: Treat possible parasite invasion, which commonly occurs in a *Candida*-overloaded colon. Wash all your produce with grapefruit seed extract liquid to kill parasites, and take grapefruit seed extract capsules when you eat out to kill possible parasite contamination on food.

Step Seven: If your *Candida* testing shows a moderate to high level of yeast growth, you need a specific antifungal medication such as caprylic acid, made from coconut oil. Caprylic acid comes in tablet and capsule form. Begin these very gradually to ensure that there are no side effects and work up to a combination of three capsules and three tablets a day before meals. The capsules help kill yeast in the upper gastrointestinal tract and the tablets affect the yeast in the lower GI tract.

In my experience, all of the above steps must be done in unison to get *Candida* under control. We can never say that *Candida* can be "cured," however, because there will always be some yeast in our bodies with the possibility of overgrowth under stressful conditions.

There are many intricacies in the treatment of candidiasis. One has to treat yeast as well as look for and treat hypoglycemia, chronic fatigue syndrome, food allergies, hypothyroidism, stress, and PMS. Therefore, the best advice is to seek counseling with practitioners knowledgeable in these conditions who can spend time sorting out your problems. Unfortunately, doctors can ill afford the luxury of taking the required hour or more to help patients with these complex situations. So, the patient must take responsibility for researching and educating himself as to what he can do in conjunction with direction from his doctors and counselors to achieve optimum health.

Canker Sores

The most common causes of canker sores in the mouth are an overload of acidic foods in the diet, hot foods, and damage to the inside of the mouth due to biting or toothbrush injury. Acidic foods include fruits, tomatoes, chewable vitamin C, and chocolate. A mechanical imbalance of the biting surface of the teeth can lead to accidental biting at the sides of the inner cheek and cause trauma that will lead to cankers.

Food allergies and candidiasis can also cause cankers. Read the sections on allergies on page 6 and candidiasis on page 40.

To treat cankers, avoid acidic foods and use acidophilus or yogurt to restore normal bacterial flora in the mouth. Rinsing the mouth with dilute hydrogen peroxide, goldenseal tea, or myrrh tea can help symptoms. Dabbing the canker with alum can relieve some of the pain. Cankers can be difficult to heal because the mouth is always moist and you cannot get a healing salve to stick to the canker.

Cankers are another condition in which people must play detective to determine the cause. Vitamin C with bioflavonoids is necessary for healing any tissue injury; food-based, organic sources are the most effective. Homeopathic Boric acid 12C can also be used for this condition. Some people have reported that their canker sores diminished after appropriate treatment for candidiasis.

Carpal Tunnel Syndrome

The carpal tunnel is an area at the wrist where tendons, nerves, and blood vessels travel from the forearm to the hand. On the palm side of the wrist, there is a band of tissue going across this tunnel that can trap the nerves and become swollen. The tendons in the wrist can then become inflamed. People who use their wrists a lot are subject to this condition, and with repetitive motions, such as in hammering, knitting, typing, writing, and massaging, the tendon can swell up. This puts pressure on the nerve that runs into the hand; the result can be numbness and tingling of the fingers, the feeling that the hand is falling asleep, and a lot of pain. Pregnant women are very susceptible to this condition. Twice as many women as men suffer from carpal tunnel syndrome. While one hand is usually symptomatic, both hands can suffer.

Medically, there is a surgical procedure to release the band over the tendons, but it doesn't necessarily cure the problem. Exercises include elevating the hands to decrease pressure on the nerve, gently rotating the wrists in circular motions, and massaging the fingers, palms, and up the wrists toward the elbows with the hand held upright. Sometimes it's merely a matter of cutting back on the amount of work you do with your hands. And whatever work you do, hold your hands so that your wrists are not bent. If you work on the computer a lot, don't type with your wrists bent backward; keep them straight. A simple readjustment of your working posture is often all it takes to remove this misery from your life.

Ice and cold packs will decrease the inflammation in the wrist, and proper sleep posture is very important. Don't lie on your arm at night and don't sleep with your hands on top of your body. Physiotherapists can fit wrist splints to help alleviate the condition. The best treatment, however, is high-dose vitamin B_6 therapy. Dr. John Ellis has been treating carpal tunnel syndrome for years, and he believes that this syndrome is actually caused by a deficiency of vitamin B_6. The dosage is from 50 to 350 milligrams per day. The symptoms can take from four to eight weeks to begin to subside, but in my experience, there is relief with this treatment. There have been reports of people self-medicating with B_6 at 2,000 milligrams and causing numbness and tingling of the nerves; however, up to 400 milligrams is thought to be safe, and even for people using 2,000 milligrams, the symptoms subsided on stopping the medication. I recommend B complex along with the B_6 to prevent an imbalance from using one B vitamin alone.

Other recommendations include calcium and magnesium for the pain and the nervous system, and possibly vitamin B_{12} injections. A multiple vitamin and mineral supplement might also be useful. For overweight women with this condition, I recommend a weight-reduction program.

Another possible cause might be food allergies leading to fluid retention, which then swells up the band of skin covering the carpal tunnel. Read the section on allergies on page 6.

Cataracts

This condition is a thickening and cloudiness of the lens of the eye. Some people feel that this is due to a toxicity in the body and a buildup of oxidation products in the lens. Microwave radiation has been known to cause cataracts, so be careful of microwave ovens. Substances that will detoxify and prevent these oxidation products are bioflavonoids, vitamin E, calcium and magnesium, B complex, and vitamin C.

Chronic Fatigue Syndrome

This condition has been called many names: Epstein-Barr syndrome and yuppie flu; the British call it myalgic encephalomyelitis (ME); but it is commonly referred to as chronic fatigue syndrome (CFS). ME is actually the most accurate name, because it identifies the muscles and brain as the target sites of symptoms. It appears to be a reactivation of an already present mononucleosis-like virus called Epstein-Barr. Up to 90 percent of the population have antibodies to Epstein-Barr, meaning they have had a previous infection. Chronic fatigue seems to be a reactivation of this virus. To most people, it seems like a normal cold or flu. Sometimes primary infection is a severe monolike infection and if the virus is re-activated, it can leave you feeling extremely fatigued and run down.

Symptoms include chronic headaches, swollen glands, periodic fevers and chills, muscle aches and pains, muscle weakness, sore throat, and numbness and tingling of the extremities. The general feeling is one of incredible fatigue, inability to do even the simplest of tasks, and an inability to cope with any stress. The cognitive dysfunction seems to be the worst part of the illness. You can't seem to write or do math or remember even the simplest things. Pain is another key to diagnosis. The pain can be anywhere in the body and often leads to multiple investigations and even surgeries in search of the elusive cause. Fibromyalgia, which means pain in the muscles, can be a complication of CFS. It seems to be due to toxins that deposit in the muscles, causing inflammation and pain. Read the section on fibromyalgia on page 80 for more information. According to allopathic medicine, in order to be diagnosed with true chronic fatigue you have to have the above symptoms for six months.

We still don't know exactly what causes CFS, but my theory is that the population as a whole, and our immune systems specifically, are excessively stressed with hundreds of drugs and chemicals in our bodies, air, water, and food; a highly refined, nutrient-poor diet; electromagnetic radiation from trillions of machines and appliances; and a focus on material and not spiritual gain. In this toxic soup of an environment, perhaps latent viruses are reactivated, and the body is not strong enough to fight them off. The toxins continue to build, and the pain and fatigue become chronic. Allopathic doctors are trying to find the one cause of chronic fatigue and the one prescription drug that will "cure" it. That's why they have such trouble with multifactorial conditions; they are used to researching one symptom at a time. In most cases of chronic disease, this tunnel vision gets us nowhere.

A composite of the typical person diagnosed with CFS is a female, thirty to fifty years of age, who works with the public as a hospital worker, teacher, or flight attendant. She is extremely overworked, was recently immunized, traveled abroad, was exposed to parasites, had surgery, has taken a lot of antibiotics over the years, and developed chronic candidiasis. She has a history of mononucleosis in her teens from which she never recovered, and developed allergies and chronic sinus and bladder infections. When she took the birth control pill, she developed chronic yeast infections.

This is much like the picture for chronic candidiasis, but there is more immune system depression, and with the potential underlying viral infection, there is a low-grade fever and much more fatigue. When the immune system is compromised, the normal yeast in the intestines overgrow, invade the surrounding intestinal mucous membrane, and cause irritation and inflammation, setting up a "leaky gut," which allows absorption of partially digested foods, which in turn creates allergic reactions. Also, an environment that favors *Candida* also favors parasites; instead of your body eliminating parasites as foreign agents, they find a home in your intestines and begin multiplying and producing toxins. Read the sections on candidiasis on page 40 and parasites on page 133 to see how to treat these conditions.

A diagnostic clue to CFS is total collapse after exercise even in its mildest form. Exercise usually helps people who are depressed and fatigued but not someone with CFS.

If you have CFS, you have probably been investigated and told that there is nothing wrong with you. Then comes the prescription for Prozac or Zoloft and a referral to a psychiatrist. It can be depressing in itself to realize your doctor doesn't believe that you are as sick as you feel. CFS is not a psychological illness, but it can be very depressing when your condition is not understood. An interesting aspect of the chronic fatigue state is the amount of time people, in general, spend worrying and thinking about problems, worrying about the past, worrying about relationships, worrying about money, or even just thinking about what they did yesterday. All this time invested in thoughts of the past means some of your energy is unavailable to you in the present;

this can be very draining. Imagining that you are well and joyful and taken care of can help attract those blessings to you.

There is no specific treatment for CFS but I suggest plenty of good, healthy, organic food to avoid pesticides and other chemicals. Check the section on diets on page 181 to determine your own regimen based on blood types. Avoid all food additives and chemicals in your diet. Aspartame (Nutrasweet) is known to cause fatigue and should be avoided. Read the section on sugar and aspartame on page 185 for more information.

Obtain your supplements from a natural source and take B vitamins, magnesium, vitamin C, a multiple vitamin, and trace minerals. Evening primrose oil and cod liver oil or fish oils seem to work to stabilize red blood cell membranes and treat the inflammatory aspects of the disease. I would also add echinacea, an herbal antibiotic that can be taken periodically during flu epidemics to avoid reinfection. Read the sections on candidiasis on page 40 and parasites on page 133 to learn if you might be suffering from these infections as well.

As I mentioned, exercise can be debilitating, so wait until you feel a little stronger from eating a better diet and taking supplements. Then start walking—even just a few steps a day—and build up slowly.

There may be homeopathic remedies that can help, but if your vital force is very low, homeopathic remedies might create a healing reaction that can make you even more fatigued, so they should be taken under the supervision of a homeopath.

Cold Extremities

Cold extremities are often due to poor circulation, yet many people who experience this condition exercise heavily. Other reasons might be low thyroid or low blood sugar. Refer to the sections on hypothyroidism on page 103 and hypoglycemia on page 102. In a food therapy book I am writing with Jeffrey Yuen, Director of the Swedish Institute School of Acupuncture and Oriental Studies, New York, Jeffrey talks about the cooling effects of a strict vegetarian diet, especially a raw-foods diet. If you are a strict vegetarian, you might have to cook more of your food and eat more spicy and warming foods.

Colds and Flus

These conditions are the body's way of eliminating mucus. They are usually preceded by excessive eating or poor eating habits, lack of rest, overwork, worry, or temperature changes as in the fall and spring. First of all, eat wholesome foods and get enough rest. At the onset of seasonal weather changes, take hot and cold showers to acclimatize the skin. Short thirty-second blasts of cold will do.

If a cold or flu begins, don't fight it and don't get angry. Take some time off, rest, and heal. If you go to work, you just end up infecting everyone else. If you take a lot of medications, you just put more toxins into your system, and the drugs won't really help. If anything, they suppress the condition and drive it deeper into your system, so it potentially can come back later in a more virulent form.

- Stop all sugar, dairy, and wheat to decrease mucus and don't eat heavy foods such as meat.
- Don't smoke.
- Take plenty of fruit and vegetable juices and chicken broth.
- If there are no contraindications, use a warm-water enema with the juice of one lemon to pull out toxins.
- Take Epsom salts baths, 2 cups in hot water, to open pores.
- Wear lots of clothing layers to encourage sweating and wrap a scarf around your throat.
- Wear a hat at all times to avoid the possible loss of 40 percent of your body heat.
- Use a vaporizer; mucus can collect at night if the air is too dry.
- Do chest clapping to loosen mucus in the chest.
- Take supplements such as vitamin C and vitamin A daily and suck on zinc lozenges.

Herbs useful for a cold are sage tea for cough (steep twenty minutes); fenugreek tea for mucus (steep five minutes); ginger grated and boiled, 2 tablespoons in 3 cups of water, gargle and use as a poultice by saturating a hand towel and wrapping around the throat, changing when the poultice becomes cool. Use garlic or echinacea herbal antibiotics as tincture, tablets, or teas at least three times a day; mullein and lobelia for chest congestion, ½ teaspoon each in hot water three times a day. These herbs can also be used as a chest poultice for pleurisy, pneumonia, or bronchitis.

Of course, if a painful sore throat or a cough persists, phone the doctor and get a throat swab or sputum culture to identify the bacteria, which may require antibiotics. When taking antibiotics, always take yogurt tablets or acidophilus, both of which are found in health food stores. These replace the good bacteria that the antibiotics kill.

To prevent germs from spreading to others, cover your mouth when coughing, don't use cloth handkerchiefs, and wash your hands before touching other people or their possessions. Also, replace or boil your toothbrush so you won't reinfect yourself.

For specific homeopathic remedies for colds, read part 4. The most common cold remedies are Gelsemium 6 or 12C, 4 drops every two hours for colds and flus due to overwork and exhaustion, and Dulcamara 12C, every two hours for colds and flus developing at the end of summer and into fall. Aconite can be used for the first signs of a cold or flu. Ferrum phos. is also used for the beginning of a cold. Kali bich. is used for colds and sinusitis with tough, stringy mucus. Hepar sulph. is used for a left-sided sore throat with a cold. Pulsatilla is used for a cold with thick yellow mucus. Oscillococcinum has undergone clinical trials for the treatment of colds and flus and comes through with flying colors. Considering that flu vaccines have side effects and the flu can cause considerable distress, it is important to have a safe remedy in the medicine cabinet.

The postinfluenza sequelae are becoming just as important as the original flu itself. In a homeopathic newsletter, Dr. Ben Goldberg lists some remedies:

For Gastrointestinal Symptoms

Antimonium crudum:	For digestive upsets from the flu. Thickly coated white tongue, aversion to food, worse from eating, worse with acidic or sour drinks. Fullness in the abdomen.
Kali bich.:	Heavy mucus, poor digestion, anorexic but craves beer.
Baptisia:	After the "stomach flu."

For Asthenia, Lethargy, and Weakness

Aurum metallicum:	Depression, weakness, hopelessness, brooding, melancholy. Thoughts of suicide, easily annoyed.
Cadmium metallicum purum:	A newly proven remedy for severe postflu depression.

Cocculus indica:	Mental and physical despair, slow recovery. Anorexia, insomnia, empty feeling. Sick headaches. Aggravated by motion, which may cause nausea and vomiting.
Picric acid:	Inability to think, as it causes headaches. Patient lies around as the least mental or physical exertion causes extreme weakness.
Phosphoric acid:	Debility and mental exhaustion, poor recovery with weakness, indifference, apathy.
Kali phos.:	Used by some physicians as a general "pick-me-up" for the depleted state following a viral illness.
Carbo. veg.:	Carries the reputation of treating "persons who have never recovered from the effects of some previous illness."
Scutellaria:	For nervous weakness after influenza, called nervous fear.

Cold Sores

This condition is also called herpes I. The herpes virus, both orally and in the genital region, sits on the nerve root underneath the skin and will be reactivated under times of stress; in women, premenstrually when the hormones are elevated or if stimulated by sun or heat. The preventive treatment is to avoid stress and too much sun on the skin, and to maintain an excellent diet and good exercise and sleep habits.

Prevention also includes using a sunblock such as zinc ointment on the lips. Zinc solution applied at the beginning of the tingling stage can speed healing. So can ice, witch hazel, or alcohol to decrease inflammation and help dry it up. You may have to boil or replace your toothbrush after the blister stage so you won't be reinfected. Some people find that two days after the cold sore is at its peak, another one pops up nearby.

When cold sores appear, begin taking lysine, an amino acid that retards the production of RNA, which is the building block of viruses. Lysine comes in 500-milligram capsules; take two capsules three times a day. The foods that contain lysine are fish, chicken, lamb, milk, cheese, beans, brewer's yeast, bean sprouts, fruits, and vegetables. Eat as much of these foods as possible during an outbreak. Arginine is an amino acid that can lower the levels of lysine. Therefore, cut down on these foods: carob, chocolate, gelatin, coconut, oats, soybeans, peanuts, wheat germ, and whole wheat flour. It is not that these are bad foods, but they provide the wrong balance of amino acids during this condition. In fact, if your diet is mostly arginine-containing foods and you are subject to herpes outbreaks, it would be a good idea to stop them for a while and see if your condition improves.

The best supplements to boost the immune system to treat herpes are B_6, B_{12}, folic acid, and pantothenic acid, all available together in a B complex. Calcium and magnesium, selenium, and zinc may be taken in a mineral complex; vitamins A and E can be found in a multiple vitamin complex.

The herbs for herpes include lemon balm (*Melissa officinalis*) and St. John's wort. Since 1978, lemon balm has been investigated as an external antiviral for herpes. It can be used as a cream made with a concentrated extract of 0.7 gram of the leaves, applied two to four times per day; or you can make a strong tea from 2 to 3 teaspoons of finely cut leaves in ½ cup hot water; cool and apply with a cotton ball several times a day. The research on St. John's wort as an excellent antiviral has been buried under all the data reporting its beneficial effects for mild to moderate depression.

The first homeopathic remedy for cold sores and also for genital sores is Herpes 200c, 4 drops three times a day for three days only during an outbreak. The second remedy is Natrum mur. 12C, 4 drops three times a day for one week after finishing the three days of Herpes 200c. Many people have found relief and if not a cure, certainly a decrease in outbreaks by using this treatment.

If there is a stress pattern or particular timing to your herpes, take lysine and more vitamin supplements around those times.

Colic

This is a smooth muscle spasm in the intestinal tract of infants caused by stress, air swallowing, or overfeeding. During a colic attack, carry the infant face down along your forearm with its head in your hand and its legs astride your elbow. This puts comforting pressure on its rumbling abdomen.

Colicky babies may need to be burped more than most and doing so relieves gas buildup. In fact, any rhythmic motion, in a car, a swing, or being carried, seems to give some relief.

Colic is also related to the stress and anxiety of the parents. A baby picks up on their nervousness immediately so parents under stress should seek help.

The formula may be at fault (see the section on baby feeding on page 156). If the infant is breast-fed, colic may be caused by the mother's diet. Breast-feeding mothers should avoid dairy products and any foods that are bitter or gas forming. If this does not relieve symptoms, the baby can be given a dilute tea or tincture of catnip or fennel. Fresh parsley tea can also be used; the dosage is 1 teaspoon of the herb to 2 cups of boiling water; let steep for fifteen to twenty minutes. When cool, give this to the infant in small teaspoons.

The homeopathic remedies for colic are Chamomilla 12C, 4 drops every few hours for fussiness and irritability, and Aethusa 12C for colic from sensitivity to breast milk; give this three times a day. Magnesium carbonate 12C and Magnesium phosphate 12C can be used for colic that seems to be better with heat and pressure, 4 drops three times a day. If symptoms persist, seek the advice of a doctor or pediatrician to make sure there is nothing more serious going on.

Colitis

Colitis is a bowel inflammation causing diarrhea. The most common cause appears to be improper food digestion, which can be brought on by a terrible junk-food diet or an intestinal infection. After the original irritation is created by a bad diet or infection, the foods that are most difficult to digest are wheat and dairy. Other substances such as cigarettes, alcohol, coffee, tea, sorbitol, and aspartame sweeteners are also implicated in bowel irritation. Another cause of colitis with diarrhea is a deficiency of digestive enzymes.

Infection can begin with sudden onset of diarrhea and can be due to bacteria, parasites, or yeast. Such infections occur commonly when traveling. A stool sample will sometimes indicate the culprit. It is very difficult to identify parasites or even *Candida albicans* from a stool sample, however. Specialized laboratories that cater to naturopathic or complementary medicine practitioners are often better equipped to find an underlying infection in cases of colitis than the local lab. They will also do sensitivity testing on the organism and indicate what medication (alternative or drug) will combat the infection.

To rule out any underlying pathology, your doctor may recommend a bowel x-ray using barium chalk and a fiberoptic examination of the colon. If nothing is wrong with your intestines, you must research dietary causes of colitis.

The first step is to avoid wheat, dairy, sugar, tea, coffee, red meat, and all food additives, especially aspartame (NutraSweet). Maintain this diet for at least one month to determine if your diet is causing your problems.

Most often people improve on this regimen. If you don't, or if only minor improvement is noted, you might have to avoid even more foods and perhaps have food allergy tests to determine the offending foods. These tests are available through complementary medicine doctors.

Elaine Gottschall has written a book called *Breaking the Vicious Cycle*. In it, she proposes that the underlying cause of intestinal inflammation and irritation is the improper breakdown of carbohydrates. Her Specific Carbohydrate Diet excludes all grains for at least one year and she claims many anecdotal successes. It is used for ulcerative colitis as well as Crohn's disease. Her book should be read by anyone with intractable colitis before resorting to surgery and strong cortisone medication.

A lactose tolerance test can determine a lactose allergy but will not indicate an allergy to any other constituents of milk. The best advice is to eliminate milk for at least two to three weeks to see if there is a change. You can also be allergic to wheat; this is often due to the gluten in wheat. Gluten is also found in oats, rye, and barley, however. This means that all four grains should be entirely eliminated for at least a month and then challenged back with several meals of gluten grains to determine if reintroduction causes more symptoms. We also find a lot of people with symptoms of colitis or irritable bowel who have an overgrowth of *Candida* in their systems. Candidiasis must be treated; read this section on page 40.

You may be suffering from a diet change that is putting too much roughage into your intestines. In trying to improve your lifestyle, you add more whole grain cereals and breads, vegetables, and beans. These foods can cause gas and cramping in the intestines on the basis of roughage and not because you are allergic to them. If this is the case, just cut back on the roughage.

Keep a food diary. Take yogurt or acidophilus to build up the good bacteria in your intestines.

Food combining is often very helpful in calming down an irritable bowel. You eat only one to two types of food at a time so that your digestion is not stressed. The simple rules are:

1. Eat fruit alone.
2. If you eat protein such as meat, fish, chicken, eggs, or cheese, eat it with leafy salad vegetables only.
3. If you eat grains or bread, eat them with root vegetables and beans.

Sometimes, in spite of numerous dietary interventions, medications, and doctor's visits, symptoms remain. Consider seeing a specialist in behavior modification. You may have developed a pattern of diarrhea and cramps under stress and specific triggers that perpetuate the problem. Each time you worry, "What if there's no washroom where I'm going, what if I can't get through my presentation?" you set off your intestinal muscles, and cramps and diarrhea result. Just as you learned how to create these symptoms, you can unlearn them.

Constipation

This condition has been alluded to in several previous sections and will be discussed again in the section on detoxification on page 178. Constipation can occur for many reasons; for instance, from poor bowel habits learned at an early age (for example, young children who fail to evacuate the bowels when they have the urge). Over time, the bowel message to evacuate is lost and the feces must build up and cause greater and greater stimulation before evacuation occurs. Sometimes it is as simple as the child not wanting to interrupt play to go to the bathroom. Parents should encourage regular bowel habits. Over time, this condition can become more serious and chronic.

One to three bowel movements a day is normal. It is the lack of fiber in our diets that makes us so sluggish. Some consider a bowel movement every three to four days normal, but this is a very dangerous concept to entertain. The longer undigested or discarded food matter remains in the large intestine, the more it putrifies and creates harmful wastes that can be reabsorbed into the bloodstream. These toxins and poisons can circulate in the bloodstream, affect the liver, and cause dozens of symptoms such as headaches, fatigue, itchy skin, insomnia, irritability, and joint stiffness. Some of these poisons are even carcinogenic.

The causes of constipation include sensitivity to certain foods such as dairy. If you drink a lot of milk, avoid it for a few weeks and see what happens.

Medications including antidepressants, codeine, certain calcium supplements, and aluminum antacids are constipating. Always take calcium with magnesium, and drink lots of water. Try to avoid the other medications.

Lots of fiber should be ingested; types of fiber are wheat, oat and rice bran, vegetables, whole grains, nuts, and seeds. Psyllium seed powder or capsules plus lots of water can be added for extra bulk. The dosage is 1 teaspoon shaken in 8 ounces of water followed by an additional 8 ounces of water taken twice a day. A little juice can be added for taste. Two extra glasses of water a day can increase your bowel movements. If you use psyllium and do not use extra water, you can actually cause constipation.

Castor oil packs can be placed on the abdomen to help stimulate lymphatic circulation of the bowel. Massage can be used; massage of the large intestine is done by massaging upward on the right side of the abdomen across to 2 inches above the umbilicus and downward on the left side of the body.

Exercise is very important for speeding up bowel transit time. The beet-transit test is an excellent way to determine how regular your bowels are. Eat a big meal of beets—three medium-sized steamed beets for lunch or early dinner. Within twenty-four hours your stool should be colored beet red. Your urine might even turn pink. Watch for a purple stool; most calls to doctors' offices about blood in the stool are really due to beets. If the red color does not come through for several days, this indicates constipation.

There are many homeopathic remedies for constipation. These can be used for a short time to stimulate the body's own vital force to improve this condition. People who need the remedy Nux vomica have a constant ineffectual urge to defecate. This remedy is also used when the stool is incomplete and unsatisfactory, as though some were left behind. This can be taken 12C, 4 drops two to three times a day for two or three weeks to see if symptoms improve. This remedy is also useful as an antidote for purgative medicines that have been used for a long time to treat constipation.

Sulphur can be alternated with Nux vomica. Sulphur treats an ineffectual urge to defecate with a sensation of heat and discomfort in the
rectum and an uneasy feeling all through the intestinal tract due to gas
and bloating. The stools are hard, dry, dark, and expelled with great
straining and often with great pain. Sulphur can also treat constipation
alternating with diarrhea. Use 12C potency, but only for a few weeks at
a time, 4 drops two to three times a day. The most commonly used
remedies are Alumina, Bryonia, Lycopodium, Natrum mur., and
Graphites. They should be studied to see if they fit your symptoms.
Most of these remedies are described in part 4 of this book.

Dandruff

Dandruff is a very common condition. It is due to buildup of skin cells
on the scalp caused by excessive oiliness. Shampoo the hair every day.
If you use over-the-counter dandruff shampoos, rotate them: some
loosen the flaky skin, some are antibacterial, some decrease the rate at
which the skin cells of the scalp reproduce, and the tar-based ones actually retard cell growth. Doctors used to tell patients that it was okay
to use cortisone creams because they were not absorbed by the skin;
now there is a multimillion-dollar market for various types of medicated skin patches. It is extremely important to only use skin and hair
products that are natural and nourishing because they will be absorbed
into the body. One of the pioneers in natural skin and hair products is
Aubrey Hampton. Aubrey's Organics are 100 percent organic; organic
products only have to be 70 percent organic to be called organic
legally! Apparently Australia's organic standards are much higher than
ours; there is a flurry of activity from Down Under as Australian companies compete for the organic market in America. I find that when
people eat a healthy diet, which includes plenty of vegetables, fruit,
whole grains, nuts, seeds, fish, and chicken, they rarely have dandruff.
Supplements that help the skin, hair, and nails include flaxseed oil,
which can be taken in salads or on hot cereals, evening primrose oil,
zinc, B complex, vitamin A, cod liver oil, and multiple vitamin and
mineral supplements.

Natural rinses for the hair include apple cider vinegar after a shampoo (¼ cup in a pint of warm water). This solution restores the natural
acid mantle of the scalp and retards dandruff. Thyme tea helps dan-

druff; it has antibacterial properties. Make a solution of thyme tea in a quart of water using several tablespoons of thyme; boil for one hour, strain, and use 1 cup of the tea over the hair after shampooing. Leave on the hair and don't rinse off.

Remember that dandruff may just be a symptom of a more general imbalance in the body, and in order to treat any symptom, we must consider treating the whole body.

Depression

Depression can have multiple causes and multiple treatments. As in all other conditions, good nutrition, proper vitamin supplementation, exercise, and sleep are the basis for any natural approach. Frequently, people facing major stress or grief are unable to sleep and will stop exercising and eating properly. This causes a vicious cycle of improper care of their bodies and can prolong their problems or deepen their depression.

Try not to get too discouraged about feeling low; this will only make you feel worse. Try to exercise or go out and do something fun, especially with other people. Sharing your dreams with a friend or counselor can often help you understand why you're depressed. You may be stuck somehow or you may be in conflict. Talking about it usually helps.

Adolescent depression can accompany the normal youth rebellion. This rebellion often takes the form of not following parental guidelines for diet, sleep, and exercise. Young people eat a large amount of refined foods, fast foods, sugar, and general junk food. This can create a zinc deficiency in the system, and low amounts of zinc can cause mood changes. Also, high sugar intake can deplete vitamin C and the B vitamins, necessary for proper mood balance. If young people take supplements, get enough sleep, exercise, and have a good diet, they can often reverse the symptoms of minor depression.

After pregnancy, women may suffer from postpartum depression. This can be treated with high doses of zinc, 50 milligrams daily for one month, then 25 milligrams daily. Ignatia 12C, a homeopathic remedy for postpartum depression, is extremely useful. The usual dosage is 4 drops three times a day. The B vitamins and multiple vitamins as well as calcium and magnesium in equal amounts can be helpful. It is important to continue these supplements while breast-feeding for proper nutrition.

The biggest news in the treatment of depression in the last several years is St. John's wort (at 0.3 percent Hypericin) for mild to moderate symptoms. In Germany a whopping 50 percent of prescriptions for depression are for St. John's wort. Sexual dysfunction is the major reason why people discontinue prescription antidepressants and why St. John's wort is so popular. Up to 70 percent of people on Prozac, both male and female, experience sexual problems including loss of libido, inability to achieve orgasm, and in men, loss of the ability to have an erection. So St. John's wort, with no history of side effects, becomes an attractive option. Another viable option for depression is tryptophan or its precursor, 5-hydroxytryptamine. Tryptophan was a top seller for the treatment of depression and insomnia when a batch of tryptophan contaminated by a genetically engineered bacterial process caused thirty-six deaths in 1989. Tryptophan was erroneously blamed, and to this day it remains off the market. Prozac came along at the same time. Unfortunately, many people have committed suicide and homicide while under the influence of Prozac and other serotonin-reuptake inhibitors (Zoloft, Paxil). The extremely safe 5-hydroxytryptamine occurs one step after tryptophan in neurotransmitter metabolism and one step closer to serotonin; it is legally available and may be even more effective than tryptophan for treating depression and insomnia. It is not genetically engineered but extracted from the African plant *Griffonia simplicifolia*, and produces a much higher level of serotonin than tryptophan.

Other reasons for depression can include cerebral allergies from food or chemical sources, hypothyroidism, hypoglycemia, and candidiasis. Read the sections on these topics to familiarize yourself with these conditions.

Diabetes

Diabetes is a chronic degenerative disease of high blood sugar that damages many body tissues including the eyes, kidneys, heart, blood vessels, and nerves and inhibits metabolic processes, such as the blood's oxygen-carrying ability. When diabetes occurs in children (Type 1 diabetes), it is usually due to damage to the insulin-producing islet cells of the pancreas, perhaps from a virus. Without insulin, the blood sugar rises out of control. Insulin's job is to open up all the cells in the body to allow blood sugar to enter and be used for energy. Most diabetes is found in adults (Type 2 diabetes), often from an overuse of sugar and simple carbohydrates throughout life. The older you get, the more likely you will acquire diabetes as insulin becomes either overworked or overused and is no longer effective in pushing blood sugar into the cells. This inability to transport sugar into the cells is called insulin resistance; the cells don't respond to insulin in the normal way. The result is high blood levels of sugar and insulin.

Several mechanisms contribute to insulin resistance; one of them is the type of fat you eat. Insulin resistance increases with consumption of omega-6 fatty acids and saturated fats from animal products and improves with consumption of omega-3 fatty acids, flaxseed, and fish oils. Too much insulin can stimulate the growth of breast cancer. Insulin levels are high in women who are overweight, particularly if they carry their weight above their waists. Contributing factors to high insulin levels include overconsumption of sugar and carbohydrates with a high glycemic index, lack of exercise, and excess saturated fat and omega-6 EFAs.

In addition to a high simple-carbohydrate diet, obesity, allergies, viral infections, and stress from surgery are prominent causes of diabetes. Up to 80 percent of adult-onset diabetics are obese. Recent reports indicate that adult-onset diabetes is on the rise in obese children, probably from overuse of simple carbohydrates and sugar since birth. The incidence of adult-onset, or Type 2, diabetes has increased a startling 30 percent from 1990 to 1998. Scientists claim they are mystified as to why this is happening because they are married to the notion that sugar is not harmful and the worst it can do is cause dental decay. Sugar is big business and pays for university research; many people won't bite the hand that feeds them, no matter how unethical or how sweet the taste.

Chronically high insulin levels themselves lead to obesity. When insulin is high and the cells are still responding, it pushes excess sugar out of the bloodstream, sugar levels drop, energy drops, and you crave more carbohydrates to bring your blood sugar levels back up. Children with high insulin levels will usually maintain those levels throughout life until insulin resistance develops. Insulin resistance increases with overuse of sugar and simple carbohydrates, lack of exercise, and high intake of omega-6 fatty acids such as margarine and animal fats, and improves with a diet low in white sugar and white flour products and high in omega-3 fatty acids, flaxseed, and fish oils.

Treatment for Type 1 diabetes is by insulin injection because there is very little insulin produced at all. Moderate exercise and an excellent diet low in white sugar and white flour will help reduce insulin requirements, however.

The focus of treatment for Type 2 diabetes should be diet. Diabetic pills to whip up more insulin are on the market and readily prescribed. They merely stimulate the pancreas to produce even more insulin, however. They do not treat the underlying condition by any means. It is still crucial to follow a diet low in sugar and simple carbohydrates and take the pills only on a short-term basis to help control blood sugar levels.

When native populations are studied before and after the introduction of refined foods, we find that diabetes was nonexistent before and rampant after the population began eating refined sugar and white flour. It does not take a rocket scientist to figure out that diet is the cause. I have seen kidney dialysis machines in Native American villages where the diet is mainly white bread and white sugar, and diabetes runs amok. It is also unfortunate that certain Native American tribes are studied like guinea pigs as scientists search for the gene responsible for diabetes when all people need to do is stop eating refined foods.

Don't be seduced by so-called research telling you that sugar is okay for diabetes; it is not, it is poison. Read the sections on sugar addiction on page 4 and sugar and aspartame on page 185. Another product undermining our health is aspartame, an artificial sweetener (NutraSweet). This substance is used in over 9,000 diet products and, according to knowledgeable medical doctors, it worsens diabetic control. Since it contains wood alcohol it poisons nerves, including the optic nerve (already sensitized by high blood sugar levels). The two amino acids used to synthesize aspartame are neurotransmitters that cause sugar cravings. These are only a few of the ninety-two side effects caused by this chemical poison.

In many instances, diabetes is either acquired or made worse by specific food allergies. These allergies create elevated blood sugar, which causes additional strain on the body's insulin supplies. Therefore, allergy testing is probably a good idea. See the section on allergies on page 6. My father developed adult-onset diabetes after the stress of surgery. I told him to avoid wheat and, when he did, his blood sugar was normal. After a second surgery the next year, he fell into the hands of a hospital dietitian who put him on a diabetic diet that allowed six slices of bread a day! Since he loved bread, he went right ahead. His blood sugar rose higher and higher and he ended up on diabetic pills. When I urged him to go off the bread again, his blood sugar returned to normal.

If you assume that your diabetes is incurable and you will need pills or insulin for the rest of your life, and you do not want to change your diet, then the diabetic industry is playing your song. If you want to take charge of your body and get it back to health, however, avoid sugar and look into allergies. Take a blood sugar test or do a finger stick reading after a meal containing one of the following: bread, dairy, vegetables, meat, fish, or fruit. You can thus determine which foods raise your blood sugar and which ones don't. Then you can eat more of the ones that don't.

As you can tell, I'm very concerned about the epidemic of diabetes. I did a search on amazon.com for books on sugar and on diabetes. I found only a few books about the dangers of sugar and simple carbohydrates, but there were literally thousands of books on diabetes and diabetic diets. It seems we just keep treating the symptoms and never want to acknowledge the cause.

There is a lot of talk about glycemic index, which is the rate at which carbohydrate foods (sugar, grains, beans, vegetables) break down and enter the bloodstream as blood sugar. Foods such as concentrated glucose have a high glycemic index and cause a rapid elevation of blood sugar; this stimulates the pancreas to produce insulin, and the excess that cells do not use is stored as fat. Foods with a low glycemic index are broken down more slowly and provide the body and the brain with a sustained energy level. Processed foods, refined white flour, and sugars have a high glycemic index; foods high in natural fiber have a low index. Sucrose, or table sugar, has a moderate glycemic index; this gave researchers the necessary ammunition to say that sucrose is okay for diabetics because it stimulates less insulin than glucose. This is another example of how a half-truth can mislead us. Sucrose is a disaccharide, which means it is made up of two sugars, glucose and galactose. It takes some time for the disaccharide bond to be broken, and so blood glucose does not rise as fast or as high as with a meal of straight glucose. But it doesn't make sucrose any less a sugar or any less dangerous for diabetics. Read the section on sugar addiction on page 4 for the real reasons why sugar is bad for you.

The best diet for diabetes includes daily portions of dried peas and beans in soups or stews; whole grains (avoiding wheat); bran, especially oat bran; lots of vegetables, preferably raw or lightly steamed; deep-sea fish; chicken, turkey, and lamb; and one or two pieces of fruit a day. Fruit juice is too concentrated in fruit sugars for diabetics and is just as harmful as refined sugar and white flour. Check out the section on diets on page 181 for what diet would be best for you and tips on increasing the fiber in your diet without getting gas.

Supplements for balancing blood sugar include chromium, which has a glucose tolerance factor; B complex and B_{12} injections to heal nerve damage caused by excess sugar; vitamin C with bioflavonoids to fight infection and for wound healing; zinc for wound healing; and calcium and magnesium. Because high sugar levels stimulate *Candida* overgrowth, take garlic as an antifungal and acidophilus, a good bacteria for the intestines. Read the section on candidiasis on page 40.

Diaper Rash
(See **Baby Tips,** page 160)

Diarrhea

For more information on this topic, read the section on colitis on page 52. Diarrhea can occur due to infection from bacterial sources, viral sources, or parasites, and is often called gastroenteritis. It can also be due to food poisoning or food allergies. With an acute onset of diarrhea, it is important to have stool tests performed in a laboratory for proper diagnosis. See a doctor immediately if there is blood in the stool. If no organism is identified, or while waiting for diagnosis, you can try the following program:

1. Avoid all dairy products, because the enzymes for the digestion of dairy are usually flushed out or otherwise unavailable. Thus, these foods can be irritating to the bowel and may prolong the diarrhea.
2. Avoid citrus and acidic fruits, which can irritate the bowel.
3. Drink lots of vegetable broth, which is high in potassium and natural minerals, to replace fluid and mineral loss. Broth can be made from celery, zucchini, beets, carrots, beet greens, or

chard; be careful to avoid sulphur-containing vegetables such as broccoli, onions, and cabbage because of their strong taste. This broth can be seasoned and taken throughout the day.

4. Intestinal flora must be replaced with good bacteria, such as acidophilus.

5. One product that absorbs toxicity is bentonite. It is a liquid clay with a very large surface area; take 1 tablespoon three times a day in water or juice.

6. Take the powder or capsule form of psyllium seed to absorb the liquid contents from the intestines and bulk the stool. Take 1 teaspoon shaken in a jar of water or two capsules twice a day with only a small amount of water.

Diarrhea can start with food poisoning or an infection; the mechanism of the bowel is to flush out the irritants with diarrhea. So diarrhea, in fact, may be a beneficial elimination of the infection. It is best not to medicate it for twenty-four to thirty-six hours. Following the advice given here will make sure it runs its course but is not prolonged. If the diet is not optimum or includes a lot of dairy and acidic fruit, the condition can continue. If you have an irritable bowel already, or if the bowel is subject to stress, it can sometimes lead to intense investigation that may be worse than the condition.

Some people, after antibiotic therapy, develop *Candida albicans*–related diarrhea episodes that may be very difficult to control. The treatment for this form of diarrhea is a yeast-free diet and the use of acidophilus to replace the good bacteria. In some cases, testing must be performed for yeast in the stool and blood. *Candida* antibody levels may be checked to determine the extent of the *Candida* and the appropriate antifungal medication needed. Refer to the section on candidiasis on page 40 for further information regarding this condition. If strong medications are needed to treat diarrhea, remember to follow up with acidophilus and an excellent diet so that the medication will not leave an imbalance of the intestinal flora.

Digestive Disorders

You may eat an optimum diet, but there is still the question of proper digestion and absorption of those foods. As we learn more and more about the various digestive processes and how they can go wrong, we are better able to educate people on digestive problems. The most important factor in digestion is proper food selection. The second most important aspect is proper chewing. If you chew each mouthful of food thirty to forty times, this stimulates the salivary amylase in the mouth and one-third of the digestion will be done there. If you hold cooked grain in your mouth long enough, it will become sweet. This is the action of the amylase breaking down the carbohydrate into glucose.

The action of chewing also stimulates stomach acid production. If you are under stress or are generally tense, the stomach muscle, like any other body muscle, can go into spasm. This spasm can cut off blood circulation in the stomach and decrease production of hydrochloric acid. This reduction in stomach acid can lead to improper or incomplete breakdown of stomach contents, especially protein. If this incompletely digested food finds its way into the intestines, the intestinal flora will feed on this food and create gas and bloating. Incomplete protein digestion can be diagnosed by a urine test called urine indicin. Most alternative medicine doctors are aware of this test, which is done in specialty labs (see the Resources section for more information).

The third most important aspect of digestion is avoiding water with a meal. Washing down each bite with water dilutes the gastric acid and leads to incomplete digestion, pushing food out of the stomach too soon. It also causes fats and oils in the food to cling together, which impedes their absorption. You may drink water ten minutes before or three hours after eating.

After the stomach, the food passes into the small intestine, where bicarbonates neutralize the pH and allow pancreatic amylase to further break down carbohydrates. Also, bile is excreted into the small intestine to emulsify fats. If there is insufficient amylase, carbohydrates will provide food for microorganisms of the gut. Carbohydrates can also become fermented in the intestine to the point that alcohol and aldehydes are produced, which, in the extreme case, may cause someone to appear drunk. If the fats are not absorbed, the stool is bulky and floats.

In treating digestive disorders, one important thing to look for is chronic stomach spasm or hiatus hernia. The stomach lies central and to the right of the abdomen directly under the sternum, which joins the ribs. If that area is hard and painful, the stomach may be in spasm. The stomach can push up between the diaphragm and even restrict the movement of the diaphragm, leading to shortness of breath or inability to take a deep breath. The pain can travel around to the back and up the front of the chest. Often, there is a reflux of acid up the esophagus because the normal sphincter between the esophagus and the stomach is stretched. The treatment for this condition is traction massage on the stomach to relax the stomach and pull it down into its proper position. Many children have this condition after vomiting. Adults who do too many sit-ups get it and women during pregnancy are susceptible, as are people with constipation, which puts more pressure on the stomach. Generalized tension in which the breathing is high in the lungs and the person is afraid or in a constant state of "fight of flight" can cause the stomach to be "hiked up."

To treat or avoid hiatus hernia or stomach spasms:

1. Avoid coffee, tea, and alcohol, which relax the sphincter between the stomach and esophagus.
2. Avoid sit-ups or do modified sit-ups. To do a modified sit-up, sit on a mat with your knees bent and back straight. Fold your arms over your chest, lean back a few inches, and sit up. Choose the number of repetitions that is best for you.
3. Do not lie down after a meal.
4. Do not drink a lot of liquids with meals.
5. In the morning, to settle the stomach in proper position, drink a glass of water, rise up on your toes, then thump down on your heels about ten times.
6. Have a professional massage your stomach hard and down and to the right to try to release the spasm; often you will hear a gurgle as stomach contents that have been trapped are released.

To treat digestive disorders, chew your food well, eat when calm, drink no more than 4 ounces of liquid at each meal so that the gastric juices are not diluted, and eat an optimum diet. If food allergies are suspected, follow the advice in the section on allergies on page 6 regarding food avoidance and food challenging or obtain food allergy tests. Candidiasis can also cause a lot of gastrointestinal upset. Read Dr. Trowbridge's book *The Yeast Syndrome* or Dr. Crook's book *The Yeast Connection,* and refer to the section on candidiasis on page 40.

Homeopathic remedies for digestive disorders include Nux vomica and Lycopodium; these can be used in the 12C potency but should be prescribed by a homeopath if they are to be used for a long period of time. Herbal remedies include Swedish bitters and mint teas. Gas with a foul odor is relieved somewhat by taking charcoal tablets. This substance absorbs toxins in the intestines and they are eliminated from the body.

Diverticulosis

Diverticulosis, a disease of the large intestine that is a direct result of a refined-food diet with a lack of fiber, is becoming almost epidemic in so-called civilized countries. Fiber is extremely important in the large intestine because it provides the bulk against which the intestinal muscles push out the waste products of digestion. If there is not enough bulk or fiber in the intestines, the areas between the muscles start to form tiny pouches, or sacks, which are called diverticuli, along the outside walls of the large intestine. When there is a lack of fiber in the large intestine, the liquid matter of the intestinal contents tends to be more completely absorbed back into the body; thus, the fecal matter becomes drier and harder. As the muscles of the large intestine try to force the hard material along and out the anus, they have to exert more and more muscular force. With all this excess (and often ineffective) pressure, constipation results and, with time, the areas between the muscles weaken and create pouches or sacks bulging out the whole length of the intestinal wall. The diagnosis can be made on barium enema x-ray. In a small percentage of people with diverticulosis, these little diverticuli can become inflamed, leading to lower abdominal pain. This is called diverticulitis. The best way to treat both of these conditions is prevention. Obviously, the first treatment is fiber. Dr. Dennis Burkitt, the "grandfather of fiber," has proved over and over again that people in countries where a high-fiber diet is maintained do not suffer conditions such as diverticulosis. The types of fiber available are bran fiber, oat fiber, and rice fiber. Of course, vegetables and fruits have a high fiber content, as well as a high water content. When you take fiber, you must increase your liquid intake—six to eight glasses of water per day is the usual recommendation. If food fibers are difficult to tolerate, or if you need extra fiber outside of the diet, psyllium seed powder or capsules are available. Once again, make sure your liquid intake is sufficient. Some people have actually made themselves more constipated by not taking enough liquid with psyllium. Beans, barley, and legumes are excellent sources of fiber. When you use these foods, be sure to soak them, replacing the water several times over a twenty-four-hour period to reduce their gas-forming potential. People with diverticulosis, and especially diverticulitis, have a lot of problems with gas pains.

Avoid processed foods and concentrate on high-fiber foods. Watch out for gas-forming foods. Check your tolerance for dairy products, and even whole wheat, to which many people are allergic or sensitive. To do this, avoid the food for a couple of weeks and then reintroduce it back into your diet. Check the sections on digestive disorders on page 63 and food allergies on page 6 for more information on these topics.

Seeds, nuts, and popcorn, especially if they are not chewed well, can be a problem for people with diverticulosis. Most people do not realize they should be chewing thirty times per bite to make sure food is completely broken down before it gets to the stomach. Do not smoke or drink and avoid caffeine. Exercise is also very important, as it stimulates the muscles of the intestines and eases bowel movements. See the section on constipation on page 54 for more information.

Dizziness

When you have a flu or cold, you can feel dizzy. If your blood sugar is low, or if there is a lack of circulation to the inner ear, it can lead to dizziness. The first two conditions can be ruled out by your doctor by examining the ear canal or eardrum, taking a history for a recent cold or flu, doing blood sugar tests, and making sure your diet is optimal to avoid low blood sugar. Dizziness due to inner ear problems should be investigated by an ear, nose, and throat specialist, a neurologist, or a vascular specialist. In older age groups, arteriosclerosis can cause hardening of the arteries and cut the circulation to the brain, leading to dizziness. Read the section on atherosclerosis on page 19.

If these conditions are ruled out and dizziness still persists, avoid mucus-forming foods such as sugar, dairy, and wheat and use teas such as fenugreek that thin mucus that may be blocking the eustachian tubes; this is taken 1 teaspoon to a cup of boiling water steeped for five to seven minutes. A homeopathic remedy called Kali mur. 12C, 4 drops three times a day, can be used for eustachian tube blockage. For dizziness itself, Bryonia can be used 12C, 4 drops three times a day.

Dyslexia
(See **Hyperactivity,** page 95)

Earaches

Earaches can be very frightening, especially in children, because the pain can be intense. Ear infections can be dramatic and parents and doctors are afraid of eardrum damage, so ear infections are often treated with antibiotics. Ear infections develop behind the eardrum from a mucus fluid buildup in which viruses or bacteria may overgrow and begin to cause pressure and inflammation. For any ear pain or suspicion of an ear infection, consult a doctor.

Not all earaches are due to bacteria; in fact, most are viral induced and self-limited. A 2000 review of thirty-six years of ear infection studies was sponsored by the Federal Agency for Healthcare Research and Quality. It found that almost two-thirds of children with acute ear infections recover from pain and fever within one day of diagnosis without antibiotics. A full 80 percent recover in one to seven days. The report also found that amoxicillin, the treatment of choice for many years, was as effective as newer and more expensive antibiotics that cause more side effects.

Some people feel that recurrent ear infections are due to food allergies. Often avoiding milk, peanut butter, and orange juice, the main culprits, can diminish or stop the infections.

Dr. Michael Schmidt, in his book *Healing Childhood Ear Infections,* gives a complete list of allergens to avoid. These include dairy products, wheat, eggs, chocolate, citrus, corn, soy, peanuts, shellfish, sugar, and yeast. What's left? Lamb, rice, squash, carrots, potatoes, chicken, and applesauce. After being on this diet for three weeks, introduce one food at a time. That one food should be eaten several times in one day along with the allowed foods. If there is an allergy, it shows up with obvious symptoms.

A wide variety of local treatments can be used while waiting for the doctor. Some midwives suggest that squirting breast milk into an infant's ear can give relief. Herbal remedies include dilute mullein oil, oil of cajeput, or tea tree oil. All these oils are diluted 1 part oil to 3 parts safflower oil and dropped into the ear. Of course, if there is an ear discharge, drops should not be used until a doctor is consulted.

Homeopathic remedies depend on the symptoms. A red-hot throbbing ear calls for Belladonna. Earache in a fussy, irritable child suggests Chamomilla. A splinterlike earache from the throat into the ear requires Hepar sulph. Use the 12C potency, 4 drops every half hour until the condition subsides. Read the section on homeopathic remedies on page 191 and obtain a homeopathic reference such as *Family Homeopathy* by Dr. Paul Callinan to have on hand for emergencies. It is also important to have a homeopathic first aid kit to use until you can get to the doctor. Michael Schmidt's book, *Healing Childhood Ear Infections: Prevention, Home Care, and Alternative Treatment,* has an excellent section on homeopathic remedies for earache. He includes Aconite, Belladonna, Chamomilla, Ferrum phos., Hepar sulph., Lycopodium, Mercurius, Plantago, Pulsatilla, and Silica. Most of these medicines are listed in part 4 of this book. A quick read can give you an idea of which remedy fits your child. You can also consult my book *Homeopathic Remedies for Children's Common Ailments,* or you may be interested in ordering homeopathic kits from companies such as Boiron. See Resources under "Homeopathy," page 220.

Eczema

Eczema is a chronic skin condition that can range from wet blisters to dry flakes. It is usually itchy and can occur on any surface of the body. It is most commonly associated with allergies, contact or ingestion, and is usually aggravated by stress. First, you must track down the allergic factor by avoiding and challenging soaps, clothes, jewelry, and certain foods. You might also investigate and treat candidiasis, which can cause or aggravate any skin condition. Once the offending substance is removed, the skin should normalize.

Most eczemas are dry. The best treatment for dry eczemas is to lubricate the body with cod liver oil. Don't put it on your skin; take it internally, 1 teaspoon or one capsule per day. Take it with meals and avoid water with your meals so that the cod liver oil and fats and oils in your food will be absorbed properly. Water in the stomach along with oil will cause the oil globules to combine together in an oil puddle, which the body will have trouble absorbing.

Avoid showers, because they strip the acid mantle of the skin. Use ¼ cup apple cider vinegar, a few drops of bath oil, and a cotton pouch of oatmeal in the bath. Clay is also helpful in a bath to treat eczema. Dry indoor air is bad for eczema; use a humidifier and external creams and lotions from organic sources. Avoid wools and use cottons. Make sure the soap you use does not irritate the skin. Do several rinse cycles on your laundry and don't use scented antistatic products in the dryer.

Supplements that promote healthy skin are evening primrose oil, flaxseed oil, and zinc. This is in addition to a multiple vitamin and mineral supplement containing vitamin A and the B vitamins.

Using cortisone creams for eczema just suppresses symptoms. If infant or childhood eczema is suppressed, the child may later develop other manifestations of allergies such as asthma. Therefore, it is important to determine and treat the cause of any new skin condition.

There are many homeopathic remedies to treat skin such as sulphur for burning, red, itchy, unhealthy-looking skin; graphites for oozing, crusty skin; petroleum for dry, cracked, rough skin; or Mezereum for painful, small bumpy eczema that is not on the face. These remedies should be properly studied and researched before using. If they do not work after a short time, a homeopath or naturopath should be consulted. If cortisone has been used for a long time, the skin may go through an aggravation or worsening before getting better. (Read the sections on allergies on page 6 and candidiasis on page 40.)

Edema

Edema is a buildup of fluid underneath the skin in the interstitial spaces between cells of the muscles and other body tissues. This area normally holds fluid as it travels between the cells and the lymphatic circulation. The lymph is an extremely important system that carries all liquid waste away from the cells, runs it through the body, and deposits it in the cisterna chylae underneath the right upper ribs. From there, the wastes go into the bloodstream and then are excreted, usually through the kidneys into the urine or through the skin or the bowels. If the lymphatic system is overloaded or clogged with too many wastes, edema can build up. With age and gravity, the lymph vessels are broken down and fluid falls to the feet, as in very old people who have swollen ankles.

The lymphatic circulation depends entirely on exercise and movement in order to pump the lymph up to the chest. There are specialists who do lymphatic massage. It is a very delicate massage that consists of light brushing of the skin in the direction of the flow of the lymph from the feet up to the chest, and from the tips of the fingers up the arms to the chest, from the abdomen down to the groin. The motion is brisk and light.

Edema in women most often occurs before the menstrual period, as hormones cause the body to retain fluid. This can be diminished somewhat by avoiding salt and sugar, which also contribute to fluid retention in the body. Diuretic herbs are parsley, watermelon seeds, uva ursi, and nettles. These can be taken in herbal tea form. Combine two or more of the above herbs and use 1 teaspoon per cup steeped for at least ten minutes. A large amount can be made at once and reheated or taken at room temperature. Actually, cool or cold teas have a greater diuretic effect than hot teas, which induce sweating. Vitamin B_6 taken a week before the period will also act as a natural diuretic. (Read the section on premenstrual syndrome on page 135.)

Emphysema

This condition can only be treated by prevention—in short, no smoking. Smoking creates a breakdown of the structure of the lung in the alveolar areas; destruction of alveoli leads to empty spaces in the lungs so air exchange can no longer occur. The treatment, once this condition has occurred, includes avoidance of allergens. Stay away from strong smells and scents. Exercise is important, especially walking and swimming.

The shallow fast breathing of emphysema may create a pulling up of the stomach, creating a stomach spasm or hiatus hernia. Learn yogic breathing; when you inhale, let your abdomen rise so that your diaphragm falls. This opens up the lungs to full capacity and massages the stomach in place.

Don't eat large meals. This puts pressure on the diaphragm. Eat small frequent meals and try to keep an optimum body weight.

Most communities have lung rehabilitation facilities that perform physiotherapy, teach people exercises for the lungs, and demonstrate the use of oxygen in the home.

Oxygenating vitamins and minerals can be used; for example, vitamin E, selenium, evening primrose oil, beta-carotene, and vitamin A. Check with your doctor regarding supplementation. Various algae and green products have been getting a lot of attention. These nutrients are good oxygenators, high in nutrients, and readily absorbed.

Endometriosis

The incidence of endometriosis is on the rise. This condition is caused by endometrial tissue, which normally lines the uterus, growing outside the uterus in the pelvic cavity. It can grow along the bowel, on the ovaries, along the fallopian tubes, or around the ligaments that support the uterus. If you have endometriosis, every month when you normally have your period, this endometrial tissue will also swell and bleed, but this blood has nowhere to go, and it stays in the pelvic cavity and causes a buildup of scar tissue. The symptoms are extremely painful periods, low back pain, painful bowel movements, and pain on intercourse.

There are many theories as to why endometriosis occurs. Tampons are a possible contributor to this condition. It is therefore advisable to use sanitary napkins; try to choose ones that aren't bleached with chlorine.

Constipation is an obvious stimulus to abnormalities in the pelvis. Toxic debris adjacent to the uterus and ovaries can tax the lymphatic drainage in the pelvis and lead to incomplete surveillance and removal of endometrial implants by the body's immune system. Detoxification is very important in endometriosis. I have found a product called Herbotox by Seroyal, which contains a combination of cleansing herbs very useful for my constipated endometriosis patients. Study the sections on detoxification on page 178 and constipation on page 54.

Endometriosis may, in fact, be an immune system deficiency. Apparently, most woman have some endometrial tissue growing in the wrong place; yet when the abnormally placed endometrial tissue bleeds, their immune systems are able to remove the debris quickly, and there is no accumulation, buildup, or scarring. An inability of certain white blood cells to engulf and eliminate foreign material may be a cause of fibrocystic breast disease as well.

During my clinical practice, I referred patients to Dr. William Ghent in London, Ontario. He was involved in some fascinating work using aqueous iodine for the treatment of fibrocystic breast disease. Dr. Ghent found that supplemental iodine stimulates the peroxidase enzymes in white blood cells which require chlorine or iodine to activate them. Activated white blood cells then become very effective in chewing up fibrocystic scar tissue in breasts and miraculously did the same thing to endometrial scar tissue. Dr. Ghent's aqueous iodine is undergoing clinical trials and will be available in the near future to treat fibrocystic breast disease and possibly endometriosis once the daily dosage and duration of treatment is defined. Dr. Ghent's patient population also had a very low incidence of breast cancer, which made me aware of the value of appropriate iodine supplementation. Natural iodine is available in various seaweeds: dulse, wakame, nori, and kombu. There are many different forms of iodine, so it is best to vary your sources and seaweeds in stews or soups, as wraps for sushi, or just eaten plain.

A good diet can also boost the immune system. Avoid caffeine, alcohol, and sugar. Eat an optimum diet of vegetables, fruit, whole grains, nuts, seeds, legumes, fish, and chicken. Fish is especially important because fish oil has anti-inflammatory properties.

Menstrual pain is treated medically with antiprostaglandin drugs, which suppress the prostaglandins that cause cramping. But natural prostaglandins found in fish oils can be just as effective. Prostaglandins that reduce cramping are also available in the form of evening primrose oil, which has proven effective in the treatment of endometriosis.

Important supplements include calcium and magnesium, which have natural anticramping properties; vitamin E, which is also useful for endometrial scarring; B complex, which is naturally calming and relaxing; and natural multiple vitamin and mineral supplements. Other recommendations include castor oil packs. Castor oil has been proven to enhance lymphatic clearing of toxins. It is used externally; an old hand towel or facecloth or layer of flannel is soaked with castor oil, wrung out and placed over the abdomen, covered with another towel, and topped with a heating pad or hot water bottle. If this treatment is done for at least an hour on a daily basis, there can be a great reduction in pain. This probably helps to stimulate the lymphatic system to clear away the menstrual discharge that occurs in the pelvis.

I have found that acupuncture helps endometriosis. This leads me to believe that there must be a degree of energy blocking in this area that would be worth exploring with someone who does body work.

The incidence of female sexual abuse, both physical and verbal, is higher than anyone is willing to admit. Inappropriate sexual behavior of an older individual, verbal or physical, with a young girl can set up fear and tension focused on the pelvic region that can lead to lifelong physical and sexual symptoms. If the emotional tension cannot be expressed freely, if the child is not protected from the abuse and is afraid to tell anyone, then physical symptoms become an outlet for the emotional pain. Pelvic tension can lead to painful periods and possibly endometriosis. Read the section on anxiety on page 14 for a description of EFT for abuse and trauma.

Homeopathy treats the physical as well as the mental and emotional symptoms. Staphysagria is the foremost remedy for treating abuse. It is best to work with a homeopath for the treatment of chronic conditions.

Epilepsy

Epilepsy is a recurrent condition of the brain, in which the firing of disordered electrical impulses is caused by one or more of the following: scar tissue due to trauma, creating a focus of irritation in the brain; imbalance of neurotransmitters; toxic chemicals, including alcohol and aspartame; medications and street drugs; vitamin or mineral deficiencies; hormonal imbalance; and low blood sugar. In infants, birth trauma, lack of oxygen, and fever are the main causes; the developing brain usually grows out of this condition. The effect on the body can be seen in extension and contraction of the arms and legs as in grand mal epilepsy (also called seizures or convulsions), or abnormal movements of the lips and staring of the eyes and loss of time in petit mal epilepsy. Often, investigations such as CT scans or brain scans find no abnormality, yet the symptoms still occur.

Diet and environment are the first things to examine. The most common causes of seizures are low blood sugar and stress. When I was in practice, occasionally someone who came in for a fasting blood sugar test would have a mild seizure because her blood sugar was low, plus she was afraid of needles. The combination of the two stresses can trigger an episode. This does not constitute epilepsy, which is a recurrent condition. Epilepsy is potentially dangerous; when seizures recur, you are usually put on antiseizure medication and adults may lose their driver's licenses. Therefore, it is crucial to explore all the possible causes.

Low blood sugar can lead to a decreased supply of glucose to the brain and trigger an epileptic episode. Eat small frequent meals of vegetables, fruit, complex carbohydrates, and protein and avoid sugar, alcohol, and food additives. Read the section on hypoglycemia on page 102.

Medications and food additives can directly stimulate seizure activity. The most notable chemical in our environment that causes seizures is aspartame (NutraSweet). It contains two amino acids that can act as powerful neurotransmitters, and wood alcohol, which is a neurotoxin causing blindness. There is concern about the phenylalanine in aspartame because of a condition called phenylketonuria (PKU) in which certain individuals who are not able to break down this amino acid develop mental retardation. It is diagnosed at birth and a phenylalanine-free diet is mandatory. Because we have no way of knowing who will be diagnosed with PKU at birth, pregnant mothers should not take anything containing aspartame.

In a 1969 study, seven infant monkeys were fed aspartame mixed with milk. One died after 300 days and five others experienced grand mal seizures. Despite this and dozens of other negative studies—such as reports that as little as one stick of sugarless gum can cause seizures in children—aspartame was pushed onto the market. Read more in the aspartame section on page 185 and don't give it to children or anyone who has seizures or epilepsy. Because aspartame has ninety-two different side effects, it is worthwhile to avoid it altogether for at least sixty days and see for yourself if you feel better without it.

Monosodium glutamate (MSG) is a food additive that makes things taste fresher and richer. It is used widely in the food industry to supplement bland foods. Up until a few years ago, it was even added to baby food. It is a potent neurotoxin and many people react to it. I feel my jaws tightening and pressure in my temples when I forget to ask about it in restaurant food. MSG can be broken down by vitamin B_6 and people with B_6 deficiency are most susceptible to its effects. Dr. John Olney, a neuroscientist at Washington University in St. Louis, found that MSG created lesions in certain regions of the brain that are not protected by the blood-brain barrier.

Since drugs and toxins are implicated in epilepsy, it is important to begin a detoxification program using Epsom salts baths and saunas. Read the section on detoxification on page 178.

There is some anecdotal information that mercury amalgams used in dental fillings might contribute to seizure activity in an individual sensitive to mercury. Read *It's All in Your Head* by Dr. Hal Huggins and make up your own mind whether to have your mercury amalgams replaced. Be aware, however, that there is a strict protocol for removal that prevents even more toxins being released.

Mineral deficiency has been implicated in epilepsy. With our food grown on mineral-depleted soil, unless we buy organic produce from mineral-rich areas we are all becoming mineral deficient. Levels of magnesium, manganese, zinc, and calcium should be investigated using hair analysis from a reliable lab ordered by a natural health practitioner. Vitamin supplements for epilepsy include B complex, B_6, folic acid, B_5, B_{12}, and choline.

Trauma is one of the predisposing factors to epilepsy. Immediately after any head injury, take homeopathic Arnica, vitamin E, and selenium to prevent bleeding, shock, swelling, and scarring that can occur inside the skull and go undetected.

The amino acids taurine and tyrosine are being studied for their antiepileptic properties. Please consult with a knowledgeable practitioner before using amino acid therapies.

An herbal treatment for epilepsy due to whiplash with consequent congestion of cerebrospinal fluid is black cohosh (Cimicifuga) in tincture form, 10 drops in water two or three times a day. Herbs such as hops, valerian, and skullcap are useful for their calming effect on the central nervous system and might be able to lower the seizure threshold. These teas can be taken in combination or as single herbs two to three times a day.

Birth trauma has been implicated in some forms of epilepsy. An assessment by a craniosacral therapist on a newborn could be very helpful to determine whether the sutures of the skull bones are jammed after a particularly difficult birth. Craniosacral therapy and chiropractic adjustments for spinal misalignment could be beneficial for adults with epilepsy, but be sure to find someone who has experience and success in this area.

Eye Problems

Good eye health depends on your general health. One of the highest concentrations of vitamin C in the body is found in the vitreous part of the eye. According to Chinese medicine, berries have an affinity for the eyes and they also tend to have a lot of vitamin C.

Red eyes can be infected or allergic. In a bacterial infection, the discharge tends to be yellow and sticky and the eyes are itchy and sometimes painful. At this point, treatment may require a sulpha or other antibiotic eyedrop, which in some cases must be applied every two hours around the clock to keep the proper concentration of drugs in the eyes. Otherwise, you just blink away the drops and the infection can come back.

In a viral infection, the discharge may be more watery. A painful eye with a watery discharge can be a herpes infection with a blister in the eye. A doctor must use a special light called a slit lamp to check your eyes for a herpes blister or a scratch or abrasion that has become infected.

To treat an eye injury caused by a scratch or abrasion, an antibiotic cream and a forty-eight-hour eye patch are used to heal the abrasion and prevent bacterial infection.

An eye allergy can be caused by external stimuli such as dust, pollens, and animal dander. Besides avoidance, you can treat the symptoms with herbal eyebright (euphrasia), homeopathic Similasin, or Optique Eye Drops from Boiron; all are available in your local health food store. Sometimes a mild eye infection responds to these remedies.

Tired, overworked eyes can be soothed with used or weak chamomile teabags. Remember, chamomile is in the ragweed family and if you have allergies to ragweed, you should avoid chamomile. Squeeze out the extra liquid and put the tea bags on your closed eyes while still warm but not hot. People with sensitive eyes should avoid chlorinated swimming pools.

Fatigue

One of the most frequent complaints brought to doctors by their patients is fatigue. The causes of fatigue are multiple and can include allergies, anemia (from iron, copper, or B_{12} deficiency), iron overload (hemachromatosis), chronic fatigue syndrome, recurrent mononucleosis, hepatitis, hypoglycemia, hypothyroidism, candidiasis, depression, insomnia, and stress. You can read about most of these conditions in various sections of this book.

Fatigue can make you too tired to exercise, which perpetuates the vicious cycle because exercise can banish some forms of fatigue. You should be content with nothing less than optimal health and should strive to obtain this with an excellent diet, good sleep habits, and regular exercise. Research and investigate the above conditions with your doctor in order to determine the cause of your fatigue.

Fever in Infants
(See **Baby Tips,** page 160)

Fibrocystic Breast Disease

Estrogen dominance before the period can cause breasts to be tender. If breasts are also lumpy, they are given the name fibrocystic breasts. But this is not really a disease and is not associated with breast cancer. Overweight women have too much estrogen in general and this can stimulate the breasts. Women on the birth control pill can be affected by the daily estrogen stimulation and may have to find another form of birth control.

Other factors that promote fibrous tissue in the breasts are salt, a high-protein diet, too much meat and dairy, and theobromine and methylxanthane in coffee, tea, and chocolate. A diet high in whole grains, vegetables, and beans and low in animal fat, especially a week or ten days before the period, helps the body excrete estrogen. Such a diet can also help with weight loss in general, especially in women who are not carbohydrate sensitive. Read the section on diets on page 181 to understand if you are carbohydrate sensitive. Detoxification and treating constipation can decrease the severity of fibrocystic breasts. Read the sections about these conditions in this book. Avoid tea, coffee, chocolate, and cola for at least three cycles to see if there is any improvement.

Oral aqueous iodine supplementation may help treat fibrocystic breasts. The mechanism, according to Dr. William Ghent of Ontario, Canada, is stimulation of the peroxidase enzymes in white blood cells to chew up foreign material, such as the scar tissue formed in the breasts by fibrocystic disease. There are ongoing clinical trials that will determine the form and dosage of iodine; this may constitute a major breakthrough in the treatment of this condition.

Other nutrients used for this condition include evening primrose oil and vitamin E. Vitamin B_6 is helpful, especially taken before the period when there is fluid retention and the breasts swell due to stimulation from the rising level of hormones. The treatment of premenstrual tension and candidiasis are also important in relieving painful fibrocystic breast disease. Read these sections in this book.

Naturally extracted progesterone is available in topical cream form to counter estrogen dominance. There are some over-the-counter brands, but only certain brands contain active progesterone. It is wise to consult your naturopath or nutritionally oriented doctor for special saliva tests to determine if you are estrogen dominant and to prescribe an active form of progesterone.

Fibroids

This is a condition of benign overgrowth of an area of muscle in the wall of the uterus. Almost a quarter of the female population has some fibroid growth by age forty, and by age fifty, up to half do. This is not a precancerous condition and the majority of fibroids do not cause any symptoms at all. But a large fibroid can stretch the uterus lining, which can cause heavy bleeding, back pain, cramping, and bloating.

We don't know very much about fibroids, except that estrogen stimulates their growth because they arise during the reproductive years, worsen during pregnancy, and regress after menopause. The allopathic treatment is usually just symptomatic; there is no medication for fibroids and a hysterectomy is usually advised if bleeding or pain are debilitating. Some feel that there are far too many hysterectomies for fibroids and that more attention should be paid to the cause; if surgery is recommended, only the fibroid should be removed, not the entire uterus and certainly not the ovaries.

Nonsurgical treatment is difficult to delineate because there is very little research on fibroids. What we do know is that fibroids are stimulated by excess estrogen and lack of progesterone. So, any treatment that lowers estrogen levels and raises progesterone is worth looking into.

A diet high in complex carbohydrates such as grains, nuts, seeds, and legumes helps reduce the body's estrogen levels. Such a diet is also low in saturated fat, and fat seems to elevate estrogen levels. Fat also stores endocrine-disrupting chemicals that can cause elevation of estrogen and stimulate fibroid growth. There is some controversy over whether it's wise to use soy if you have fibroids. According to Tori Hudson, N.D., soy phytoestrogens do not have an estrogenic effect on the uterus. She says soy foods may be part of a new class of drugs called selective estrogen receptor modulators. They act selectively, and it seems that, in the uterus, soy isoflavones have an antiestrogenic effect. Read the section on soy on page 184.

Dr. Hudson recommends inositol and choline to promote the removal of fat from the liver. Nick Gonzalez, M.D., uses a pancreatic enzyme treatment for eliminating cancer tumors. Similar results may result from using pancreatic enzymes in benign tumors such as fibroids. To work best, they are taken between meals.

Unsaturated fatty acids such as evening primrose oil and fish oils, as well as vitamin E and vitamin A, are recommended. These are taken in conjunction with a good multiple vitamin and mineral supplement.

Naturally extracted progesterone may balance the dominance of estrogen and inhibit the growth of fibroids. Yet, a report from Brigham and Women's Hospital in 1995 argued that progesterone itself may stimulate fibroids. Therefore, it is possible that some women may have more progesterone receptors in the uterus (as they may have in the breasts) than estrogen receptors that respond to excess progesterone by stimulating growth. There are reports of a handful of women who experience breast enlargement and fibroid growth after introduction of natural progesterone or synthetic progestins. Go slowly and be alert to changes, good or bad.

External castor oil packs can help the pain and congestion created by fibroids.

Fibromyalgia

Many rheumatologists and arthritis specialists don't "accept" fibromyalgia as a real disease and just consider it a painful condition of the muscles and surrounding fascia (fascia is a thin layer of tissue that encloses muscles and tendons). They say that fibromyalgia has no known cause and no known cure. Diagnosis is based on a chart of trigger points.

I consider fibromyaglia closely related to chronic fatigue syndrome and candidiasis. It seems to be the painful endpoint after years of stress, fatigue, infections, and a bad diet. Read the sections on chronic fatigue on page 45, candidiasis on page 40, and parasites on page 133, as well as allergies on page 6, hypoglycemia on page 102, diets on page 181, and detoxification on page 178. The toxins from viruses, yeast, parasites, and a bad diet find their way to the joints and muscles. The painful result, according to classical Chinese medicine, is actually accomplished in order to protect your internal organs from receiving the brunt of these pathogens. And it is also a wake-up call to reduce your various stressors.

Begin by cutting back the toxins you put into your body such as coffee, sugar, alcohol, and diet products sweetened with aspartame. You may be using them as stimulants to rise above your fatigue, but it's obvious that "what goes up must come down" and stimulants just make your life a roller coaster.

Do some stretching exercises to get the blood flowing into your muscles to move out some of the toxins. Sauna therapy is an excellent, relaxing way to sweat out toxins. See the description of how to take a sauna in the section on detoxification on page 178.

Diet is next. Add whole live food into your diet. Use bean sprouts and beet kvass, described on pages 177 and 178. Try to eat organic vegetables to avoid pesticides and herbicides and use hormone-free, antibiotic-free meat and poultry, depending on your blood group. Read the section on diets on page 181.

Supplements from natural sources are the easiest to absorb and assimilate. There are fantastic, elaborate, and expensive new supplements on the market. Start with the basics, however, to get a good grounding in all the essential trace minerals, vitamins, and nutrients from whole plant and animal sources. Read the section on supplementation in the Introduction.

When I was in practice, people would come to me at the end of a long journey of illness and doctor's visits. Whether they had candidiasis, chronic fatigue, fibromyalgia, or even HIV, their underlying problem was chronic infections. I spent the last seven years investigating solutions to these multiple layers of infections. The solutions include detoxification, diet therapy, and specific herbal formulations. In time, I will make the protocol available to the public.

Flat Feet

You have flat feet when the arch of your foot loses its elevation and touches the floor. People who have this condition can be miserable, with chronically sore and achy feet. You can diagnose yourself by stepping out of a pool or tub onto a surface that will show the outline of your sole. If the whole foot imprint shows, then you have flat feet. An elevated arch will not touch and wet the surface at all.

Flat feet seem to be hereditary and possibly can't be avoided. If children grew up wearing proper shoes with proper supports, this may be prevented. Sneakers with arch supports can help maintain good foot structure.

Podiatrists and some chiropractors offer orthotic devices to help people with fallen arches or flat feet. These are leather or plastic inserts that are placed in the shoe and are usually constructed from a mold of your foot. They are quite expensive, but some insurance companies cover them and for many people they are indispensable.

Gallbladder Disease

The gallbladder stores and concentrates bile that is used to emulsify fats. There is an intricate balance between cholesterol, lecithin, and bile acids in the production of bile. If the diet is high in saturated fats, then those fats that become liquid at 149°F and solid below that temperature will clog the bile flow and lead to a buildup of cholesterol and subsequent stone formation in the gallbladder. If there is insufficient lecithin, gallstones can also form. The pain from gallbladder attacks is from sludge or stones in the gallbladder that are trying to exit through the narrow bile duct under the stimulation of fat in the stomach. A fatty meal stimulates the gallbladder to excrete bile for fat digestion but will only cause pain if there are stones present.

An interesting avenue of research is the allergic component of gallbladder attacks. There are many people who have had gallbladder surgery but continue to have pain. Dr. Jonathan Wright, in his book *Dr. Wright's Guide to Healing with Nutrition,* has a section on foods that have been shown to stimulate gallbladder pain. Other than medications, the biggest offenders are eggs, pork, onions, fowl, milk, coffee, and oranges. Try avoiding these foods before having surgery. The treatment for gallbladder problems also includes avoiding animal fats and eating a more vegetarian diet.

There are many herbal remedies for the liver and gallbladder that can be taken in tea or tincture form. These include herbs such as burdock, parsley, garlic, onion, black Russian radish, and horseradish. Some doctors advise vitamin E, copper, taurine, and lecithin. A diagnosis of stones can be made by having a gallbladder ultrasound. If there are no stones, a gallbladder flush with a drink of olive oil and lemon juice might be helpful. This type of flush should be done under the supervision of your naturopath and only after you are sure there are no large stones that can get stuck in your common bile duct. This is a medical emergency and often necessitates surgery.

Gas

It's something we all have, some in more abundance than others. In certain people, gas results in belching, and in others it causes flatulence. Flatulence can occur due to lactose intolerance or as a result of eating various foods high in sulphur, such as the cruciferous vegetables (broccoli, brussels sprouts, cabbage, and cauliflower), onions, dried legumes, and wheat products. Sometimes it occurs because of poor digestion, ranging from improper chewing, to lack of hydrochloric acid in the stomach, to drinking too much water with a meal and allowing incompletely digested food into the intestines where gas-producing bacteria have a field day.

If you lack the enzyme to digest the lactose in milk, there are Lactaid enzymes that you can put in milk or take after eating dairy products to help you digest this food. Beans and legumes can be soaked for twenty-four hours, removing the water and replacing it several times to reduce the gas-forming substances. Beano is a product that also provides a missing enzyme and can be added to the first mouthful of a bean dish. Avoid foods to which you are allergic or sensitive. Eliminate suspect foods from the diet and then reintroduce them; see if flatulence returns to determine the foods you should avoid.

More fiber introduced into the diet for health reasons can actually promote gas because the body is not used to it. Go slowly when introducing fiber.

Treat gas with various products such as acidophilus bacteria. This is the good intestinal bacteria; if there is a proper amount of good bacteria, the gas-forming bacteria won't have as much chance to grow. Activated charcoal tablets absorb gases in the intestines and may treat symptoms. Bentonite clay absorbs gas. Again, gas is just a sign of a possible imbalance, so before using a remedy, try to get to the root of the problem and cure it entirely. Read the sections on digestive disorders on page 63, constipation on page 54, beet kvass on page 178, and detoxification on page 178.

Gout

In gout, uric acid builds up in the big toe. Gout has long been considered due to a high intake of heavy protein foods. Foods to avoid are coffee, tea, alcohol, chocolate, cocoa, wheat germ, pastries, cookies, cream, cakes, beef, lamb, pork, all fried meat, fried potatoes and potato chips, bouillon, consommé, meat stock, soups, gravy, and yeast. If this diet is strictly adhered to, the incidence of gouty attacks diminishes greatly.

For acute symptoms, soak the foot in Epsom salts and clay. Put a clay pack on the affected area to draw out the inflammation. Use ice, not heat, for relief and keep the foot elevated. Drink lots of water to flush out the uric acid.

Supplements that can help are cherry juice taken daily, folic acid, and B_{12} injections. The latter two supplements are given after B_{12} and folic acid blood tests are performed to ensure that these supplements will not mask an underlying condition of B_{12} deficiency called pernicious anemia.

Gum Disease

Gum disease, or gingivitis, may be the result of inadequate dental care. The teeth will build up plaque or tartar, another name for the food debris that coats the teeth, which becomes a breeding ground for organisms, usually bacteria. To deal with this plaque and tartar, brush and floss your teeth properly. Plaque can also occur at the gum line and cause irritation of the gums, leading to bleeding and infection of the gum line, pyorrhea, and receding gums.

The correct way to brush is with a soft toothbrush at a 45-degree angle to the gum line, using small side-to-side motions down the teeth, so that the gum and the tooth are both cleaned. Rinse with half water, half 3 percent hydrogen peroxide to remove bacteria from the mouth. Baking soda also works to change the pH of the mouth and create a less hospitable environment for bacteria. Eating raw vegetables can certainly help; they clean the teeth and stimulate the gums at the same time. Some people use oral irrigation units to flush debris away from the gums and teeth. Cigarettes and alcohol have a negative effect on the mouth and can also deplete your body's vitamins and minerals.

Gum disease is a precursor to osteoporosis in the jawbones, so calcium-rich foods are recommended: dark green leafy vegetables, nuts and seeds, sardines, salmon, and organic dairy products. If you take a calcium supplement, use it along with magnesium. Vitamin C and bioflavonoids are also recommended; one of the first signs of scurvy (vitamin C deficiency) is bleeding gums. Bioflavonoids are especially important for capillary healing.

What's missing in general recommendations concerning gum disease is the awareness that yeast organisms also make their home in the mouth. A coated white tongue or white patches along the inside of the mouth that can be scraped off indicate oral thrush. Yeast organisms will overgrow when sugar and alcohol intake are high and in people who use oral cortisones, cortisone nasal drops, or even cortisone air-puffers for asthma. It also occurs in those who take antibiotics.

Many dentists recommend antibiotics prior to teeth cleaning if you have mitral valve prolapse (MVP). More and more people are being diagnosed with MVP, probably because of increased use of ultrasound technology. It is unfortunate that so many people are being prescribed antibiotics to prevent the possibility of a very rare infection of the heart valves after dental work. I cannot tell you to avoid these antibiotics; each person has to decide for herself. Where there is a severe allergy to the recommended antibiotics, patients have used high doses of echinacea, 20 drops in 4 ounces of water, taken four times per day a few days before, and five days or so after dental work. (Please read the section on candidiasis on page 40 for more information about yeast overgrowth that can affect the mucous membranes of the mouth, just as it can the gastrointestinal tract and the vagina in women.)

I see cases in which people have thick, raw, beefy tongues; bleeding, sore, burning mucous membranes; and indentations along the tongue from the teeth. This condition responds to *Candida* treatment and B vitamins. Burning mouth syndrome can be amenable to B vitamins, but because *Candida* is often a factor, the B vitamins should be from a nonyeast source. Aspartame also causes burning tongue.

Parasites are another class of organism often forgotten by dentists and periodontists. These can only be seen by direct microscopy. Fresh swabs from the mouth must be viewed immediately under a microscope to see these organisms. Treatment is usually an antifungal agent; however, most oral antifungal agents are very harsh and there are many side effects, one of which is an overgrowth of yeast in the body. The most natural remedy for oral parasites is a new product in health food stores made from grapefruit seed extract. This extract is a very viscous liquid, the more thick and viscous, the stronger. It is extremely bitter, and sometimes, for intestinal parasites, it can be put in capsules, but for use in the mouth it must be dissolved in water, 2 or 3 drops in 3 ounces of water. Gargle and rinse the mouth for several minutes, but don't swallow the solution. Do this twice a day and you can probably eliminate parasites from the mouth.

The health of the whole body is important, because the cause of gum disease, or gingivitis, may be a deficiency of a number of vitamins or minerals. An optimum diet should be followed, including lots of vegetables, a moderate amount of fruit, nuts, seeds, whole grains, beans, legumes, fish, and chicken. Avoid sugar, alcohol, and coffee. Use the following supplements: vitamin C, calcium and magnesium, beta-carotene (very important for the mucous membranes), and a good multiple vitamin and mineral.

Hay Fever
(See **Allergies,** page 6)

Headaches

The most common types of headaches I see are hypoglycemic, tension, post-motor vehicle accident, migraine, allergic, and chronic fatigue headaches.

Headache is one of the many symptoms of hypoglycemia. (See that section on page 102 for a full discussion.) If a meal is skipped and the brain is deprived of glucose, a hypoglycemic individual will feel foggy or dizzy; if the warning signal is not heeded and food is still not eaten, a full-blown headache can result; some people get tension headaches and some get migraines. The treatment is obvious—keep the blood sugar up with small frequent meals and avoid sweets.

Stress headaches can start the vicious cycle to chronic tension headaches. Physical and emotional stress can both contribute. Physical misuse of the body, such as sitting too long at a desk without taking a break, can cause muscle cramping and tightening. Periodic stretching is recommended. Yoga is also an exceptionally good exercise to help keep the whole body flexible.

Poor sleep position can also lead to neck pain and consequent headaches. Lying on the stomach is especially harmful. Keeping the whole body in alignment is the key. The head should not be propped up on several pillows. You can purchase special neck posture pillows, or try rolling up a small soft towel and placing that under your neck with the back of your head on a flat pillow. If you lie on your side, the towel should be under your neck as well. Adequate support of the neck, in this way, prevents neck tension and spasm.

Emotional stress is a major cause of headaches. It can occur suddenly or creep up insidiously over time. Most of us have received some shocking news and immediately the heart raced, the adrenaline poured out, the blood rushed to our heads and pounded in our ears, and a headache was born. Crying often intensifies the pain, although for some it can release tension. Relief may come with a quick resolution to the situation, but if stress is ongoing, natural measures can be taken.

A cold pack on the forehead, eyes, and/or the neck relieve symptoms. A hot shower or soothing bath or footbath may calm the whole body, since headache is a whole-body reaction to stress. A neck and head massage is helpful and also comforting.

Chronic emotional stress can lead to chronic tension headaches, which must be treated more aggressively. Tension headaches can occur from a progression of long-standing muscle spasms of the neck and shoulders that over time begin to encroach on the muscles of the scalp. This causes pulling and strain on the scalp and also can begin to jam the underlying sutures of the cranial bones. Muscle spasms can be extremely powerful, to the point of actually dislocating bones. In the upper back and neck, a muscle spasm can cause rotation of the vertebrae of the neck or a rib dislocation and severe pain. A muscle spasm will create decreased blood flow in the center of the spasm. The lack of circulation will allow buildup of waste products in that area, which can lead to scarring and calcification. When a muscle spasm becomes chronic, it is called fibrositis, or fibromyalgia. The treatment of fibrositis is very deep muscle massage to try to break down the calcification, increase the circulation to the area, and return normal function.

TMJ, or temporomandibular joint syndrome, is a commonly overlooked cause of headaches. The joint between the cheekbone and the jawbone can be off balance and create constant pressure on sensitive nerves around the joint every time you chew or talk. Under stress and tension, you can grind your teeth at night, leading to TMJ. Holding your jaw open for long periods of time at the dentist can also cause this problem. Your dentist should be aware of this and allow you to take "jaw breaks" periodically if you are having a long treatment. Poorly aligned teeth, infection, or gum disease can also throw your "bite" off. Treatment for TMJ often involves wearing a specially molded appliance called a "bite plate" at night over your bottom teeth. This stops you from grinding your teeth and encourages relaxation of the jaw. See the section on temporomandibular joint syndrome on page 151 for more information.

Whiplash or other head and neck injuries can progress the same way. Treatment for these headaches begins with an optimum diet, adequate rest, gentle stretching exercises, massage, and sometimes deep massage for the calcified, scarred areas of the muscles, plus craniosacral massage if tension has jammed the cranial bones. Craniosacral massage is a highly specialized type of body work in which the practitioner must be able to feel and influence the subtle rhythms of the cerebrospinal fluid in the spinal canal and brain. Look for someone who is very skilled in this modality. A good treatment can release pressure and tension in the head and neck by an almost imperceptible movement of the cranial bones. Chiropractic adjustment may be necessary to release the cervical vertebrae, but adequate attention must be paid to the muscle component. It is often muscle spasm that is pulling the vertebrae out of alignment, and frequent adjustments are not going to help if the muscles are still in spasm. Some patients find that chronic neck and back problems after back injury are helped by cleansing programs such as aloe vera gel, 1 tablespoon each morning in juice or water. (See the section on detoxification on page 178.)

Migraines can be triggered by fluorescent lighting, especially if the lights are old and buzzing at a particularly nasty frequency. Light sensitivity, changes in vision, nausea, and sometimes vomiting that come before the pain, are called "the aura," which heralds a migraine attack. Therefore, a darkened, quiet room is helpful to reduce heightened sensitivity and lessen the severity of a migraine.

Research done in England on migraines shows that up to 85 percent of subjects become headache free with the elimination of cigarette smoke, pork, oranges, wheat, eggs, chocolate, dairy, sugar, beef, tea, and coffee. Avoid these possible allergens or irritants for a sufficient period of time to determine if they might be causing your migraines. Keep a food diary, since any food or additive could be the culprit. In fact, an insidious brain irritant in our food supply is aspartame (NutraSweet), which has crept into over 9,000 products worldwide. Among the ninety-two physical symptoms it causes, headache is number one. Anything labeled "diet" is suspect. Read the section on sugar and aspartame on page 185 for more information.

Inhaling chemicals that cause neurologic pain, or irritation of the mucous membranes of the respiratory tract, can also cause allergic headaches. Food allergies can create antigen-antibody complexes that circulate in the bloodstream and trigger reactions in the brain, causing spasm and pain. An allergic reaction to yeast and mold is a good example; their metabolic waste products include aldehydes and alcohol, which can cause severe headaches.

When diagnosing allergic headaches, the timing of onset is very important. If you only get these headaches in a particular environment or after a particular meal, you can begin to narrow down the causes and avoid them. If you eat the same things every day, you may build up an intolerance to these foods. Read the section on allergies on page 6 for a more in-depth discussion and to learn why you should rotate your foods.

Sinus headaches are often quite painful and difficult to diagnose and treat. During a cold, if bacteria take up residence in your sinus cavities, they can cause a swelling of the mucous membranes with a buildup of mucus and lots of painful pressure. If bending over makes the throbbing pain in the forehead and face worse, that is one clue to diagnosis. There are sinus cavities above the eyes, beside the nose, and in the cheekbones. Finger pressure over these areas usually elicits pain. Treatment for the underlying infection is aimed at draining the sinuses and eliminating the bacteria involved. This will resolve a sinus headache. Read the section on sinus infections on page 142 for a full discussion.

Remember, sudden onset of a new type of head pain, not relieved by sleep, which wakes you at night, or is associated with blood coming from the eyes, nose, or ears must be investigated immediately by your doctor.

Because headaches are most often a symptom of another health condition, treatments for headaches are varied and include investigating the various conditions mentioned above.

Lack of physical exercise, poor posture, and poor sleeping habits can all contribute to chronic headaches. Yoga is probably the best form of stretching exercise and can improve your posture. Sleep on a hard mattress and use a special pillow that supports your neck. The simplest treatment of all may be just to drink lots of pure water. Dehydration and consequent thickening of the blood can cause platelet aggregation and constriction of blood vessels leading to pain. Hydrotherapy in the form of swimming, whirlpools, hot baths, steam baths, and saunas help relax the body plus eliminate toxins that may be contributing to the pain.

Specific headache treatments include various vitamin, mineral, herbal, and homeopathic preparations. Vitamins C and E and niacinamide act as antioxidants and improve circulation. Calcium and magnesium relieve pain. The essential fatty acids found in evening primrose oil and fish oils are anti-inflammatories and stabilize the blood vessels.

Feverfew is the most notable herb used in the treatment of migraines. It appears to have anti-inflammatory properties and can be taken as a preventive on a daily basis. Dosage is two to six 300-milligram capsules per day. Attempts are being made to standardize it to 0.2 percent parthenolides or 125 micrograms of parthenolides per day. Culinary herbs such as ginger and garlic gently thin the blood and relieve platelet aggregation. Hops, valerian, and skullcap are relaxants and sedatives and in this way lessen pain. Specific herbs for pain in the head and neck are Cimicifuga and Pueraria. Herbalist Matthew Wood calls Cimicifuga the "whiplash remedy."

Homeopathy has a lot to offer a chronic headache sufferer. *Homeopathy for Musculoskeletal Healing*, by Asa Hershoff, D.C., N.D., is the best resource for homeopathic remedies. He recommends Cimicifuga for head and neck pain shooting down the left arm; Chelidonium for pain down the right arm; Bryonia for stiffness and pain in the neck and trapezius muscles; and Nux vomica for neck pain from the back of the head to the shoulder. The best potency to use is 12C in frequent doses (every few hours). If these remedies don't work within a few days, don't continue them on your own but have a proper consultation with a homeopath to find your constitutional remedy.

Heartburn

A protective muscular sphincter normally separates the esophagus and the stomach. If for some reason that sphincter is weakened, acidic stomach contents can be pushed up into the esophagus, causing burning pain. This is called "heartburn" because the area of pain lies close to the heart. People with heartburn can be misdiagnosed with angina or heart pain. It is also called gastroesophageal reflux disease (GERD).

The stomach lining is designed to handle very strong digestive acid, but the esophagus is not. A large meal can stretch the esophageal sphincter and allow a reflux of acid, especially if you lie down afterward. Avoid large meals, and don't lie down after eating. Small frequent meals move out of the stomach quickly and don't cause reflux.

The substances most apt to relax the esophageal sphincter are alcohol, coffee, tomatoes, tobacco, and physical factors such as bending forward while lifting (instead of bending at the knees), overdoing sit-ups, or going to bed shortly after eating. Stress can also weaken the sphincter because, under stress, we tend to breathe shallowly; this means that the diaphragm is not moving in a rhythmic motion that also massages the abdominal contents and keeps the stomach in place.

When you are under stress, the stomach and abdomen tend to get tense, which can lock the diaphragm in place so that it can't move with breathing, and the breathing is shallow. This can lead to stomach spasm, which can mimic a hiatus hernia and create problems with digestion. If you try to eat a big meal, spicy food, or a carbonated beverage when your stomach is in spasm, it will not be able to hold much and will start looking for a way out. If, at the same time, you're drinking coffee or alcohol, the esophageal sphincter will weaken, and the stomach contents will push up into the esophagus.

Another way heartburn can begin is after gastroenteritis with nausea and vomiting. When the esophageal sphincter opens up during vomiting, the esophagus may become irritated or burned, and the esophageal sphincter weaken. In this case, gastroenteritis will be followed by stomach spasm and heartburn (which you might think is part of the gastroenteritis). The treatment is to gently massage the stomach from the tip of the xiphoid process, which is at the bottom of the sternum (that little space between the ribs where they attach to the sternum, or breastbone), down along the right-hand side of the rib cage. Massaging in one downward movement to the right several times will often take the spasm out and direct the stomach back into place. See the section on digestive disorders on page 63 for more information on stomach spasm and hiatus hernia.

The best dietary advice is to avoid the foods and drinks already mentioned. Herbal remedies include ginger, as a tea or in capsule form. Herbs such as catnip and fennel are also useful for heartburn. Slippery elm and DGL licorice can help soothe the esophageal sphincter. An old folk remedy prescribes 1 teaspoon apple cider vinegar in 4 ounces of water, taken throughout a meal to help digestion. Mint teas seem to make the problem worse, even though there are many after-dinner mints on the market; in fact, mint actually weakens the esophageal sphincter. I do not recommend antacids, although they do coat the esophagus and stomach and settle the stomach fermentation, helping to push things through. They interfere with digestion, eliminate necessary hydrochloric acid, and only offer symptomatic relief; they do not get at the root of the problem.

Heart Disease
(See **Angina Pectoris,** page 12)

Heat Exhaustion

Heat exhaustion occurs when body fluids are lost through sweating and not replenished. Salt can also be lost through the skin; it's not just water that comes out. When you think of the surface area the skin covers, you can understand the potential for enormous loss of fluids over a period of time.

I see this condition when people stay out in the sun too long, don't drink enough water, forget simple measures such as wearing a hat in the sun, and stay out in the direct sun between eleven o'clock and two o'clock. You should have water with you at all times if you're going to be outdoors. Eating lots of fruits and vegetables is helpful because of their high water content. Salt tablets should be avoided because they take water away from the extremities and bring it to the stomach to dilute the salt. The best way to get salt is by eating vegetables because they have natural sodium. High-sugar drinks are counterproductive for the same reason—the sugar must be diluted in the stomach first. Fruit is a much better way to keep your blood sugar up and to hold water. Obviously, you should avoid coffee, alcohol, and smoking: these dehydrate the body and cause blood vessel constriction. Suspect dehydration when urination slows down or stops completely.

When heat exhaustion is leading to heatstroke, there can be headache, neck pain, dizziness, nausea, and disorientation. If heatstroke is suspected, the best place to be is in the hospital. Otherwise, a cool, dark room with air conditioning or fans is sufficient, and cool water can be applied with a spray bottle or cool towels, which is better than total immersion. Water is the best fluid to take in, and the next best is water with lemon and a bit of honey. This replenishes the sodium and sugar. Then take vegetable juices or vegetable broth.

Hemochromatosis

Hemochromatosis is also called iron overload disease. It is the most common genetic disorder in the United States. It is a metabolic disorder that increases absorption of iron, which is deposited in various body tissues and organs, and can cause damage.

It is an inherited condition and those at risk are predominantly of Scottish, Irish, or English descent. Symptoms vary according to which organs are most affected and include lethargy, joint pain, bronze or yellowish skin color, loss of body hair, impotence in men, amenorrhea in women, irritability, and depression.

Untreated or severe hemochromatosis may lead to an enlarged liver, an enlarged spleen, diabetes, abnormal heart rhythm, and congestive heart failure.

Hemochromatosis is usually discovered through a routine blood test that shows high iron levels and high iron storage levels, called *serum ferritin*. Further diagnostic procedures for hemochromatosis may include a transferrin saturation (TS) test and a liver biopsy. Dr. Paul Cutler is the leading North American expert in the diagnosis and treatment of hemochromatosis. See the Resources section.

One treatment is bloodletting; become a blood donor and help someone else while you drain excess iron from your system. The treatment for severe cases is intravenous chelation, not unlike the treatment for heart disease that pulls out excess minerals from the body's tissues and arteries. People with iron overload should avoid taking supplements that include iron and cut back on iron-rich foods such as red meat. Read the section on liver disease on page 116 to learn how to heal the liver from iron overload damage.

Hemorrhoids

Hemorrhoids occur in the anal canal and can be internal or external. They are weakened, swollen veins that can swell and even bleed due to pressure from the liver's portal circulation, pressure from constipation, or straining the abdomen in any way. They can cause a fair amount of disability and irritation.

They are also exceedingly common in both sexes, in women due to pregnancy and in men due to constipation and inactivity. In fact, this was my topic when I first appeared on the television show *The View*.

When we rehearsed the segment I had a huge audience of the show's crew, mostly men, who seemed very interested in hemorrhoids. After rehearsal, one of the producers remarked that she hadn't seen such a turnout since Pamela Lee Anderson's rehearsal!

On that show, I demonstrated that hemorrhoids are like a cluster of grapes that pop out of the anal canal. Meredith Vieira, one of the show's hosts, said hers were even bigger than grapes after giving birth; her mainstay was a donut cushion to take the pressure off the area while they healed. We can't stop pregnancy and the pressure that puts on the veins, but we can avoid constipation, increase our exercise, and strengthen our veins.

Treatment begins by eating an optimum diet and avoiding alcohol, cigarettes, and drugs. Avoid constipation with a high-fiber diet, including bran and beets. Foods that help veins regain elasticity are garlic, onions, lecithin, okra, green leafy vegetables, and whole grains. Use plenty of liquids and avoid straining when passing stool. Veins are strengthened by bioflavonoids, which are part of the vitamin C complex. These nutrients help treat varicose veins, uterine hemorrhage, and strokes. Food sources are buckwheat or citrus pulp.

Local treatments include baking soda to take away the itch, witch hazel in a sitz bath, and vitamin E oil on the area to relieve swelling. To ease swelling and pain, coat a piece of potato the size of your small finger with vitamin E and insert into the anus. For swelling, bleeding, and pain, apply comfrey ointment. For pain and to assist shrinking of the swollen tissues, apply plantain and yarrow ointment. Homeopathic Witch hazel by mouth 12C, 4 drops three times a day, is also helpful.

Sitz baths are very effective. Use one or a combination of witch hazel, plantain leaves, comfrey root, or white oak bark. These herbs are all strong astringents. Use 2 ounces of dried herb and ½ gallon of boiling water. Steep for one hour, strain, pour some into a shallow pan, and sit in it for fifteen minutes.

Zinc ointment and vitamin E are very good for healing fissures, which may occur along with hemorrhoids. Most of the above suggestions for hemorrhoids are useful for fissures.

With both conditions, pay special attention to cleaning the anus after a bowel movement; tiny sharp particles in the feces can cut the anal skin. A bidet is the best solution, allowing you to wash the area immediately after a bowel movement. Otherwise use soft, undyed, unscented toilet paper. Wet some paper and try to clean the first inch of the anal canal. A thin, wet washcloth and neutral pH soap help.

Surgical treatment can be very simple for single hemorrhoids. A very tight rubber band is placed at the base of the hemorrhoid to cut off circulation; the hemorrhoid is then absorbed or sloughed off.

Hiatus Hernia
(See **Digestive Disorders,** page 63)

Hyperactivity/ADHD

There is no doubt that some children are more active than others. Hyperactivity appears to have many causes: our electric environment, television, fluorescent lighting; chemicals in our water; a highly refined diet containing sugar and white flour; and a chemical diet of thousands of food additives. Even peanut butter can be highly allergenic due to a common mold; its oily nature makes it go rancid quickly, but it is often highly sweetened with sugar so you don't taste the rancidity. I visited a young couple with a two-year-old boy and witnessed the proverbial Dr. Jeckyl/Mr. Hyde. Within minutes of spooning out peanut butter from the jar this adorable young man turned into a head-beating, rampaging monster. I shared the above information, which at first shocked the parents but helped them adjust their son's diet; he became a normal person again.

In some cases, there is a muscular imbalance of the eyes, leading to a form of dyslexia that can trigger symptoms of hyperactivity or lack of coordination between the right and left sides of the brain. All these various causes might have to be investigated for each individual child.

Since the medical management of attention deficit/hyperactivity disorder (ADHD) includes the prescription drug Ritalin, it is extremely important that we look for alternatives. In 1995 the U.S. Drug Enforcement Agency warned doctors about the shared chemistry of cocaine and Ritalin; it is classified in the United States as a class II substance along with heroin, morphine, barbiturates, and cocaine. Yet, the multibillion-dollar sales of Ritalin have increased by 400 percent since 1995.

In the United States, 330 million doses of Ritalin are taken daily, while the rest of the world only consumes 65 million pills daily. As soon as a child reaches puberty, the effect of Ritalin changes under the influence of hormonal surges to act like true "speed" with such devastating effects (violence, suicidal depression, and so on) that the child may be put on Prozac—"the frying pan into the fire routine," as Dr. Ann Blake of the International Coalition for Drug Awareness describes it. In January 2000, the American Medical Association expressed alarm that children as young as two years of age are put on Ritalin and five-year-olds are on Prozac. The long-term effects on the growing brain are unknown as no long-term studies have ever been conducted. Evidence does, however, exist to show that long-term use of Ritalin significantly reduces blood flow to the brain, disrupts growth hormone, and can cause depression and insomnia.

There is a light at the end of the tunnel, however. Research by Dr. David Horribon, with whom I worked on his initial trials using evening primrose oil for colitis and PMS, and Dr. Jacqueline Stordy shows a deficiency in essential fatty acids (EFAs) as the underlying cause of ADHD, dyslexia, and dyspraxia (severe clumsiness).

They were assisted by Vicky Colquhoun and her daughter Sally Bunday in the United Kingdom who founded the Hyperactive Children's Support Group. They observed that ADHD children are more thirsty than other kids, and they drink more but produce a lot less urine. They also have a higher incidence of asthma and much more dry skin and brittle hair. Since skin is waterproofed through the action of essential fatty acids, which must be replenished daily through food, it appears that ADHD children lose water rapidly through their skin—EFAs are somehow chronically depleted. EFAs from food are converted through the liver and gut metabolism into polyunsaturated fatty acids (PUFAs). These PUFAs supply vital brain food without which perception, cognition, memory, attention, spatial behavior, and the eyes simply cannot work properly. And to top it all off, ADHD appears to be due to a deficiency of EFAs that begins in utero if the mother is nutritionally depleted during her pregnancy.

The British government followed up on this work and studied 17,000 children from the time they entered school for several years; objective blood tests and extremely reliable predictive behavior tests were developed to identify which kids developed these learning disabilities. Remedial action with EFA supplementation was taken with immense success.

In 1995 in the United States, Purdue University did controlled studies providing undeniable proof of the EFA hypothesis. When research showed that human breast milk is rich in EFAs, but infant formula contained virtually none—resulting in highly significant differences in

IQ—the American Society for Nutritional Sciences submitted a report to the FDA in 1998 that resulted in EFAs finally being put into infant formulas.

These EFAs can be obtained from fish oils, flaxseed oil, evening primrose oil, and borage oil. The overuse of inferior, rancid, fried, fake oils to the exclusion of EFAs explains why so many brains are slowing down, both young and old. A tablespoon or two of flaxseed oil on salad or cooked cereal, and a tablespoon of cod liver oil every day can provide most of the necessary essential oils. Check in your health food store for special formulas containing omega-3, omega-6, and DHA. Go to www.efamol.com (the Efamol nutraceutical company Web site) for information on specialized supplements for ADHD and taped lectures by Professor Stordy.

Regarding the electric environment connection, make sure your child's desk and bed are 3 feet away from any electrical outlets. There have been huge debates about whether high-voltage electrical outlets cause cancer and there is now a consensus that they are harmful. When studies only focus on cancer as an endpoint, they look at a condition that takes many years to develop and is multifactorial; this distracts us from looking at day-to-day concerns. It also forces the victims to prove that they are harmed rather than forcing an industry to prove that what it is doing is safe.

Let's look at diet. Children should not be given sugar or junk food, and the most allergenic foods such as dairy and wheat should be avoided to see if the child's behavior changes. Foods with coloring or additives are very suspect. The worst ones to date are aspartame and MSG. They play havoc on the developing brain from the fetal stage on into adulthood. Aspartame is an artificial sweetener made from two amino acids and wood alcohol. It should be entirely banned because of the adverse reactions of laboratory animals producing seizures, brain tumors, and ninety-two other side effects. Chewing a single stick of aspartame-sweetened gum has induced seizures in susceptible children.

I first became aware of the toxicity of aspartame back in 1988 when I was writing a book on sugar. I read all the studies on sugar and hyperactivity and I came across these bizarre studies that used aspartame as the placebo, or so-called inert substance, to compare with sugar. The results of these studies were that the effects of aspartame and sugar on the behavior of children were the same; the conclusion was that sugar does not cause hyperactivity. When I researched aspartame, however, I found that it is a neurotoxin and can cause hyperactivity and aberrant behavior. The researchers assumed that aspartame was benign so there were as many or more incidents of hyperactive behavior due to aspartame, making sugar look good. See the sections on sugar addiction on page 4 and sugar and aspartame on page 185 for more information.

Monosodium glutamate (MSG) is a modified form of glutamic acid with one sodium atom added to the molecule. It is called an excitotoxin, because it literally excites neurons to death. Dr. John Olney, a neuroscientist at Washington University in St. Louis, found that MSG is toxic to the retina, and a single dose can destroy specialized cells in the hypothalamus. Dr. Olney went public with his findings and spent many years trying to convince the FDA to remove MSG from baby foods. Be sure to read labels for MSG and avoid hydrolyzed protein, which also contains MSG.

Books by Dr. Ben Feingold (*Why Your Child Is Hyperactive*) and Dr. Doris Rapp (*Is This Your Child? Discovering and Treating Unrecognized Allergies in Children and Adults*) are useful to investigate and understand the role of allergies in ADHD. Dr. Feingold really hit gold with his theory about food additives causing hyperactivity. Thousands of children have benefited from following his diet. Doubt was intentionally cast on his approach when the food industry funded studies to show that food additives were not responsible for ADHD. They claimed they found no hyperactive behavior in children by only studying ten food additives and using chocolate as the placebo. These were considered legitimate studies by the food industry in spite of the fact that there are thousands of food additives children can be exposed to and chocolate itself can cause hyperactive behavior. When the media was given spin-doctored conclusions of these "fake" studies, parents were led to believe that there is no harm in the thousands of chemicals in their children's diets. The same whitewash is performed with sugar. The food industry would have us believe that the damage caused by sugar is only to our teeth and ignores the rampant escalation of diabetes and numerous other diseases of civilization.

Let's look at ADHD and adolescence. There is a common misconception that ADHD improves with age, which has led to a lack of acknowledgment and support for teens in high school with this problem. In girls, talkativeness, inattention, and truancy is not viewed as ADHD but as a lack of discipline. In boys, impulsive behavior, drugs, truancy, and vandalism may, in fact, be due to ADHD. One of the symptoms of

ADHD is a constant need for stimuli, mostly sound. So if the music isn't blaring or if they aren't on the telephone, teens conduct a nonstop monologue to fill up acoustic space. The added stress of puberty worsens an existing ADHD problem because the hormones have their own way of creating mood swings. For girls, it is especially bad before the menstrual period.

Researchers using positon emission tomography (PET) scans and specialized electroencephalograms (EEGs) on ADHD speculate that the problem of ADHD is a "slowing of the brain waves." Whether this is true or not, it still doesn't explain what is causing the slowing, which is probably a combination of nutrient deficiencies, especially of EFAs, and environment toxicity.

The need for brain balancing in your hyperactive or dyslexic child can be determined by finding out if she is using the same dominant eye as her dominant hand. Do this experiment: Punch a hole in a piece of plain paper with a pencil. Simply ask your child to look through the hole at a distant object. Give no further instructions. He will obviously have to look through one eye and the eye he chooses will be his dominant eye. If he is right handed and chooses his left eye, the right and left sides of the brain have to work a lot harder to pass information between the two sides. *Brain Gym,* by Gail Dennison, is a wonderful brain exercise book that helps balance the right and left brains and enhances communication across the corpus collosum that divides the two brains. One theory on why boys have more ADHD than girls is that the male brain is left brain dominant while the female uses both brain hemispheres equally and has a larger corpus collosum.

Some children may be deficient in certain vitamins and minerals. If dairy is avoided, calcium and magnesium should be provided. The section on osteoporosis on page 130 contains a list of calcium- and magnesium-rich foods. In puberty, the mineral zinc could be called an essential mineral. Zinc deficiency can be found using a zinc taste tester in your naturopathic doctor's office. Hair analysis can also provide this information. Zinc is required for sexual development and often becomes deficient at puberty if not introduced in the diet with foods such as sunflower seeds, pumpkin seeds, and oysters. Zinc supplements might be necessary through early puberty. EFAs and zinc are necessary for healthy skin; perhaps one of the reasons kids have acne is that these nutrients are deficient. The B vitamins are also important as cofactors for thousands of metabolic functions in the body, including the complex functioning of the brain. They also help control mood swings at puberty. A natural multivitamin and mineral rounds out the supplement picture. Try to choose a brand in which the ingredients are at least partly derived from organic or natural sources and not completely synthetic. Strictly avoid vitamins sweetened with aspartame; many of them are. Companies such as Standard Process have supplements in powdered form so they can be blended in a protein or fruit shake for the family.

Herbs that calm the nervous system include hops, valerian, skullcap, wild oat, and St. John's wort; they can be found in tea bags at your local health food store. Developing a habit of drinking calming herb teas will keep your teens away from the stimulating effects of tea and coffee.

Read *Ritalin Free Kids,* by Judith Reitchenberg-Ullman, for the scoop on how to treat ADHD with homeopathy.

Hypertension

This is elevated blood pressure. The top reading of blood pressure is called systolic pressure, and is the force of blood that pushes up against the blood vessels. The lower reading, called diastolic pressure, is the back pressure on the heart. The diastolic is the more important reading in terms of heart disease. Blood pressure rises with age only in so-called Western civilized countries. It is a consequence of lifestyle: coffee, alcohol, cigarettes, heavy-metal toxicity (including mercury dental amalgams), stress, a junk-food diet, and the wrong kinds of fats, all of which lead to hardening of the arteries, weakness of the heart muscle, and deficiency of potassium, magnesium, and a plethora of other nutrients mandatory for healthy heart function.

Treatment for these conditions begins with diet, especially because diabetics are prone to hypertension. Read the section on diabetes on page 58 and lock up the sugar bowl. There are two schools of thought on the optimum diet for hypertension: some say high protein and some say high carbohydrate/low fat. This seeming disparity is obvious if you look at blood group diets; if you have O type blood you need more protein; if you have A type you need a high-carbohydrate diet. Read the section on diets on page 181 for a more thorough explanation. Foods that alleviate hypertension include garlic, onions, fish, lots of green leafy vegetables, root vegetables, and oatmeal. Potassium broths are an excellent way of getting this important mineral. The recipe includes potato skins, celery, and zucchini cooked in a big pot of water for at least one hour. Drink the seasoned broth, throwing out the spent vegetables.

Blood pressure can become elevated due to mineral deficiencies. When you eat a poor diet, you just don't get the necessary nutrients. Calcium, magnesium, potassium, and trace minerals, along with a good multiple vitamin and mineral supplement, are all very important. Essential fatty acids are also useful in hypertension to heal the arteries and bring the fats in the body into balance. These are obtained from flaxseed oil and fish oils. Coenzyme Q10 is an important heart supplement; read more about it in the sections on angina on page 12 and atherosclerosis on page 19.

Stress and tension are also known causes of hypertension. You can benefit from relaxation exercises as well as physical exercise and biofeedback.

If your doctor feels that you have to go on antihypertensive medications, ask for a twenty-four-hour blood pressure monitor test. This enables both doctor and patient to understand if this condition is present at all times or only during stress. This test will prevent the overuse of medication and alert you to the presence of "white-coat hypertension," which is hypertension whenever your doctor takes your blood pressure.

Hyperventilation

Hyperventilation is caused by breathing too fast, usually because of anxiety. When you are afraid or anxious, adrenaline and fight-or-flight mechanisms start taking over. The blood pumps faster, the heart pounds, more anxiety builds, and you start breathing too quickly. As part of the primitive fight-or-flight reflex, if you needed to run away from something threatening or fight somebody, this extra oxygen would be necessary. When you're standing still and having an anxiety attack, however, this rapid breathing can be frightening.

The best treatment is breathing into a paper bag; the carbon dioxide exhaled and lost during hyperventilation will be absorbed back into your body and will shut down the mechanisms perpetuating the rapid breathing. It also helps to have someone with you who can coach you to take slower breaths and help you relax.

Coffee, alcohol, and cigarette smoking exaggerate anxiety and hyperventilation. Read the section on anxiety on page 14 for more information on this condition.

Hypoglycemia

Hypoglycemia means low blood sugar. Medically, it is only recognized if the blood sugar drops below a certain range (50 mg% or 2.7 grams/dl glucose); however, the level can vary depending on the individual and the circumstances. Ideally, blood sugar should stay within a certain normal range. If you eat a highly refined diet, however, your blood sugar will quickly become elevated as this food is rapidly absorbed into the bloodstream. When the blood sugar reaches a certain maximum, insulin is stimulated to enter the bloodstream and take the excess glucose away into the body's cells. The amount of insulin released is dependent on the rate of increase of the blood sugar. If a great amount of insulin is released, the blood sugar may fall dramatically. When the blood sugar falls in a precipitous manner, adrenaline is stimulated to make sure the blood sugar does not fall too low, rendering you unconscious. Adrenaline stimulates the sugar stores (glycogen), but it can also produce a fight-or-flight reaction. You may feel a sense of anxiety or impending doom for no apparent reason. At this point, if you eat a meal of refined foods or coffee and a donut, you may feel better quite quickly, but the cycle of rapid elevation of blood sugar and then rapid decline repeats itself—you can go through life as if on a roller coaster. We call it the "crash and burn syndrome."

It is important to diagnose this condition properly. This can be done with a glucose tolerance test, although there is much controversy about this testing. You must keep a journal of your symptoms while having a glucose tolerance test. After twelve to fourteen hours of fasting, you are given a sugar drink and blood is taken every hour for five hours to document what happens to your body's blood sugar over this period of time.

The treatment for hypoglycemia is small, frequent meals of complex carbohydrates (vegetables, whole grains, seeds, nuts) and protein. Some suggest either one or the other, but it is important to balance both protein and complex carbohydrates in the diet. Sweets, refined foods, and alcohol must be avoided. Don't make the mistake of switching to artificial sweeteners to avoid sugar. The most common sweetener, aspartame (NutraSweet), is found in over 9,000 diet products. It is a neurotoxin and causes sugar cravings, headaches, and seizures among its ninety-two FDA-documented side effects. Read labels and avoid it. Read the section on sugar and aspartame on page 185 for more information. It may be worthwhile to sit down with a nutritional counselor to devise proper diet management of this condition.

Supplements that are helpful in treating hypoglycemia are B vitamins to support the nervous system; a good multivitamin and mineral; and pantothenic acid, a B vitamin that supports the adrenal glands. Chromium, a mineral, has been shown to assist glucose tolerance and balance. For people whose adrenal glands are exhausted, desiccated adrenal can also be used for a short time, at midmorning and midafternoon.

Hypothyroidism

The thyroid gland is located on either side of the trachea in the neck. It controls the metabolism of all the cells of the body. If the thyroid is low, or hypo, the metabolic rate is lowered. Symptoms are widespread and include sluggishness, fatigue, difficulty waking up in the morning, obesity, coarsening of the hair and skin, constipation, frequent infections, heavy menstrual periods, and poor wound healing.

Because these symptoms overlap with many other conditions, it is important to make an accurate diagnosis. Unfortunately, blood tests for the thyroid tend to be inaccurate and can miss an early case of low thyroid.

Many practitioners think there is an epidemic of hypothyroidism in the present population. Hormone-disrupting chemicals such as pesticide pyrethroids may interfere with the immune and endocrine systems, especially the thyroid. According to toxicologists, animal tests showed that chronic exposure to resmethrin (a synthetic pyrethroid) could increase thyroid weight and cause thyroid cysts. In animal studies, it was found that exposure to pyrethroids can suppress both the thyroid's T4 and T3 levels and raise thyroid stimulating hormone (TSH) levels, in addition to a variety of other health effects. There is much outrage around the world as hormone-disrupting chemicals create an epidemic of feminization in male animals and fish. Why would humans be immune?

Recent testing on perchlorate, a fertilizer leaking into our groundwater, shows that it affects the function of the thyroid gland. Researchers have stated that the hormonally active isoflavones in soy are capable of suppressing thyroid function and causing or worsening hypothyroidism or, in some cases, causing goiter. While soy may be good for the symptoms of menopause, consider the millions of women with abnormal thyroid function and to what extent soy may be harmful to them. Studies indicate that radiation exposure to the thyroid gland can cause hypothyroidism and thyroid tumors. Mercury is another common cause of hypothyroidism.

It's becoming more and more obvious that when the government finally gets around to studying the effects of chemicals on our health, it will find they are responsible for a great deal of illness and disability. A crucial mineral for the proper functioning of the thyroid is iodine. There is a theory that I learned from an industrial chemist friend that the amount of iodine we require is set at the time we are in the womb by the amount of iodine in our mothers' diets. In other words, if your mother lived by the sea and ate fish and seaweed containing a lot of iodine, then you will require a similar amount of iodine throughout your life. If you don't get enough, you will be hypothyroid. If your mother had very little iodine when pregnant, then you need very little, and if you take too much for your needs, you can develop hyperthyroidism. Try to make an assessment of how much iodine you need based on where your mother lived when she was carrying you. If she was near the ocean and ate a lot of seafood, you should consume foods that are high in iodine, including fish, seaweed, and root vegetables. Avoid foods that contain substances that suppress the thyroid, such as broccoli, brussels sprouts, mustard greens, kale, and spinach.

Read Dr. Broda Barnes's excellent book, *Hypothyroidism: The Unsuspected Illness.* Dr. Barnes suggests that basal body temperature can be a way of assessing metabolic rate and thyroid function. Keep a basal thermometer on your night table. When you wake up in the morning, before you move, put the thermometer under your armpit for ten minutes. For women, the temperature is best taken at the end of the menstrual period. If your temperature is under 97.6°F, you may have a thyroid problem. Dr. Barnes suggests desiccated thyroid or Armour thyroid to supply the thyroid gland with the essential building blocks to support its function. Armour thyroid is a dessicated thyroid from pork thyroid that is standardized to a specific dosage. It supplies both T3 and T4 and is far superior to synthetic varieties. It is made by Forest Pharmaceuticals and is available by prescription. Doctors either don't know about it or don't prescribe it because they were told in medical school that the dosage could vary from batch to batch and it was an unreliable drug. Times have changed, however, and Armour thyroid, a very reliable drug, is the treatment of choice for hypothyroidism.

Medically, doctors wait until the thyroid is very weak and damaged before using replacement thyroid therapy with synthetic thyroid hormone. Nutritionally, the supplements for a weak thyroid include dessicated thyroid, Thytropin by Standard Process, tyrosine (an amino acid), vitamin B_6, zinc, iodine, and kelp. The dosage of supplements has to be individualized for each patient and should be taken under the supervision of a naturopathic doctor.

If you take too much iodine or too many thyroid supplements, usually the first sign of excess is a rapid heart rate and hearing your heartbeat pulsing in your ears when you lie down. Iodine is used to "paint" wounds to disinfect them; it turns the skin brown temporarily. Using this property of iodine, some practitioners suggest painting iodine on the soles of the feet at night. If the color is gone by morning, this means the iodine was necessary and was absorbed. You can then continue to eat iodine-containing foods and take thyroid support. Every week or so, paint on the iodine and when the stain remains on the feet overnight, you have enough iodine and you should cut back on your intake. As you can see, the proper monitoring of your thyroid requires you to be tuned to your body and its shifts and changes and to practice using your own intuition.

One last thought on thyroid: Dr. E. Denis Wilson claims he has discovered another form of thyroid disease, which he calls Wilson's disease. His protocol is based on taking your temperature and trying to get it to normalize by using a T3 thyroid preparation as opposed to the usual T4 thyroxine, or eltroxin. There is much dispute over his work. It seems that Armour thyroid with its balance of T3 and T4, however, should help people who are deficient in either of these hormones. Explore more about thyroid with Mary J. Shomon on the Web site www.about.com.

Incontinence

Urinary incontinence is the involuntary loss of urine. Some consider it to be a normal consequence of aging, but this is not so. Women are more susceptible to this condition, probably because of the weakening of their bladder sphincter muscles during childbirth or pressure on the bladder from uterine prolapse. Men are susceptible as they get older because the prostate at the base of the penis enlarges and puts pressure on the urethra, causing urinary frequency. (Read the section on prostate problems on page 137.)

Many things can help this condition; you don't have to run out and buy incontinence pads right away. Regard this as a symptom of an underlying problem that can be reversed in many cases. First of all, avoid alcohol, which is a great irritant to the bladder sphincter. Avoid caffeine, which causes increased urination. Caffeine is not just in coffee; it's also found in cola beverages, chocolate, and many over-the-counter medications. Make sure you're not taking caffeine in any form. Smoking also causes bladder irritation, and "smoker's cough" can cause bladder leakage when the whole body goes into reflex spasm from the cough. Aspartame, found in over 9,000 products, causes burning and irritation of the bladder and urethra and can bring on incontinence. Read labels and avoid this product. It is even included in certain vaginal creams and gels—I can only imagine why!

Maintain an optimum diet, which will help you lose excess weight; this in itself will help take the pressure off the abdomen and the bladder to reduce incontinence. Your diet should also help you have normal bowel movements; the pressure from constipation can irritate the bladder. The proper diet is high in fiber, with enough fluid to keep the fiber from making you more constipated. It includes lots of vegetables, moderate amounts of fruit, whole grains, nuts, seeds, legumes, fish, and chicken. Keep a food diary of what you eat and drink, the times that you urinate, and when you experience incontinence. After a week or so, you may see a pattern: a relationship between what you eat and how often your bladder leaks. It may be a simple matter of drinking too much fluid. Dehydrating yourself is not the answer to this condition, however.

Urologists advise "double voiding" for incontinence: after you urinate, remain on the toilet and wait for any excess urine that remains to leave the bladder. You can apply gentle pressure over the pubic bone, run the water tap, or bend forward a bit to encourage all the urine to run out of the bladder. Some people hold back when they have to urinate. At a seminar, meeting, or social event, they ignore nature's call and hold their urine until the bladder becomes too full. If this is done too frequently, it can weaken the sphincter muscles. Some people don't even know they have to go to the bathroom until they start to feel pain in the abdomen above the pubic bone.

Those at risk for incontinence should begin a "bladder drill," using the toilet at regular, structured intervals. This will help awareness of what it feels like to have smaller amounts in the bladder instead of the big, stretching pain that comes when the bladder is overfull. Retraining the bladder like this seems to set the bladder capacity to a better level for emptying. We urinate an average of every two and a half to five hours. In the bladder drill, try to void every hour, then over the next month or so, increase the time between voiding.

Kegel exercises are especially important for the bladder. Pretend you're tightening the muscles around the anus, and then pretend you're holding back the urine; this identifies the two groups of muscles that you're going to be working on. Starting at the anus, tighten those muscles, and then proceed forward, tightening the muscles at the urethra; hold this to a count of four, then release. This should be done for two minutes at least a dozen times a day. You can do the Kegel exercise when you're waiting at a traffic light or for a bus, or anywhere at all. No one knows when you're doing Kegels, and they are very helpful.

Infections

Read the sections on colds and flus on page 48, bladder infections on page 27, bronchitis on page 29, diarrhea on page 62, earaches on page 68, chronic fatigue syndrome on page 45, kidney disease on page 111, prostate problems on page 137, gum disease on page 84, sinus infections on page 142, and vaginitis on page 153.

The first aid section on page 168 includes treatment for skin and wound infections, and also for burns. The single most important treatment for wounds is proper cleaning. To clean a dirty wound, use dilute hydrogen peroxide, which will bubble on contact with pus. After all the dirt is removed, calendula, echinacea, hypericum, or goldenseal tincture diluted (about 10 drops per 4 ounces of water) can be used to wash and pack a wound. If a wound is producing a lot of pus, like a boil, it is wise to try and keep it open to maximize draining. The best way to accomplish this is to obtain sterile gauze from the drugstore, dip it in the above herbal water, and pack it into the wound. As the wound is cleaned of debris, fresh live tissue is formed so that it will heal from the base up.

Soak a dirty wound in hot water with added salt or Epsom salts. Poulticing is even more powerful than soaking because you can apply the poultice to the skin for a longer period of time. Bread, clay, and herbs are the three best substances to use. Moisten a piece of bread (this is the only time that white bread is useful), and place it over an infected area, boil, cystic acne, or an inflamed wound. Cover it with gauze or thin cotton cloth and tape it on for several hours, even overnight. Do the same with clay; first make it into a paste. The best herb poultice is comfrey; use fresh cooked herb or dried herb made into a tea.

If there are red streaks going away from a wound, suspect blood poisoning and seek medical advice and maybe an antibiotic. If you take an antibiotic, be sure and use acidophilus by mouth to replace the good bacteria.

Infertility

Female

In the 1930s, Weston Price, D.D.S., and Francis Pottenger, M.D., did an interesting study on cats that may have implications for human infertility. The cats who were fed an optimum cat diet of raw meat and milk fared well, but the cats whose food was cooked and pasteurized could produce no live births by the third generation. I'm not suggesting that mothers eat raw meat and milk, but consider how much "live" food you do eat. By making a substantial part of your diet raw fruits and vegetables, sprouts, whole grains, nuts, and seeds, you are passing on the beneficial nutrients and enzymes of live foods to your child.

In modern society, there are many causes of infertility: a junk food diet; environmental pollution of the air, water, and food supply; drug intake—including prescription drugs (the birth control pill) and street drugs; and food additives, especially aspartame (NutraSweet). Dr. H. J. Roberts in *Aspartame (NutraSweet): Is It Safe?* explains that excessive prolactin production by the pituitary gland is a significant cause of menstrual changes or loss in women. Phenylalanine (which makes up 50 percent of aspartame) is one of the most potent stimulators of prolactin secretion by a single amino acid. On the aspartame Web site, www.dorway.com, there are many reports of infertile women who conceive when they give up their addictive habit of using NutraSweet. See the sections on sugar addiction on page 4, sugar and aspartame on page 185, and pregnancy on page 169 for more information on aspartame.

In my practice, I have counseled teens whose friends have gone to birth control clinics and been freely handed the pill. These girls may not have even started their periods, yet they are given a daily hormone that basically tricks the body into thinking it is pregnant. We may now be seeing the result of this practice. After ten years of artificial hormone intake, the body may not be able to jump-start its own hormonal cascade. The daily levels of estrogen and progesterone have long since shut down the pituitary gland's production of FSH and LH, which prepare the follicles in the ovaries to become eggs.

Quite often, these women are then given huge doses of fertility hormones to jolt the pituitary into action. Multiple births can result, with unknown repercussions on the children's health.

Vitamin and mineral imbalances may also be created by the use of the pill. The B vitamins, including folic acid, are depleted, since they are used as coenzymes in the biochemical breakdown of the hormones in the pill. Most of this processing occurs in the liver. The liver is thus diverted from other work to perform this function.

Because long-term use of the pill is often to blame for infertility, give your body at least six months to rebalance before trying to conceive and especially before going on any fertility drugs. We still don't know the long-term side effects of those hormones, although they have been associated with an increased risk of cancer. If you have been on fertility drugs, be very careful about taking more synthetic hormones in your lifetime; go for the natural ones.

Folic acid is crucial to prevent neural tube defects in the newborn, but it is even more crucial to create the neural tube in the first place. Many first-trimester miscarriages may occur due to nonviability of the fetus from folic acid deficiency. Folic acid can be found in all green vegetables.

When you study the nutrient requirements for conception and pregnancy, almost every known nutrient is implicated. Therefore, the best advice is to maintain an excellent diet of whole foods, as close to their natural state as possible. Also make sure you have no underlying allergies, candidiasis, or mineral deficiencies by having blood tests and a hair mineral analysis. Avoid coffee, alcohol, and cigarettes for obvious reasons of toxicity. Don't do more than an hour of strenuous exercise a day, because it can burn off too much fat (necessary for proper hormone production and ovulation). Douching should be avoided, as it changes the normal vaginal pH.

Of course, the usual tests for infertility must be done to rule out any anatomical abnormalities. Make sure there is no underlying reason that your body might not be able to sustain a pregnancy. If you are chronically ill or chronically allergic, your body might not direct its energies toward creating new life until it has a strong, viable life force to sustain it.

Male

It is very important to understand that males contribute 50 percent to fertility and that diet and lifestyle can have an effect on semen and sperm count. This means you should avoid smoking and decrease sugar, coffee, alcohol, and refined foods in the diet. An excellent diet will achieve optimum results.

You should also avoid tight underwear. The testicles are meant to hang away from the body and they make more viable sperm at a lower temperature than body temperature. Hot tubs should also be avoided.

If the sperm count is low, several supplements can be used. A low sperm count can be increased with zinc. Agglutination of sperm can be balanced with vitamin C, and sperm motility can be enhanced with arginine, an amino acid found in soy, peanuts, wheat germ, and coconut.

Insomnia

These days, people are often so wound up before going to bed that it is difficult to settle the mind or the body into sleep. If this is the case, it is important to relax before bedtime. Avoid coffee or alcohol or a late dinner. Don't do strenuous exercise at this time (although sexual intercourse often helps you sleep). Take a hot bath with Epsom salts, or play some quiet music. Perform this type of ritual before bed so that your mind begins to slow down and turn off as a prelude to sleep. You can also play a relaxation tape while lying in bed. Daily exercise is also very important to achieve good sleep.

Sleep specialists recommend that you change beds if sleep has not come within a half hour, or get up and leave the bedroom to read or engage in similar activities until fatigue or tiredness sets in. Then return to the bedroom to sleep. Don't use your bedroom for anything else but sleep. Set your alarm and get up at the same time each morning. Don't nap during the day. Go to bed at a reasonable hour each night. These instructions, followed to the letter, should reprogram your body to sleep properly.

An excellent supplement for insomnia, anxiety, and depression is tryptophan; or, I should say, *was* tryptophan. This amino acid was used for decades until 1989, when it became the scapegoat of the first genetic engineering deaths. A Japanese company producing tryptophan began using a genetically engineered component in its process. As a result, over a thousand people became ill, and thirty-nine died. Tryptophan itself was blamed and was withdrawn from the market. However, 5-hydroxytryptamine, which follows tryptophan in the chemical cascade to serotonin, is available and is as effective as tryptophan for anxiety, depression, and insomnia. Research indicates that 5-hydroxytryptamine is actually more powerful than tryptophan in producing serotonin. Serotonin enhances mood and sleep, effects that have became synonymous with Prozac. Was it just coincidental that Prozac hit the market at the same time? Too many people have committed suicide and homicide while under the influence of Prozac and other serotonin-reuptake inhibitors (Zoloft, Paxil) for it to be a viable medication for most people. See more about Prozac in the section on depression on page 57.

For better mineral absorption, chew calcium lactate pills, or take calcium powder or calcium liquid at bedtime to enhance sleep.

Herbal remedies include tinctures of skullcap, 10 to 15 drops in a few ounces of water, or capsules combining hops, valerian, and skullcap, one to two at bedtime. One of the many homeopathic insomnia remedies is Coffea 12C, 4 drops, one to two doses at fifteen-minute intervals before bedtime to quiet an overactive mind.

Kidney Disease, Chronic

Chronic kidney disease or kidney failure is brought on by such conditions as severe kidney infections, uncontrolled diabetes, or severe hypertension. It is only when your kidneys are working at two-thirds of their capacity that you begin to have symptoms and signs of kidney disease, and, in the beginning, these symptoms are vague and not specific to the kidneys. They include urinating at night, fatigue, headaches, and nausea. On lab testing, there might be a protein spill in the urine, or blood tests may show a high BUN and creatinine. By the time the kidneys themselves are symptomatic with pain, kidney disease may be well advanced.

Kidney disease may also result from toxic medications or drugs or by precipitation of minerals as kidney stones. Beyond the treatment and prevention of underlying conditions or the avoidance of drugs and medications, there are dietary principles, herbs, and homeopathic remedies that can be used in kidney disease, but most of these treatments must be individualized.

The diet for kidney disease should be low in protein and high in complex carbohydrates, vegetables, and fruit. A good natural multivitamin and mineral supplement along with bioflavonoids are useful in supporting the kidneys. Strengthening treatment of the kidneys includes herbs such as nettle, parsley, uva ursi, and juniper berries. A classical Chinese medicine practitioner can prescribe herbal formulas and perform acupuncture for chronic kidney disease on an individual basis. Similarly, a homeopath can prescribe remedies for this condition after taking a detailed case history. See the section on kidney stones below.

Kidney Stones

Kidney stones are mostly seen in men with a family history of stones. Women can have a rare form of stone called struvite, caused by proteus bacteria that infects the bladder. Stones often cause no symptoms unless they block some part of the kidney or ureter. Then they cause severe pain that ebbs and flows and can cause a shocklike state. The pain is usually in the back and may radiate around the front to the abdomen and into the groin.

This condition, once it has occurred, has a high probability of recurring. An actual kidney stone attack is best treated in the hospital, but often it is only treated with painkillers, rest, and time. There are new methods of removing kidney stones surgically that are less invasive than earlier ones. A small instrument can be inserted up the urethra into the kidney area, and the stone visualized on x-ray. The instrument can then crush the stone and the debris can be urinated out. There are also ultrasound machines that can be directed at the area of the stone; in this case, sonic waves break up the stone.

Prevention is obviously the best treatment. Some people get kidney stones through dehydration in times of stress or from just not drinking enough water. A kidney or bladder infection can be a warning signal. Drink plenty of fluids to prevent buildup of the minerals that can cause kidney stones.

Over 80 percent of all kidney stones are made up of calcium or calcium combinations. Prevent these from occurring not by limiting your calcium foods, but by taking in enough magnesium to balance out the calcium. We seem to eat more calcium-rich foods than magnesium-rich foods. Calcium is found in dairy products, green leafy vegetables, nuts, seeds, and fish. Magnesium is found in whole grains, green leafy vegetables, legumes, nuts, and tofu.

Over 50 percent of all stones are calcium oxalate stones; oxalates are found in foods such as rhubarb, raw spinach, parsley, chocolate, and tea. These foods should be limited. A high protein intake can increase calcium plus phosphorus in the urine, which may lead to calcium stones. Salt can also cause precipitation of calcium in the kidneys. A rare, possible source of overproduction of oxalates is thought to be high doses of vitamin C. This has been researched by many, but even with extremely high intakes of up to 100 grams of vitamin C per day in AIDS patients, there has been no incidence of kidney stones.

The supplements for kidney stone prevention include magnesium and vitamin B_6. B_6 can lower the amount of oxalate in the urine and is a natural diuretic that increases flushing of the kidneys. Vitamin A and beta-carotene are very helpful for mucous membrane production and healing, so they help maintain the urinary tract lining. Simply eating a carrot or two a day will provide you with enough beta-carotene.

Lactose Intolerance

Some people believe that cow's milk is only for baby calves and that humans should not consume dairy products; they say we are the only mammals who take milk past the age of weaning. This may be good advice, especially for those millions of adults who do not have the necessary lactase enzymes to digest milk. Africans are especially apt to be lactose intolerant and over 80 percent cannot digest milk. I have always been struck by the terrible irony of sending dry, powdered milk to people suffering from famine, or after catastrophes in Africa, when this product will actually make these people sicker. As many as 30 percent of whites are also lactose intolerant. The diagnosis is through blood tests or by a breath test. These tests will often confirm symptoms in the gastrointestinal tract, such as diarrhea, cramps, gas, or constipation.

Another reason people are turning away from milk is because it is being contaminated with genetically engineered bovine growth hormone (BGH) injections given to cows to increase their milk production. BGH causes udder infections, for which cows are given massive amounts of antibiotics; pus cells and antibiotics find their way into the milk. BGH also increases the levels of insulin-like growth factor (IGF-1) in milk by about 80 percent. IGF-1 is implicated in prostate cancer and lung cancer—so far. The "Got Milk?" ads have sprung up in an attempt by the dairy industry to counter the truly negative effects of BGH. Canada blocked the introduction of BGH into that country based on scientific evidence of its carcinogenic potential.

Certified organic milk, however, has important nutrients for those who can digest it. In fact, proponents of organic and natural products say that it is the excessive processing that milk undergoes that makes it indigestible, not the milk itself. Check out the Web site on organic milk at www.realmilk.com. An antimilk Web site can be found at www.notmilk.com.

If you suspect dairy upsets you, do a little experiment. Avoid it for a few weeks. If you have eaten dairy on a daily basis, your body may have developed a certain tolerance to it and you may have gotten used to the gas and bloating, dry skin, excess mucus, and other symptoms. When you go off dairy, your body finally gets a chance to detoxify. Then drink a few glasses of milk and have a large portion of cheese and see if your symptoms return. This type of testing lets you know if you are allergic to any component of milk, not just lactose.

I personally don't eat dairy because I get excess mucus from it. With all the public speaking I do, I cannot afford to be gagging and clearing my throat all the time, so I avoid it. In 1979, I became aware of the D'Adamos' blood group diet theory with Type Os requiring a high-protein diet, Type As a vegetarian diet, and Types AB and B thriving on a combination of each. I considered that with my Type O blood group, I just wasn't able to assimilate dairy. Check the section on diets on page 185 to learn more about blood group diets.

Eating yogurt can be an effective way to take dairy products if you have mild lactose intolerance. Yogurt is a fermented product with a reduced lactose content. If you make your own yogurt, instead of incubating it for only twelve hours, continue for twenty-four hours so more of the lactose is broken down.

If you decide to avoid dairy products, take a calcium/magnesium supplement. Taking excess calcium without magnesium might be a cause of future kidney stones. Avoid supplements such as Tums, which have antacid properties that greatly decrease the absorption of the calcium. Foods and supplements rich in calcium are listed in the section on osteoporosis on page 130.

There is an enzyme product on the market called Lactaid, available in tablets or drops, to put in your milk. Lactaid-treated cheeses are also available with up to 90 percent of the lactose broken down. For people who are extremely allergic to milk, the 10 percent that is left over could still be a problem, however. Remember, lactose is not the only component of milk. You could be allergic to casein, to whey, or to the antibiotic and hormone residues given to dairy cows.

One of the conditions you can develop with lactose intolerance or the overconsumption of dairy products is candidiasis. Lactose is a disaccharide made up of glucose and galactose. When this breaks down, you then have glucose sugar available, which can have the same effect on yeast organisms as refined sugar. The section on candidiasis on page 40 might be useful. You may find that avoiding dairy eases your symptoms, especially if you also avoid sugar, yeast breads, and fermented foods.

Leg Cramps

A condition commonly called a "charley horse" can cause excruciating pain, usually in the calf of the leg or the foot; it is associated with a calcium or magnesium deficiency. Vitamin E can help prevent a condition called restless legs. This occurs in bed at night when the legs twitch and jump almost uncontrollably, causing insomnia and fatigue. Poor circulation can aggravate both of these conditions. Poor circulation in the calf muscles leading to chronic pain is called intermittent claudication. (If blood vessels in the heart are blocked, the pain is called angina; blocked vessels to the penis lead to impotence.) An acutely inflamed, swollen, and painful calf can be caused by a blood clot, which needs emergency care.

For chronic intermittent claudication, first stop smoking. Next, start walking. Alternating warm and cold footbaths can help. For poor circulation that results in cold feet, don't use hot water, heating pads, or hot water bottles, because you could burn your feet. Choose proper footgear and take good care of your feet. When the circulation is poor, cuts and infections don't heal.

In children, leg cramps or pains are sometimes related to growing pains. Vitamin E supplementation will often alleviate this problem.

Osgood Schlatter's disease in children is a painful condition of the knee bone or patella. Some specialists feel it is caused by growth spurts in the leg and thigh muscles that put a strain on the patella. Selenium seems to alleviate this condition. Food sources of selenium include Brazil nuts, snapper, halibut, salmon, swiss chard, oats, and orange juice.

Liver Disease

The liver has the awesome responsibility of detoxifying every chemical that we encounter. According to Dr. Sam Epstein, this amounts to at least 500 different foreign chemicals in each cell of the body. With thousands of food additives and pesticides, herbicides, industrial chemicals, and radiation breakdown particles in our environment, our livers and immune systems are very much overworked.

Does an overworked liver make it easier to contract hepatitis, a viral infection of the liver leading to degeneration? It's possible. There are at least four types of viral hepatitis; each new variant is given an alphabetic designation. Hepatitis can also be caused by mononucleosis, alcoholism, and drug exposure.

Hepatitis A is the most common form of infectious hepatitis. It is a viral condition contracted by eating or drinking something contaminated with the virus from someone's urine or feces. Because hepatitis A is contagious during the incubation period of two to six weeks before symptoms show up, it can be easily spread and epidemics occur frequently. Fortunately, hepatitis A does not create a carrier state and does not lead to chronic liver disease. It is seen mostly in children and young adults.

Hepatitis B is a more deadly form of hepatitis; it includes a carrier state, acute hepatitis, chronic hepatitis, necrosis, and, potentially, liver cancer. Hepatitis B is spread by puncturing the skin, usually through infected needles, or during sex with an infected partner. Medical personnel are at risk when they treat someone with hepatitis B. The incubation time ranges from one to five months.

Hepatitis C is assumed to be caused by an infection, but this has not been identified, and there are at least six variants. In general, it presents with a similar incubation time and biologic and clinical pictures as hepatitis B. It is also spread by puncturing the skin, most commonly through transfusion or shared needles, and may lead to a chronic carrier state. There is an epidemic of hepatitis C among boomers who had flings with drugs in the 1960s and are discovering that they have this disease. Research in 2000 indicates that there is a much lower risk of chronic disease or cancer in patients who have hepatitis C than previously thought.

The symptoms of hepatitis A may be so mild as to go unnoticed but there can be fatigue, malaise, dark urine, headache, and jaundice. For hepatitis B and C, these symptoms are more severe, including enlarged liver and spleen; blood tests reveal severe liver enzyme elevation. Antibody testing is done to determine the type of hepatitis.

In the treatment of all forms of hepatitis, protein in the diet is important. It appears to be difficult for strict vegetarians to overcome hepatitis. But you also need a wide variety of fruits and vegetables, organic if possible. Avoid sugar, alcohol, all caffeine products (coffee, black tea, cola, and chocolate), fried foods, food additives, and drugs to decrease the stress on the liver.

Supplements should include a natural multivitamin and mineral without iron. See the section on hemochromatosis on page 93. Dessicated liver or liver protomorphogen extracts (Hepatrophin PMG from Standard Process) are uniquely derived nucleoprotein-mineral extracts that supply building blocks to the liver; you may want to talk to a naturopath about obtaining these.

Milk thistle has been used as a liver tonic for a long time. Research confirms that it protects liver cells and can reverse toxic liver damage as well as protect the liver from toxic chemicals. Most studies have been done using a standardized extract (70 to 80 percent) of silimarin, which constitutes a dosage of 400 milligrams twice a day. Herbal Black Russian radish, in tincture form, 10 drops in water twice a day, is effective for mild forms of liver disease. Turmeric (curcumin) is an Indian spice that strengthens the liver.

Homeopathic Cheladonia 12C, 4 drops three times a day for several weeks, is specific for the liver. For mononucleosis, which can affect the liver, use homeopathic Cistus canidenses 12C, 4 drops three times a day.

Castor oil packs can be placed over the liver to enhance the lymphatic clearing of toxins. Soak a flannel cloth with castor oil and cover the liver, which is located below the right lower front ribs. Cover the cloth with a plastic bag and wrap a towel around you to hold it in place.

Rest for at least one hour. You don't even need to apply heat. Castor oil will stimulate the lymphatic circulation in the liver to begin to clear debris and start the healing process.

Menopause

Menopause is a natural occurrence. The female hormones normally decline after the age of forty-five and periods cease between ages forty-five and fifty-five. Unfortunately, due to a combination of chemical endocrine disrupters, weakened immune systems, and massive stress, women can undergo premature menopause. Cleaning up both our bodies and our environment is the only answer to this new epidemic.

A frequently overlooked function of the monthly period is to flush toxins from the body. I wonder if the absence of the period may be one reason why more women develop arthritic-like symptoms during menopause because they are retaining more toxins, which can then deposit in joint spaces. That's why I think it is extremely important for women in the menopausal years to start some form of regular detoxification. See the section on detoxification on page 178.

In Asian countries, women do not seem to experience the same symptoms of menopause that women do in North America. They have little incidence of hot flashes, depression, and mood changes in this normal phase of their lives. Perhaps it is because in these countries elders are respected and honored, whereas in the West we worship the "cult of youth," and menopause for many women means the loss of the status of youth.

Attitude plays a great role in any of life's transitions. If menopause is a time when your children have left home, you can now pursue a career or goal that may have been impossible before because of responsibilities at home. You may look on this time with renewed vigor, interest, and excitement. It should be a carefree time when you can do what you want to do, not what family or society dictates. Many female baby boomers are becoming activists on environmental issues in their communities. I predict that this group of women is going to have a huge impact on cleaning up the environment.

As far as treatment goes, I am not an advocate of either Premarin or synthetic hormone replacement. Premarin is made from pregnant mare's urine. If the barbaric conditions under which horses are kept to collect their valuable urine were made public, women would flush their pills down the drain immediately. Compounding this inhumane practice, Premarin itself is fit for horses, not women; it contains many other hormones that have never been tested on women. And Premarin causes uterine cancer.

When the high incidence of cancer due to Premarin was finally acknowledged in the mid-1980s, the answer from the pharmaceutical companies was to add another drug, synthetic progesterone, to the hormone replacement protocol. At that time, I was not in favor of this move. I was already reluctant to give estrogen because of the cancer risk. I always reasoned that because estrogen is considered so dangerous that a woman is immediately taken off it when diagnosed with cancer, how was I to know if there was a submicroscopic or subclinical cancer lurking that would be boosted by my prescription? It was not a risk I was willing to take, ethically or morally. This stand led me to explore options and alternatives to hormone replacement therapy.

As it turns out, combination hormone replacement therapy using synthetic estrogen and synthetic progesterone was proven in January 2000 to increase the incidence of breast cancer. The presumed solution to uterine cancer causes yet another cancer! We have to realize that all synthetic drugs overload the liver and can cause more problems than they cure.

Diet is extremely important in menopause because women gain more weight around this time. There is an epidemic of obesity in America and countless women are seduced by advertising to purchase diet products in the hopes that these products will help them lose weight. The synthetic sweetener aspartame is found in over 9,000 products worldwide. In his book *Aspartame (NutraSweet): Is It Safe?*, Dr. H. J. Roberts explains that aspartame triggers excessive prolactin production by the pituitary gland, which is a significant cause of menstrual changes or loss of periods in women. Aspartame also stimulates food cravings, causes fluid retention, and in general is a very bad joke on the women who are taking it in good faith in order to lose weight.

Foods that are very high in phytoestrogens (natural plant estrogens) include soy, as soy milk, soybeans, tofu, and tempeh; ground flaxseeds, (use a small coffee grinder and put on cereal or in juice and eat immediately [this is my personal favorite]); sprouted mung beans (another favorite) and clover seeds (see the section on bean sprouts on page 177); and pumpkin seeds, raw or lightly roasted. By focusing on one or two of these foods every day you can often eradicate hot flashes.

Plant estrogens work by providing tiny amounts of plant hormones that adapt to the needs of the body; they either increase your hormones if you have too little or decrease them if you have too much. Mother Nature knows best. Another important aspect of diet is to avoid hot, spicy foods and herbs when you are going through menopause. In my own case, avoiding cinnamon on my daily breakfast cereal made a big difference in my hot flashes.

Soy is on the tip of everyone's tongue now as the cure for menopause. Unlike Asian women, however, we did not grow up on soy and we may not have developed the necessary enzymes to digest it. If you get gas from soy products, eat them only once or twice a week, or use soy supplements that contain genistein and diadzein and check your tolerance of these products. Also, don't go for megadoses of genistein; the body was not designed to deal with such high amounts. If you get gas from soy products, assume you are not digesting and assimilating them and they are just being eliminated. Read more about soy on page 184.

If you are a heavy meat eater, it is important to cut back because digestive enzymes decrease with age. You can increase natural enzymes with the use of high-enzyme foods such as bean sprouts, papaya, and pineapple or take enzyme tablets to aid digestion and food breakdown. Remember, exercise and detoxification are very important practices to continue as you get older; they can make you feel younger. Exercise is important for the bones, heart, and circulation; we are finding out exercise is probably just as important as hormones for these conditions.

Women who have spent several decades as vegetarians may actually need to *increase* their protein intake. In fact, several vegetarian friends find themselves going into early menopause. All I can say is balance and individualization is the answer in choosing your diet. Read the section on diets on page 181 to try to determine what's best for you.

For specific symptoms, such as flooding that can periodically occur with blood clots and heavy bleeding, take bioflavonoids. They can be taken during the flooding or before an expected period. This supplement heals the capillaries lining the uterus. If heavy bleeding comes after having missed a period for many months, see your doctor.

Hot flashes are related to hormonal shifts as they affect the blood circulation. One treatment is to make sure the adrenal glands are supported in their production of female hormones as they take over from the ovaries. Many women in the West are under considerable pressure to juggle a career and a family. And there is no question that women do most of the work of child rearing compared to their spouses. The chronic lack of sleep common in mothers drains the adrenal glands. By the time of menopause, the adrenal glands are unable to supply the hormones required to make up for the decline of the ovaries.

Support for the adrenals can be given in the form of dessicated adrenal or Drenatrophin PMG (Standard Process), taken midmorning and midafternoon; pantothenic acid, a B vitamin that supports the adrenal glands; and vitamin C, which also supports the adrenal glands. Dr. Robert Atkins has successfully used folic acid as a precursor to hormone production for many years. He uses very high doses, which have to be prescribed by a doctor. Vitamin E aids circulation and supports the liver. Calcium and magnesium are very important, even before menopause, to prevent osteoporosis. They can be introduced and used at any time after age thirty but should be continued indefinitely. See the section on osteoporosis on page 130 for high-calcium and high-magnesium foods. Boron is a mineral that promotes hormone production; it is best taken in a trace mineral formula and not in high doses.

Exercise should be mentioned again. Yoga, tai chi, swimming, and walking are the best forms of exercise. All types of exercise are important for bone building, not just weight-bearing exercise.

Ginseng as well as black cohosh can be useful herbs for menopause. The best form of ginseng is red Korean. The dosage of black cohosh in tincture form is 10 drops in water, two to three doses per day. Vitex herb enhances progesterone production.

Homeopathic remedies such as Sepia and Pulsatilla are very useful for menopausal symptoms, including hot flashes. Go over the descriptions of these two remedies in part 4 of this book and see if they fit your case. If neither is a match, consult a homeopathic doctor for an individualized prescription.

For vaginal dryness, try progesterone cream to build up the mucous membranes and vitamin E oil for vaginal healing. Some vaginal preparations in the health food store include evening primrose oil, vitamin A, and vitamin E. For more information on the natural treatment of menopause, refer to my book *Menopause Naturally*.

In the event that none of the above recommendations give you the relief you are seeking, natural hormone replacement is becoming more widely available. Compounding pharmacies extract natural estrogens and progesterone from plant sources. On the other hand, synthetic hormones are constructed from petroleum-based carbon, hydrogen, and oxygen. They are said to be the same chemical structure as natural hormones, but they are mirror images that try to fit backward into receptor sites. Candace Pert, chief of brain sciences at the National Institutes of Health (NIH) for thirteen years, did the definitive work on hormone receptor sites. She says that synthetic hormones, because they are a mirror image and not the exact conformation of natural hormones, essentially "rape" receptor sites and render them useless for normal functioning, which leads to many side effects, including cancer.

Another important factor in the hormone controversy is the use of estradiol by pharmaceutical companies, because it is the most powerful estrogen but also the most harmful compared to estrone and estriol. All three can be extracted from plants, but using mostly estrone and estriol can reduce a woman's chances of stimulating cancer growth. Also, progesterone is often more deficient in women than estrogen; both need to be given in a balanced fashion. For some women, testosterone may even be required in small amounts. These hormones are available by prescription, but you should insist on a thorough hormonal panel, including testosterone, to determine your needs. Testing can now be done using either blood or saliva.

Read Dr. Serafina Corsello's wonderful book, *The Ageless Woman*, for a detailed description of the endocrine system and balancing the female hormones.

Menstrual Pain

The medical term for this condition is *dysmenorrhea*, and it affects half the female population. Menstrual pain can occur as a result of fibroids and endometriosis, both of which are dealt with in separate sections on page 79 and page 72, respectively. Painful periods with no underlying organic cause can be extremely debilitating. Dysmenorrhea tends to lessen after childbirth, so young women suffer most. One of the proposed causes for menstrual pain is an imbalance in the level of prostaglandins in the uterus. Prostaglandins are hormonelike substances that are manufactured from fatty acids. If the fatty acids are predominantly from arachadonic acid (meat and diary), this encourages prostaglandins, which stimulate excessive bleeding and uterine cramping. These findings have led to treatment with antiprostaglandin drugs.

Natural treatments include evening primrose oil and fish oils, which enhance those prostaglandins that inhibit uterine contractions. Calcium and magnesium also help stabilize muscle spasms in the uterus and can be taken throughout the day. Make sure there is no vitamin D added to the calcium-magnesium combination.

Eliminating coffee, alcohol, meat, sugar, dairy, salt, and white bread seven to ten days before the period can be extremely helpful in reducing menstrual cramps.

Castor oil packs and a hot water bottle on the abdomen can be very soothing. Use several tablespoons of castor oil on an old hand towel. Soak oil into the towel, cover the lower abdomen with the towel, and top it with plastic. Heat with a hot water bottle. Leave the pack on for at least one hour at a time. Hot baths with Epsom salts are also helpful. Exercise is very important to help stabilize contractions, so swim, walk, or stretch during the pain. Sexual intercourse can help as well.

There are several useful homeopathic remedies for painful periods. Use Mag. phos. 12C for the type of pain that is better when you are curled up in a ball with a hot water bottle pressing against your right side. The dosage is 4 drops every half hour. Colocynthis is for more intense, sharp, stabbing pain better with pressure than with heat and more on the left side; your mood is bitter and irritable. Cimicifuga 12C is for severe cramps across the abdomen and down the legs, and for backaches; you are hysterical, irritable, and achy. This is taken 4 drops every hour while in pain. There are many remedies for this condition. A homeopathic book or, better still, a homeopathic doctor should be consulted if the first few remedies do not achieve the desired result.

Mononucleosis

Mono is called "the kissing disease"; it is a virally transmitted infection that affects the lymph glands and the liver. Because it is a viral illness, there is no conventional medical treatment for mono, aside from rest. In my practice, however, I have used natural and homeopathic remedies with great success.

Viruses usually affect you when you are run down and your immune system is vulnerable. So you have to get lots of sleep and eat an optimum diet. Specific remedies include high doses of vitamin C with bioflavonoids and liver herbs such as milk thistle (*Silybum marianum*) in tincture form, 10 to 30 drops in 1 cup of water taken three times per day. The homeopathic remedies I prescribe include Cistus canadensis, which is specifically for mono, and Cheladonia, which is for the liver and the spleen. The potency for these remedies is 12C. Take both remedies three or four times per day until you start to feel better. Then gradually cut back the frequency.

I've seen teenagers go from being flat in bed to the ski slopes in three weeks on this regime. If not treated properly, mono can go on to become chronic fatigue syndrome.

Multiple Sclerosis

Multiple sclerosis (MS) is caused by degeneration of the myelin sheath surrounding the nerves and can occur in any nerve of the body, leading to widespread, nonspecific, and confusing symptoms. The cause of MS is unknown and, at this point, the medical treatment or cure is unknown. There is a consensus in naturopathic medicine that there is no one treatment for MS but a variety of treatments that can help alleviate some of the symptoms.

Often, the diagnosis can take several years to confirm. In that time, a patient can experience eye, bladder, and muscle symptoms. If the bladder is affected and you get bladder symptoms, antibiotic overuse can lead to an overgrowth of yeast in the entire body. The toxins from the yeast will irritate the nerves even more, thus increasing the symptoms of MS.

Anxiety about what is causing your symptoms and not getting a diagnosis can also mimic MS symptoms. For example, hyperventilation can cause tingling and numbness in the extremities, just as MS does. Some research has shown that allergenic foods can cause antigen-antibody reactions in your system that can further irritate the nerves, muscles, and joints. An avoidable cause of MS symptoms is aspartame (NutraSweet) intake. This synthetic chemical contains wood alcohol (methanol), phenylalanine, and aspartic acid. Read the section on sugar and aspartame on page 185 to understand the potential toxicity of aspartame and why it should be avoided if you are having any symptoms of numbness, tingling, weakness, blurred vision, joint pain, or insomnia.

The natural treatment for MS entails dietary manipulation to avoid the major allergenic foods: dairy, wheat, and perhaps all the gluten grains, which include wheat, rye, oats, and barley. Sugar and alcohol are also excluded. Roy Swank, M.D., has been treating MS patients for over forty years and has concluded that avoiding wheat and dairy can stabilize a person and prevent progression of the disease. His book is called *The Multiple Sclerosis Diet Book.*

People who have been treated with cortisone for their flare-ups and antibiotics for bladder symptoms are advised to go on anti-*Candida* treatment. (See the section on candidiasis on page 40.) With a hypo-allergenic diet, an anti-*Candida* diet, and avoidance of aspartame, a great many MS symptoms can be relieved or alleviated. Homeopathy seems to have a place in the treatment of MS, but the proper treatment includes constitutional remedies, which can only be given after a complete history has been taken by a homeopathic doctor.

Nail Abnormalities

Nails and their abnormalities are related to many different deficiencies. Brittle nails indicate an iron deficiency and decreased circulation. Brittle, ridged, thin nails indicate Raynaud's syndrome, in which there is decreased circulation during cold weather or during periods of stress. Spoon-shaped, concave nails indicate an iron deficiency. Brittle nails can also indicate overuse of solvents and detergents. White spots on the nails indicate zinc deficiency or, more rarely, a loss of protein in the urine. In teenage diets, zinc is very low and it is required to metabolize the junk food that so many young people eat. Yellowish nails indicate lymphatic congestion, respiratory congestion, or deficiency in vitamin E. Yellow toenails and red patches and bruising around the nails indicate diabetes. Dark nails can indicate a B_{12} deficiency. A white cuticle with a dark tip is an indication of chronic kidney disease. Whitish nails indicate liver or kidney disease or anemia. Horizontal ridges on the nails indicate protein or zinc deficiency. Vertical lines on the nails indicate iron, calcium, or magnesium deficiency.

Nausea

In my practice, I see many people with nausea, often because of candidiasis. (See the section on candidiasis on page 40.) It can be from the toxicity that can occur when the body is completely overloaded with toxins. Imagine a barrel filled to the top with oil, dirt, and debris; anything else that goes in assumes the character of the debris. Sometimes people are so toxic that any food they take in just adds to their toxicity and makes them feel sick. In this case, people have to detoxify and cleanse before they do anything else. Good food and excellent supplements are useless in the face of a toxic overload. Read the section on detoxification on page 178 to help with this. If the nausea is due to pregnancy, read the section on pregnancy on page 169. A common cause of nausea among healthy people who take vitamins is taking zinc on an empty stomach. If you want to know what morning sickness feels like, eat zinc tablets for breakfast.

The best remedy for nausea while exploring the above sections or for nausea caused by motion sickness is ginger tea or ginger capsules. Acupuncture is also very helpful because it can work on the vagus nerve, which may be irritated by stomach acidity and give a constant nausea reflex. In most cases, however, nausea is only a symptom of a bigger problem.

Neck Pain

The problem of neck pain is extremely common among North Americans. It has to do with the way we sit at our desks with our necks bent forward, our shoulders slumped, and our brows scrunched up in concentration. It starts in the shoulders and moves up into the neck. It feels like we have just been in a motor vehicle accident and suffered whiplash. Muscle spasms in the neck can be very severe. The best treatments are heat or ice, and if both give some relief, they can be used alternately. Massage is very helpful; you can do a self-massage that can relax the neck. Lying on two tennis balls tied up in a sock and positioned at the base of the skull can relieve pressure. Do this carefully so that you don't cause more pain. To avoid neck pain, make sure you sit with good back support. I personally find that the kneeling chair is helpful. It has two levels of cushioning: one you kneel on, and the other you rest your buttocks on. By kneeling forward on your knees, you redistribute your weight, which produces a new, forward center of gravity. This maintains your body in an upright posture. When you're working at a computer, as so many of us do today, make sure your computer is at eye level and that you have to look neither up nor down. An accessory is available that elevates the computer screen, or you can stack up several telephone books.

When you lift any heavy object, be sure that you're bending at the knees and not putting a strain on your back and neck. Sleeping for six to eight hours in the wrong position can aggravate neck problems. Choose a firm mattress. Use a rolled-up towel under your neck, or find a neck pillow or cervical pillow that puts proper support under your neck. Never sleep on your stomach; the best position is either on your back or curled up in the fetal position. If your neck is very stiff or you feel tenderness in certain areas, you might want to check with a qualified chiropractor for treatment. You might be advised to get x-rays to diagnose any problems with your vertebrae. Read the section on x-rays, page 175. If your neck pain comes from a motor vehicle accident, be sure you are under the care of a medical doctor.

Night Blindness

Night blindness is due to vitamin A deficiency so the treatment is very simple: take vitamin A or beta-carotene. The best sources of beta-carotene are yellow vegetables such as carrots, yams, and squash and green leafy vegetables, such as kale, spinach, and broccoli. Vitamin A is found in fish liver oils. One teaspoon of cod liver oil or halibut liver oil a day supplies essential fatty acids, including vitamin A. When you take fish oils, check the label and don't take more than 10,000 IU of A or 400 IU of D per day on a long-term basis.

Nosebleed

Nosebleeds occur more often in the winter months due to drying of the nasal membranes, which leaves them susceptible to cracking and bleeding. To avoid this, humidify your living space, especially your bedroom, so that you have more moisture in the air.

Nosebleeds are often connected with more than dryness alone; a winter cold can bring on a lot of nasal mucus and irritation, with the consequent nose-blowing that sets the stage for dryness, cracking, and bleeding. Also, allergies to inhaled dust and mites, and even food such as dairy and wheat, can cause extra mucus in the nose. Therefore, a vicious cycle is set up that results in breakage or tears in the membranes inside the nose, which can take up to a week to heal. Usually, people can't leave their noses alone for more than an hour without blowing out the mucus or even picking at the crusts, and it will require much longer periods in order to heal a damaged area in the nose. The more you stick your fingers in your nose and pick at it, the more you are susceptible to nasal boils. These are usually staphylococcal bacterial infections that start with a very painful swelling in the nose, form pus, and then dry and crust.

The nose is very sensitive, and the treatment for this vicious cycle is to leave the nose alone except for using vitamin E oil or comfrey cream, several times a day, to help lubricate the nose lining and heal the scabs. If you do get a staphylococcal boil, you might need an antibiotic ointment, used several times a day, to kill that bacteria. The underlying cause for these boils may be candidiasis; read about this condition on page 40.

The vitamin and mineral treatments for nosebleed include vitamin C with bioflavonoids, zinc, calcium, and magnesium. Drugs that interfere with clotting include aspirin, as well as drugs that are taken specifically to thin the blood. Sometimes the side effect of these medications is nosebleeds, but you can overcome this if you follow the above recommendations. Not everybody taking these medications has nosebleeds.

Obesity

Since I wrote the first edition of this book over ten years ago, the incidence of obesity has skyrocketed. Over half the adult population is overweight, and kids are catching up fast. Besides putting a strain on all your joints because you carry extra weight, obesity puts a strain on your heart. What's not talked about is the way fat cells hold on to toxins to try to protect the body from being poisoned. Toxins abound in our culture and environment. We allow thousands of chemical additives in our food, air, and water, and the liver has to process all of them.

Because a lot of these chemicals end up in fat stores, this means when we try to lose weight these toxins are released into the bloodstream. In fact, when you go on a fast or diet, you can feel so sick within two to three days that you quit the program and all your good intentions fly out the window. Like caffeine or cigarette withdrawal, when you stop eating foods to which you are addicted or which are poisoning you, your body starts flushing the poisons or toxins from those foods out of your system. As these toxins are released, especially from fat cells where they are stored, you can feel really terrible, with headaches, cramps, diarrhea, and fatigue.

What's the answer? Any diet must be started slowly; drink lots of water to flush out poisons and above all, avoid constipation. Take saunas when you diet to use your skin as "your third lung" to eliminate toxins by sweating. If you don't sweat right away, rub sea salt all over your skin to pull out the sweat. Clay body wraps are an excellent way to pull toxins from fat cells; read more about cleansing in the section on detoxification on page 178. Also, drink lots of purified, filtered water, and eat good oils and fats such as fish oils, flaxseed, olive, and coconut, avoiding margarine and processed vegetable oils.

The low-fat, high-carbohydrate diet seems to have backfired and there is now a big swing to high-fat diets! What is the answer? First, read the section on diets on page 181 and try eating according to your blood group. Then read the section on diabetes on page 58 to learn about insulin resistance, which is why sugar builds up in the blood, causes diabetes, and increases fat stores. Read about sugar addictions on page 4 to understand why you are addicted to sugar. The section on sugar and aspartame on page 185 will round out your education when you learn that artificial sweeteners such as aspartame (NutraSweet) stimulate the brain and actually cause carbohydrate cravings. This means that when you take any of the over 9,000 diet products laced with aspartame, you are ironically gaining weight, retaining fluid, and causing neurological damage to your body all at the same time.

According to Drs. James and Peter D'Adamo, if you are an O blood type and you continue to eat bread and flour products you will gain weight and you may also become allergic to wheat and gluten products. You retain fluid in order to dilute the toxins from this allergic reaction. Food allergy testing may be helpful to sort this out. Avoiding the gluten grains, rye, oats, wheat, and barley, is the first step.

If you are an A blood type, a high-meat diet may be causing your weight gain. You may not be digesting the meat and may need to cut back and eat more complex carbohydrates such as root vegetables, beans, legumes, nuts, and seeds to lose weight.

Eating small, frequent meals may be important for your weight-loss programs. Don't starve throughout the day and make up for it with one large meal at night. If you only eat one large meal a day, you can actually gain weight because the body is designed to have a meal and metabolize, digest, and break down the excess in the few hours following the meal. If one large meal is consumed, only a portion of the food will be metabolized and utilized and the excess will go into fat storage. You are also triggering the mechanism leading to insulin resistance when you only eat one meal a day. Read the section on diabetes on page 58 to learn more about insulin resistance.

Another weight loss tip is exercise. If you are an O blood type, you require lots of exercise to help metabolize the heavier animal protein diet. A good exercise program for you includes vigorous walking, swimming, or bicycling, with yoga thrown in for flexibility and relaxation. As an A blood type, you do better with yoga, tai chi, and walking because on a vegetarian diet you have fewer heavy foods to metabolize and eliminate.

People often ask about fasting to achieve weight loss. This is not the best route to take; it is important to change lifestyle and habits rather than depending on such extreme methods. During a fast, a lot of metabolic mechanisms slow down and you don't necessarily lose weight. If you are allergic to foods and they are contributing to your weight problems or you want to detoxify, you can go on a modified fast that includes hypoallergenic protein powder with psyllium seed as a bulking agent, plus vegetables, for a period of three to ten days in order to get rid of excess fluid weight and to clear the body of possible allergenic foods. Then you can begin an elimination diet. See the section on allergies on page 6. Ultrabalance/Ultraclear protein powder or algae protein powders are available at your health pharmacy or through your naturopathic doctor; see the Resources section at the back of this book for more information.

Osteoporosis

Osteoporosis is more and more in the news, probably because our population is aging. Also, there is a big push from pharmaceutical companies to use estrogen replacement therapy to help strengthen the bones. Others are stressing calcium supplementation. All this information is varied and complex, often not completely researched, and leaves the public not really knowing how to proceed.

Osteoporosis means a thinning of the bones. If a bone is not exercised, it will automatically begin being reabsorbed. Space astronauts discovered this when they were in weightless flight. The most important advice is to maintain an optimum level of exercise to avoid bone resorption. Avoid alcohol, which interferes with bone formation. Smoking lowers estrogen, which adds to osteoporosis risk. Coffee also affects the bones adversely; it hastens calcium excretion, probably by its diuretic action.

In countries with low protein intake, osteoporosis is not a problem. Protein, especially meat with its high phosphorus content, causes calcium loss. Phosphates in soft drinks also seem to be a concern, as they bind calcium and take it out of the body.

In regard to calcium replacement therapy for osteoporosis, it must be acknowledged that bones are made up of a multitude of minerals and nutrients and treatment should include all of them. These include calcium, magnesium, zinc, copper, boron, mucopolysaccharides, chondroitin sulphates, and many of the B vitamins that are important for the enzymatic production of bone. Most of the studies of osteoporosis take one nutrient or modality and try to see if it prevents bone loss. In the individual case, it is important to assess and maintain all modalities. With regard to estrogen replacement, again, there is no one thing that will help bone loss. When someone has true and obvious estrogen deficiencies and can only be helped with estrogen supplementation, the natural hormone should be used. Menopause is a natural transition in one's life and need not be medicated. (See the section on menopause on page 118.)

Another drug that should be avoided is Fosamax. It is a popular bone-resorption inhibitor (actually, it kills bone resorption cells) used in the prevention and treatment of osteoporosis. Some of its known side effects are gastric and esophageal inflammation, renal failure, ocular damage, skin reactions, hypocalcemia, hepatitis, and brittle bones.

Many people avoid dairy because of lactose intolerance, bovine growth hormones, allergies, diarrhea, constipation, or its toxic fat content. The table on page 132 lists food sources of readily absorbed calcium.

If you don't feel you are getting enough dietary calcium and you need to take supplementation, calcium lactate is the most readily absorbed form. Other types of calcium may require up to a dozen metabolic steps to make it recognizable to the body for absorption. Calcium lactate requires only one step. This means supplements claiming to contain 500 or 1,000 milligrams, if they are only 10 to 30 percent absorbed, will merely give you 50 to 150 milligrams or 100 to 300 milligrams of

CALCIUM CONTENT OF COMMON FOODS

Food	Mg. Calcium
Vegetables	
½ cup cooked spinach	88
1 cup cooked dried beans (white, kidney, soy, and so on)	95 to 110
½ cup cooked kale	103
½ cup cooked collards	110
1 cup cooked turnip greens	126
½ cup cooked dandelion greens	147
½ cup cooked beet greens	157
1 medium stalk broccoli	158
1 cup bok choy cabbage	252
Baked Goods	
1 slice whole wheat bread	50
1 medium waffle	76
1 medium corn muffin	96
½ cup soy flour	132
1 tablespoon blackstrap molasses	140
Seafood	
¾ can clams	62
6 scallops	115
½ can salmon with bones	284
20 medium oysters	300
7 sardines with bones	393
Nuts and Seeds	
½ cup sesame seeds	76
½ cup Brazil nuts	128
½ cup almonds	175
Fruit	
½ cup rhubarb, cooked	200

From Joy Underwood's *Calcium Content of Common Foods* (out of print).

available calcium. This is yet another incredibly frustrating hurdle for the health product consumer.

Magnesium can also be deficient in osteoporosis because it is deficient in the standard American diet. Magnesium is present in legumes, tofu, nuts, whole grains, and green leafy vegetables, and lacking in fish, meat, and milk. Magnesium lactate is the most readily absorbed form of magnesium.

Parasites

The World Health Organization (WHO) estimates that half the world's population is infected with parasites. In the West, we pretend we are not susceptible. The New York City water supply occasionally harbors *Giardia lambia*, a common parasite. It used to be picked up by travelers to foreign countries, but it is common in mountain streams in any country. Epidemics of *Giardia* periodically affect day-care centers and fast-food establishments. On a daily basis, people eat contaminated restaurant or packaged food that causes intestinal reactions they may not attribute to parasites.

Parasites are not killed easily with just soap and water. Some health advocates even advise washing food in a basin of water to which is added one or two capfuls of bleach. Fortunately, there is another product that does not have the potential for its own side effects that bleach might have: bitter grapefruit seed extract, sold in stores as citricidal. Soak all your fruits and vegetables in a basin of water and add several drops of the extract. It can be taken internally in capsule form to kill parasites in food when eating out.

Parasites have the potential to cause multiple symptoms, just like *Candida*. They can cause gas, bloating, and more diarrhea than constipation, and the toxins from parasites can cause symptoms of fatigue and irritability. Pinworms in children are notorious for causing grinding teeth, ravenous appetite, and itchy bottom. Parasites have a life cycle that makes them especially active during a full moon. Women sometimes mistake parasite symptoms for premenstrual tension.

When parasites cannot be ruled out, they may be treated on speculation. This line of reasoning is offensive to allopathic medicine, which contends that you have to have a diagnosis before you can treat anything. There is no blood test for parasites, however, and stool testing for parasites is notoriously inaccurate. There is a whopping 50 percent chance of missing parasites when a stool sample is placed in a preservative and sent to a lab. The stool may not be collected properly, leaving the stool in a clump and not adequately mixed with the solution, and the parasite decomposes before analysis. The stool may not contain any parasites at all because they live in the mucous membranes of the intestine, not in the stool. The best stool sample is a direct swab of the anal canal, which is read immediately by a skilled technician.

In Europe, you often hear of children and animals being regularly dewormed with potions of garlic and herbs. We do not follow that practice in North America because we somehow have the notion that parasites cannot affect us. Consider this scenario: A migrant farm worker may not have hygienic sanitary facilities in the field. If the worker has parasites, they may be passed onto the produce being picked and end up on your table. Produce does not undergo any effective washing or cleansing process to deal with parasite contamination. Unless it is cleaned with grapefruit seed extract or bleach in your kitchen, you have to assume it has parasites.

If you don't eat organic produce, wash all your fruits and vegetables in VegiWash to remove the majority of pesticide surface residue.

Phlebitis

This occurs when a blood clot forms in a deep vein of the legs. The reasons for it include the birth control pill or long periods of immobility, such as during air travel or bed rest following surgical procedures or accidents. The best treatment is prevention, of course, by eating an optimal diet, which keeps the blood from becoming too thick with cholesterol and triglycerides, and getting plenty of exercise. If you have a family history of phlebitis or have had an occurrence already, you must not smoke. Read the section on atherosclerosis on page 19 to get more information on how to take care of your veins and arteries.

Poison Ivy

Avoid poison ivy by knowing what it looks like. Once you have contacted poison ivy, every effort should be made to isolate that area of the skin and not touch, rub, or press it up against any other area of the skin or clothing that can retain the resin and pass the allergic reaction along. I have even had cases of patients who blistered after handling an old, dried, pressed specimen of poison ivy.

The treatment, if it can be accomplished on the spot, is to locate a jewel weed plant and rub the plant over the affected area. If you live in a poison ivy region, make sure you learn how to identify both plants. At home, wash the area with warm, soapy water and never touch the blisters without washing your hands afterward. Also, take Rhus tox. by mouth, a homeopathic remedy for poison ivy, either 12C or 200C hourly. Keep the area dry and apply calamine lotion.

Premenstrual Syndrome

Premenstrual syndrome (PMS) is a condition of hormonal imbalance and inappropriate fluid retention that occurs seven to ten days before your period and can cause bloating, swelling, and weight gain as well as psychological distress such as poor concentration, depression, irritability, anxiety, and anger. Some women can become so irritated that they become suicidal or homicidal. Of course, these cases are as rare as they are extreme. In the early 1980s, I was treating PMS with diet, vitamin B_6, vitamin E, and for the worst cases, progesterone suppositories before it was even recognized as a true medical condition. Suppositories were necessary because oral progesterone was destroyed by the liver. Now progesterone is available in both transdermal cream and in oral micronized forms that are not immediately broken down by the liver. Over time, PMS has been accepted by the medical mainstream and types of PMS as well as its mechanisms and causes have been researched and described.

There are four types of PMS. PMS-A causes anxiety; PMS-C causes cravings; PMS-D causes depression; PMS-H (for H_2O) causes water retention. There are over a dozen known contributing factors or causes of PMS, including estrogen dominance and low progesterone; faulty nutrition and excess salt, coffee, and alcohol; hypoglycemia; candidiasis; hypothyroidism; adrenal exhaustion; food allergies; environmental toxicity, including mercury fillings; infections, both viral and parasitic; stress, including sexual abuse; and lack of proper sleep and exercise. Examine these conditions in various sections in this book to understand the underlying factors that worsen your PMS.

My advice is to use a charting system in which you keep a record of your cycle and your symptoms to determine whether indeed you are experiencing PMS. Symptoms must occur from ovulation to the period and disappear at the onset of menses to be true PMS. The mere identification of your symptoms as cyclical can help to alleviate some of your frustration about what is going on. And perhaps, with simple rest and acknowledgment, you may realize that your symptoms can be expected to subside in a few days and you won't get too caught up in them.

In the Native American culture, women at the time of their moons were honored; they spent their moon time in a special longhouse where they were fed and waited on. They shared their visions and dreams with other women. The premenstrual time for all women is one of greater dreaming, intuition, and vision. These aspects of our inner knowing and spirit have been ignored or rejected in our society in the past but are being more accepted as greater numbers of women reach maturity and publicly honor our gifts.

Regarding diet, avoid foods that cause fluid retention, such as salt and sugar. Avoid chips, candy, desserts, alcohol, tea, coffee, and soft drinks (especially aspartame-sweetened drinks) and try to eat an optimum diet of whole grains, nuts, seeds, vegetables, legumes, fish, and chicken. Most women with PMS have not been following a good diet and require detoxification to unburden the liver, which is responsible for making our hormones. Read the section on detoxification on page 178 for simple cleansing instructions.

The next step is to use supplements, starting with vitamin B_6 to decrease fluid buildup. I used to advise high doses, but these are mostly from synthetic sources. So I recommend B_6 (pyridoxine hydrochloride) mixed with natural factors. Instead of 300 milligrams per day you might just need 100 milligrams per day. Another supplement deficient in premenstrual tension is magnesium. Take it as magnesium lactate, 200 milligrams per day; this is especially important if you suffer painful periods. Evening primrose oil is used for many premenstrual symptoms, especially breast tenderness, and can also be used for painful periods. Take this at a dosage of four to six capsules per day. A good natural multivitamin and mineral supplement is also an asset, especially for its B vitamin content to help balance the use of extra B_6.

The next step I suggest is homeopathic remedies. The three simplest ones follow.

1. Sepia is for dark-haired women who are angry and irritable and push people away, feel better when they are dancing, feel their uterus is heavy and falling, and suffer leg pains prior to and during the period. This can be taken, 12C, 4 drops three times a day, seven to ten days before the period.
2. Pulsatilla is for blonde women who are weepy and inconsolable but who also may be changeable; that is, they may appear angry and irritable one moment like a Sepia, and the next minute be in a flood of tears. The same dosage, 12C, 4 drops three times a day is used, seven to ten days before the period.
3. Nat. mur. is a good remedy for women who crave salt. These women retain a lot of fluid and they are "shut down"; that is, not wanting to get involved with anyone and quite often have suffered a heartache or major grief that keeps them behind a protective barrier. They are often good listeners and try to help others but never get involved. Again, this remedy is 12C, 4 drops three times a day, for seven to ten days before the period.

Usually these remedies are used for three to four cycles. Many symptoms abate, and after that the remedies are only used as needed.

If you don't entirely respond to the treatments suggested above, you may require progesterone cream. Estrogen dominance can be determined by blood or saliva testing. If estrogen is high and progesterone is low, you can usually get relief for PMS with creams that contain progesterone. Some of the pure wild yam creams contain no progesterone. Dosage varies from ¼ to ½ teaspoon once or twice a day and should be discussed with your naturopathic doctor.

Above all, don't fall victim to the propaganda that PMS is a mental condition requiring Prozac, even if the name is changed to Serafem and it is advertised for PMS.

Prostate Problems

The prostate gland is located at the base of the penis and helps produce prostatic fluid, which carries semen. Zinc is the main mineral that helps the prostate function. Oysters, pumpkin seeds, and sunflower seeds contain large amounts of zinc. In supplement form, zinc should be taken in a multiple mineral along with trace minerals. Too much zinc can deplete copper, so it is wise to not overdo it.

Prostate cancer is reaching epidemic proportions because of the many hormone-disrupting chemicals in our environment. We cannot escape them. They end up in our drinking water, our food, and the air we breathe. Our bodies reach a state of overload and the immune system cannot detoxify all the poisons as well as keep the body free of cancer cells.

Herbal prostate formulas are available in most health food stores. They may include saw palmetto berries, cornsilk, pumpkin seeds, uva ursi, and buchu. The homeopathic remedies used for the prostate are Thuja, Coninum, Medorrhinum, Staphysagria, and Baryta carb. All of these remedies are constitutional remedies and it is best to work with a naturopath or homeopath when using them. They are usually taken in the 12C potency for one month to see if your condition can be improved.

There are far too many men having prostate resection for benign enlargement. The side effects of this operation may include impotence, so this surgery should not be taken lightly. As well as the basic supplements mentioned, it is also important to have an optimum diet and avoid heavy, fried, spicy, rich foods that can increase the toxic burden on the body. Read the section on detoxification on page 178.

PC-SPES is a Chinese medicine formulation for prostate cancer that has a remarkable track record. It is a unique blend of herbs that contain specific properties that enhance the immune system, especially of prostate cancer patients. *PC* stands for "prostate cancer" and *spes* is Latin for "hope." A group of eight herbs developed by chemist Sophie Chen, Ph.D., it contains certified organic herbs harvested at the best time to ensure maximum potency and quality

Psoriasis

Psoriasis occurs when the skin cells reproduce up to a hundred times faster than normal. When this occurs, the skin builds up in dry, flaky patches and causes a lot of irritation, itching, and embarrassment. Unfortunately, product advertisements for treating "the heartbreak of psoriasis" make the public think of it as a horrible disease, and for some people it is. But those with mild to moderate cases can actually aggravate their psoriasis by fretting and worrying about the appearance of a new skin lesion.

Number one, try not to worry. Sunbathing helps a lot; even sun-lamps are helpful, but be careful because too much sun has side effects. Use sunscreen on the nonpsoriasis areas to prevent sun damage in those exposed parts. Tar soaps sold at drugstores seem to help slow down the production of psoriatic patches. Sea clay body wraps are fabulous for psoriasis. Read the detoxification section on page 178 and see Resources.

One supplement that helps this condition is zinc, which is depleted by the excessive cell production. Supplements should also include high doses of vitamin A, vitamin E, B complex, trace minerals, alfalfa tablets, calcium, magnesium, and bioflavonoids with vitamin C. Lecithin is also beneficial as well as the essential fatty acids in evening primrose oil and marine lipids. These oils have anti-inflammatory properties and nor-malize body tissues, including skin.

I have found in my practice that when people are treated for can-didiasis or allergies, their psoriasis begins to clear up. Check the sec-tions on these conditions on pages 40 and 6 for more information. It seems that almost any skin condition can be aggravated by *Candida* overgrowth.

The diet that is important in the treatment of psoriasis includes lots of vegetables, moderate fruit, lots of nuts, whole grains, legumes, beans and peas, fish, and chicken. Avoid saturated fats and refined foods such as pork, beef, and baked goods. You must pay attention to the body's acid balance and avoid oranges, which can cause an overalkaline reac-tion. Use cranberry juice, prunes, and plums, which are a bit more acidic. Avoid alcohol, smoking, coffee, and sugar.

Pyorrhea

This gum inflammation results from inadequate dental hygiene. If plaque and food build up between the teeth, they can irritate the gums and lead to gum inflammation. Dental floss or tape is helpful, as well as a Water Pik. Edgar Cayce recommended Glycothymoline, which contains a solution of boric acid. In the acute stages, rinse the mouth with a dilution of 1 part Glycothymoline to 3 parts water. In the chronic stage, or once the acute stage has passed, 2 to 3 drops of

Glycothymoline in 8 ounces of water shaken fifty times can be used as a homeopathic mouth rinse every night to prevent plaque buildup and pyorrhea. See the Resources section for more information. Calcium and magnesium are important for the proper maintenance of the gums as well as bioflavonoids, vitamin C, and zinc. An optimum diet is also beneficial.

Raynaud's Syndrome

Raynaud's is the name given to a condition that causes blue or white discoloration of the fingers due to lack of sufficient oxygen and blood supply. There is no known cause for this condition. Treatment is designed to keep the fingers warm and improve circulation in the hands. Always wear gloves in cold weather; swinging the arms like a windmill to force blood into the fingertips is helpful. Have your doctor check your hemoglobin and iron to see if you have a hemoglobin deficiency, which can decrease your oxygenation. People with low thyroid can have a lower body temperature, so read the section on hypothyroidism on page 103. Smoking is not recommended for people who have Raynaud's because it constricts the blood vessels.

Avoid alcohol, even though you feel it may be warming to the body; it actually creates heat loss and results in chilling of the extremities. Coffee and caffeine products in over-the-counter pain medications, in chocolate, and in cola drinks should be avoided because they, too, constrict blood vessels. Be sure you drink enough warm fluids, especially herb teas. Eat an optimum diet: plenty of vegetables, moderate fruit, and lots of whole grains, nuts, seeds, beans, legumes, fish, and chicken.

An important supplement for this condition, besides iron when indicated, is evening primrose oil. This oil is especially important because one of its properties is to produce, strengthen, and maintain the actual membrane of the red blood cell. If this membrane is strong and flexible, the red cells are able to conform to the shape of the very tiny capillaries at the tips of the fingers and toes. Perhaps Raynaud's is a deficiency of this nutrient. I don't think that there have been any clinical trials of this supplement yet, but theoretically it should help. Gamma linolenic acid, which is the major active ingredient in evening primrose oil, is not found in a typical North American diet. The only known side effect is headaches in people who are susceptible to alcohol-induced migraines.

You can get a headache from evening primrose oil if your liver is toxic or overloaded and not able to process or metabolize either alcohol or oils and fats. If this is the case, read the section on liver disease on page 116.

Other helpful supplements include the B vitamins, which are important for the nervous system and help heal the nerves of the fingers; vitamin E for thinning the blood and oxygenation; calcium and magnesium for their effect on cramping; and a good multivitamin and mineral combination.

Rectal Itch

This condition can be caused by food allergies, acidic and spicy foods, candidiasis, or anusitis, an inflammation of the anus. The avoidance of food allergens and treatment for candidiasis should be undertaken. If the condition does not completely improve, treatment with an instrument called Anurex is available; this is a cold suppository that is reusable. It is kept in the freezer and inserted into the anus to freeze the mucus-forming glands that keep producing irritating mucus around the anus, which can perpetuate this problem. Local creams that can be used include antifungal medications, zinc ointment, or vitamin E oil. Zinc ointment can be applied in a thick layer and act as a barrier against irritation while the skin is healing. Cortisone creams should be avoided because they can cause thinning of the skin.

Shingles

This is also known as herpes zoster. It is the reactivation of the chicken pox virus, usually in older people, and occurs with stress. The treatment is with B vitamins; vitamin E, 400 IU one to two capsules per day; B_{12} injections; and acupuncture. At times the pain is so severe that cortisone and strong painkillers must be used so that you can rest and sleep. The homeopathic remedies for herpes zoster are Ranunculus for the neuralgia, and Mezereum for the itching and burning. Rhus tox., Apis, Arsenicum, Natrum mur., Cantharis, and Clematis have also been used. Any of these can be taken in a 12C potency, 4 drops hourly, but consult part 4 of this book or a homeopathic manual to match your symptoms more closely with a specific remedy.

Sinus Infections

The sinuses are small cavities in the bones of the head that prevent the skull from being too heavy. The cavities are lined with mucous membranes; these membranes can be irritated or become inflamed and swollen from inhaled or food allergies or from infections. It is important to determine what is allergy and what is infection. With swelling of the mucous membranes, the channel between the sinus cavities and the nose becomes blocked and mucus builds up in the sinuses, causing great pressure and considerable pain. You know you have a problem with blocked mucus in your sinuses if you get face, nose, or head pain when you bend over to touch your toes. This clue should propel you toward a mucus-free diet and astringent herbs such as goldenseal, barberry, and dandelion. An infection starts if bacteria trapped in the cavity can live and grow on the mucus. Temperature and heat identify an acute infection, but sometimes there is no temperature with a chronic infection.

To treat a chronic condition, try hot compresses on the face or lymphatic massage. (See the section on edema on page 70.) Avoid mucus-forming foods and treat allergies. Saline nasal douches are very helpful. Get saline water at a drugstore or use a pinch of salt in boiled warm water; hold in a shallow cup under the nostril, inhale gently, then blow out. The salt will help constrict the mucous membranes so that mucus trapped in the sinuses can flow out. Health food or yoga supply stores carry a *neti pot*, which is specifically designed with a spout that fits into one nostril allowing saline water to flow through the sinuses and out the other nostril. I also add a few drops of tea tree oil as an antiseptic. Make sure you use a humidifier or balsam steam inhalation to keep the mucus flowing. Lots of fluid intake is important. My personal favorite for flowing mucus is eating spicy foods such as chili peppers, garlic, curry, or horseradish—a different spice for every day of the week. Exercise also seems to help. The best one is swimming in salt water.

For acute infections, a homeopathic nasal spray called Euphorbium can be used as well as hot compresses, shiatsu massage on pressure points around the face, and oral homeopathic Kali bich. 12C, which is for tough, stringy mucus. For severe and painful sinusitis, take Mercuralis 12C by mouth. If bacteria are involved, the above treatments can be used, but antibiotic therapy is sometimes necessary. When on antibiotic therapy, it is important to take acidophilus to replace good bacteria in the intestinal tract that the antibiotics are killing off. A homeopathic remedy can be made from the antibiotic if there are any side effects or if you feel the antibiotic remains in your system (see the section on making your own remedy on page 207).

Skin Conditions

Acne

Acne can be caused by or aggravated by dietary and hormonal factors. Young men get acne around puberty with surging testosterone, and young women's acne is stimulated by the elevation of estrogen before the period and while on the birth control pill. There is no way to stop hormones, but young women can slow down puberty and put if off for a year or two by eating soy products. Soy contains phytoestrogens (plant estrogens) that balance the hormones at both puberty and menopause. We are experiencing an epidemic of early puberty and acne, due to synthetic hormones injected into and fed to cows and chickens, and xenoestrogens (chemical estrogen mimickers) from pesticides and herbicides in our food supply. Soy partially blocks their action at hormone receptor sites.

Greasy, sugary foods can cause or worsen acne by stimulating the secretion of oils on the facial skin. The oils then plug up skin pores, allowing the bacteria that naturally live on the skin to infect the plugged pores and create blemishes.

For some, simply avoiding sugar, chocolate, refined foods, and artificial sweeteners (such as NutraSweet) can change the picture. Others may have to avoid fried foods and cut back on meat consumption, especially beef and pork. Try eliminating both for a while and see what happens. You have nothing to lose but your acne! An added bonus is that you are eliminating a lot of junk food from your diet and you will actually feel healthier.

If you have blemishes on your back and buttocks as well as your face, especially if they are cystic in nature, this can mean a food or drug allergy. Dairy products and iodine are the most common causes of cystic acne. Look for sources of iodine in your diet (iodized salt and seaweed). Avoid dairy products for a period of three to four weeks to see if your acne clears up. If it doesn't subside, investigate other foods in your diet. Start with foods you eat every day as the possible culprits.

Avoid a suspected food for two to three weeks, then challenge your body by eating it for a two-day period to investigate whether the food is indeed causing your problem. A good natural skin cleanser and facial mask such as clay can be used on a regular basis. When beginning this treatment, sometimes the acne will appear to get worse as the underlying pores are cleaned and debris comes to the surface. Oil-based makeup creates acne by blocking pores.

If you have acne with dry skin, not oily skin, be sure to use a neutral pH soap from the health food store that won't dry out your skin. Dry skin treatment includes cod liver oil and flaxseed oil. Use one capsule or 1 teaspoon of cod liver oil and 1 tablespoon of flaxseed oil per day, which will give you several essential fatty acids (EFAs). Your skin, hair, and nails will love you for it.

Supplements that help heal acne include zinc, which is very deficient in a junk food diet. You can get zinc from sunflower seeds and pumpkin seeds or a natural zinc supplement. Zinc supports healthy skin, hair, and nails. Evening primrose oil and borage oil contain essential omega-6 fatty acids, and flaxseed oil and fish oils contain essential omega-3 fatty acids, necessary for healthy skin. Both omega-6 and omega-3 fatty acids tend to be deficient in young people and can result in skin problems. Use a tablespoon of flaxseed oil every day as a source for both. Vitamin E and wheat germ oil are also beneficial for healing the skin, both taken by mouth and rubbed into acne scars. Cod liver oil will also give you the vitamin A you need for healthy skin. You can round out your supplements with a good natural multivitamin and mineral supplement. Remember, high potency is not what you are after; what you want are supplements that the body recognizes as natural so they can enhance normal body function and metabolism.

Internal cleansing is an important factor with regard to acne. The body detoxifies chemicals or excess toxins through the liver, and the end products of this detoxification are eliminated through the intestines, the kidneys, and the skin. If the kidneys and intestines are overloaded with toxins, then skin conditions can develop as too many waste products are being eliminated. Therefore, general cleansing can help the skin condition. The simplest form of cleansing is to increase the intake of fresh, pure water and fiber.

If bowel movements are increased from one to two per day by drinking more water, we are sure that excess toxins are being released. Other gentle forms of cleansing include aloe vera gel, which can be taken in juice once a day, and psyllium seed, taken as a bulking agent. Acidophilus bacteria should be replaced if psyllium is used for more than one month at a time. Psyllium is taken either as a powder or capsule. The powder is stirred in a glass of water and followed by a second glass of pure water so that the bulking agent will not cause constipation. Psyllium can be used for people with irritable bowel syndrome because it bulks up stools that are too loose or too solid. Take acidophilus as powder or capsules, two doses per day, or as plain yogurt. Acidophilus is the "good bacteria" of the intestines. (See the section on detoxification on page 178.)

Homeopathic treatments useful for acne are Hepar sulph. 12C for painful acne that resembles tiny boils and Graphites 12C and Antimonium tart. 12C for acne that scars. There are many other homeopathic acne remedies, but a personalized prescription requires a constitutional assessment by a homeopathic physician.

Above all, in the treatment of acne, it is important to realize that the use of oral antibiotics should be avoided if at all possible; the side effects of antibiotics can cause more problems than the acne itself. Oral antibiotics will kill the bacteria that cause facial blemishes, but they also kill all intestinal bacteria, creating an extreme imbalance in the intestinal flora, which can lead to the overgrowth of yeast or *Candida* in the intestines. (See the section on candidiasis on page 40.) *Candida* also overgrows when you are on the birth control pill and before the menstrual period, as these hormones encourage yeast growth. Staphylococci bacteria on the skin plus *Candida* create boil-like acne blemishes. Treatment of *Candida* often decreases acne outbreaks.

Acne Rosacea

Acne rosacea is a chronic acnelike eruption of unknown origin that occurs on the face, mostly over the nose and cheeks. It is three times more common in women than men and usually begins in middle age. It is also accompanied by facial flushing, broken capillaries, pustules, and dry skin, but not blackheads. In men, it is more common to have an unsightly, red, swollen, and inflamed nose. Rosacea can also cause inflammatory eye symptoms.

Avoid spicy foods, alcohol, coffee, and cigarettes, which can all irritate the skin and worsen symptoms. Initiating factors for the condition may include vitamin B deficiency, food allergies, low stomach acid, low thyroid, and a family history or tendency toward dry skin and dermatitis.

The medical treatment for rosacea often includes antibiotics. Antibiotics encourage yeast and fungal overgrowth, however, even on the skin. So there is a vicious cycle at work: an antibiotic can kill off some of the organisms that are causing rosacea, but it can also encourage more fungus to grow, which perpetuates the very problem. Another aspect of skin health is that overuse of antibacterial soaps and creams diminishes the natural immune protective layer of the skin. Patting the skin with cotton balls soaked with 3 percent hydrogen peroxide after washing with a neutral pH soap will help gently clean the skin.

In order to treat rosacea and restore "good bacteria" to your body, especially if you have been using antibiotics, a yeast-free program is necessary. A yeast-free diet will exclude the three most common food allergens: wheat, dairy, and sugar. See the section on candidiasis on page 40 for full details.

Make sure you have enough B vitamins, which should probably come from supplements. You know you have enough B vitamins when your urine turns yellow; they are water soluble and any excess will be eliminated in the urine. Zinc is important for wound healing, and you can get it from sunflower seeds, pumpkin seeds, and oysters.

If there is undigested food in your stool, or you feel that your food is not digesting well, add a digestive supplement containing hydrochloric acid at the end of each meal. The usual dosage is a 5-grain tablet, one or two per meal. Incompletely digested food can be absorbed and create allergic reactions that can manifest as skin conditions.

To investigate a possible thyroid connection, you should take your morning temperature several days in a row. Women should do this around their period, because at midcycle your temperature will show an ovulatory temperature elevation. If your temperature is a degree under the normal 98.6, you may have to ask your medical doctor or naturopath for advice on supporting your thyroid gland. Read the section on hypothyroidism on page 103 for more information.

If there is a family history of dermatitis, the usual deficiencies are of the essential fatty acids (EFAs) found in flaxseed oil, evening primrose oil, and fish oils. Simply adding cod liver oil can be very helpful; there are mint- and fruit-flavored brands on the market and a teaspoon or two a day can supply vitamins A and D as well. Take no more than 10,000 IU of vitamin A and 400 IU of vitamin D per day. Flaxseed oil or mixed omega-3 and omega-6 oil blends are available at health food stores and can be used 2 tablespoons a day on cooked cereal or in salad dressing.

Allergic Skin Reactions

There are thousands of food additive chemicals in our diet, any one of which may cause an allergic reaction in a sensitive person. If you have skin breakouts and don't know the cause, try a very clean diet of free-range, organic chicken, brown rice, and organic vegetables for a few days and see if your skin clears.

One common cause of skin rashes and hives is aspartame (Nutra-Sweet). Some people have suffered for years from this condition only to discover it is caused by this synthetic substance found in over 9,000 products. Neurosurgeon Russell Blaylock, M.D., says that aspartame reactions are not necessarily allergic but toxic and poisonous.

Dry Skin

Most people think that dry skin should be treated by external cream applications. Attention to your diet is probably more important, however. The essential fatty acids (EFAs) such as evening primrose oil and fish oils, three or four capsules a day, are crucial. In fact, a sure sign of deficiency of EFAs is dry skin. Dry skin is very common in kids and adults with attention deficit/hyperactivity disorder (ADHD), and the cure is EFAs. Zinc supplementation can be very important for skin, hair, and nails. This is in addition to a good general multiple vitamin and mineral supplement. In terms of skin care, too many showers and baths may strip the skin's normal acid mantle and allow dehydration and drying. This can be treated by putting a few tablespoons of apple cider vinegar in the bath and by using neutral pH skin creams.

Drinking lots of water is vital for dry skin. Do not take water with your meals, however; this means up to ten minutes before or three hours after. Water and oil from your food don't mix, causing the oil globules to stick together and impede food absorption.

Seborrhea

This condition occurs around the edges of the scalp, over the eyebrows, around the eyes, and at the lateral corners and to the sides of the nose. It is a flaky, yellowish skin discoloration that sometimes becomes red and bumpy. It is referred to as skin dandruff and is worsened by stress. It responds to treatment with B vitamins. Clean your skin with neutral pH soap, avoiding either extreme of alkaline or acid. The skin would rather be a little more acid, however, and alkaline soaps tend to dry out the skin, strip the acid mantle, and allow irritations and dryness. (Read the section on dry skin on page 147.)

Smell and Taste Problems

These two functions are very much controlled by the mineral zinc. If zinc is lacking in the diet, your taste buds can no longer distinguish the four primary tastes: sweet, sour, acid, and bitter. If you no longer taste your food, the mechanism of feeling satisfied (not necessarily of feeling full) is lost. This can lead to binge eating and overeating. Also, you will go for more and more sweet foods, again to try to reach some kind of taste satisfaction. I use zinc for people who are binge eaters, sugar cravers, or even anorexics or bulimics who don't seem to have a good sense of taste. There is a zinc sulphate hydroxide solution that can be used as a taste test to determine the amount of zinc in the body. This can be administered by a doctor or naturopath. The treatment for zinc deficiency begins with diet. Oysters, pumpkin seeds, and sunflower seeds are high in zinc. Zinc is best taken in a multiple mineral along with trace minerals. We know that too much zinc can deplete copper, so it is wise to not overdo it.

Sore Throat
(See **Colds and Flus,** page 48)

Sprains

The most common type of sprain is an ankle sprain; however, any group of muscles, tendons, or ligaments can be strained or sprained. A sprain can be as serious as a broken bone, so it should not be treated lightly. First, an assessment must be made to see if indeed there is a broken bone, including x-rays, then a thorough examination should be done to look for a torn ligament or tendon.

If you hear a "snap, crackle, and pop," you probably have sprained your ankle. First the tendon snaps from its attachment at the protrusion at the side of the ankle bone; then, if the force is strong enough, it can crack a bit of bone off at the tendon attachment and finally pop it, resulting in a break in the bone. So if you hear or feel something snap, it's important to head for a hospital emergency room where x-rays may be taken. You may be strapped or even put in a cast depending on the severity of sprain. There must be some support to the ankle.

After taking Arnica for the trauma, use Rhus tox. for the stiffness or Ruta if there is more tendon injury to be healed. The dosage is 12C, 4 drops every hour while the pain is severe. Use less as the pain lessens.

Massaging olive oil or castor oil from the toes up to the calf will help clear the swelling. Be sure to use ice for forty-eight hours, elevate the foot, and stay off it as much as possible. Other strains or sprains can be treated similarly.

Stress

Stress today is a favorite media topic. Without stress of any kind, however, we would be comatose or sleeping. There must be some stress in our lives to keep us activated. The book *Joy of Stress,* by Peter G. Hanson, M.D., does a good job of balancing the positive and negative aspects of stress. In other words, it is not all negative. Stress can be used to cover many definitions of distress in a person's life. If you are overly busy, feel that you are being pulled in many directions, and worry that you cannot meet your commitments, then you are no doubt under stress.

The best advice for this situation is to set goals and priorities, recognize your individual limitations, and not overextend yourself. Often good stress counseling will help teach you how to deal with external causes of stress that are then internalized. Conflicts in personal relationships can also be stress inducing.

I find that people, particularly women, place too much pressure on themselves to perform in too many roles. They take on a full-time job while maintaining a family and caring for both partner and children. Most women feel that they should be able to "do it all" and feel guilty if they can't. Cut back on your workload and take better care of yourself before you become ill and are forced to take time off. Often illness is a subconscious way of cutting back. The issues in allowing yourself to overwork are complex and multiple and it would be wise to sit down with a stress counselor to work out your conflicts, your sense of self-worth, and your goals and priorities in order to lead a more balanced life.

Exercise can be an excellent stress reducer but it is very individualized and can be according to your blood group. See *Eat Right 4 Your Type*, by Dr. Peter D'Adamo. O blood types need heavy exercise, while A types need more gentle relaxation types of exercise such as yoga and tai chi. What works for one person won't necessarily work for another.

The best supplements for stress are the B vitamins. For depression and stress, 5-hydroxytryptamine can be taken; it is the precursor to tryptophan, which is the precursor to serotonin. Prozac is a serotonin-reuptake inhibitor that does the same job of elevating serotonin but has some nasty side effects, like homicide and suicide.

Calming herbs include hops, valerian, and skullcap; they are also good for insomnia.

Sunburn

The treatment for sunburn depends on the degree of injury. Above all, do not break any blisters that form. Use sunscreen to prevent future sunburns. If a burn does occur, use aloe vera gel or vitamins A and E creams immediately and lavishly. Milk of magnesia was recommended by a patient who used it successfully for sunburn. Some people have even used mud or clay to take out the stinging pain of a sunburn. The homeopathic remedies for burns in the section on first aid on page 168 can be taken by mouth.

Teeth Problems

For information on pyorrhea, see the section on gum disease on page 139. Also, read the book by Dr. O. Nara, *How to Be Dentally Self-Sufficient*. The biggest controversy in dentistry is about mercury amalgam fillings. Sweden has banned mercury fillings, considering them a definite health hazard. More and more people are inquiring about having their amalgams removed. The composites that replace the mercury are a little less stable, may break down a little more easily, and may require earlier replacement. It is best to see a specialist in this work who has spent a lot of time researching the best technique and the best products to use.

Also read the book *It's All in Your Head* by Hal Huggins. Amalgam removal should follow a very specific protocol to avoid creating even more mercury absorption by your body. When having amalgams removed, be sure to use oxygen during the procedure. Also take extra vitamin C before and after removal. Your dentist may advise other supplements. Ear acupuncture in the dental points and relaxation points is very helpful for anesthetic purposes and for faster healing.

Good dental nutrition includes avoidance of sugar and refined foods. With proper brushing and flossing and a good diet, most cavities can be avoided.

Dental terror is a common complaint that is easily treated with doses of homeopathic Aconite. Use the 12C potency and take one dose every hour before visiting the dentist. It is a remarkable remedy and can really calm down the nervous system.

Temporomandibular Joint Syndrome

The temporomandibular joint lies between the jawbone and the cheekbone. Out of balance, it can cause nighttime teeth grinding that leads to clenched jaw and head muscles; this can cause the worst pain you have ever known. A visit to a good dentist to assess grinding (your teeth will be worn down in back) is crucial; you may have to wear a specially molded bite plate at night. Hot and cold packs; relaxing herbs such as hops, valerian, and skullcap; calcium and magnesium for muscle relaxation; the B vitamins for stress relief; and relaxation techniques will all help. Read the section on headaches on page 86 for more information on TMJ.

Tendonitis

Tendonitis most commonly occurs at the elbow, as in tennis elbow, but in squash players the overworked tendon is in the wrist. It can be quite debilitating, causing every movement of the arm to be painful.

To prevent tendonitis, first of all, avoid overuse. If the elbow or wrist is starting to hurt, don't push it. Use castor oil packs at night. Put 2 to 3 tablespoons castor oil, at room temperature, on an old cloth and wrap around the affected area. Tie on with a scarf and wrap in plastic to prevent an oil spill. This often helps to take out the inflammation. Regular icing at the onset of tendonitis or when the area becomes inflamed is beneficial. After the tendonitis has cooled down, heat will help. Use a whirlpool, put a heating pad over the castor oil pack, and use hot compresses.

The remedies that help are Rhus tox. for stiffness and Ruta, which is specifically for tendons. The dosage is 12C, 4 drops every two hours for acute pain and less for moderate pain.

Acupuncture can often help this condition. Medical doctors prescribe physiotherapy and ultrasound. Chiropractors use ultrasound and sometimes adjust the area.

Ulcers

Over the years, there have been many different theories on the cause of ulcers and as many different treatments. Research now shows that ulcers have an infective basis due to an organism called campylobacter that causes ulceration of the stomach lining. If you have an ulceration due to campylobacter, the organism has to be killed before the ulcer can heal. There is a blood antibody test to determine if you have this infection. Gastroscopy, looking into the stomach with a fiberoptic scope, can also include a biopsy of the stomach to identify an infection or other abnormalities. If campylobacter is found, Pepto Bismol may be the cure; it is now being researched. Ask your doctor. Investigation by barium swallow will identify an ulceration and the usual antacid treatments are instituted, along with antibiotics.

A diet for ulcers used to be low fiber and bland, but the best diet advice is to observe what makes the pain worse and what makes it better. Smoking and alcohol certainly are contraindicated for people with ulcers. Milk may cause problems by increasing stomach acid. Antacids and ulcer medications might themselves cause problems in the long run since they interfere with food digestion.

Cabbage juice (use young cabbages), 4 ounces per day, helps ulcers with a constituent that has been labeled vitamin U. Supplements that may help heal ulcers are B vitamins for stress; zinc for wound healing; vitamin A to heal mucous membranes; and herbs such as comfrey, slippery elm, and aloe vera. Herbal antibiotics such as echinacea, goldenseal, olive leaf, and barberry may be substituted for an antibiotic under the supervision of your naturopath. If you do use an antibiotic, be sure and add acidophilus to your regime to replace the good bacteria in the gut.

Homeopathic Nux vomica and Lycopodium are often used to treat ulcers if you have the constitutional characteristics that go with these remedies. The usual dosage is 4 drops, three times per day. Read about these two remedies in part 4 of this book to see if they match your picture.

Vaginitis

Vaginitis is most often due to yeast overgrowth rather than bacteria. The diagnosis is made clinically, especially in the case of yeast, and confirmed by vaginal swab, although the positive yield of yeast identification in a laboratory is very low. Doctors often must go by the clinical impression plus the history; that is, vaginitis prior to the period, worse after overindulgence in sweets, bread, or fruit. The discharge is white, cheesy, itchy, and irritating. There is also a history of being on birth control pills and antibiotics. Bacterial vaginitis can usually be diagnosed by a swab. If it is a common gardnerella, strep, or hemophilus bacteria, the infection is not in the fallopian tubes, and there are no fever or chills, then a local douche with Betadine is often acceptable. If the bacterial infection is gonorrhea or chlamydia, the treatment is with oral antibiotics. Remember to take acidophilus with the antibiotic to prevent yeast infection.

To prevent yeast vaginitis, avoid tight jeans and wear loose cotton underwear (which may have to be boiled, microwaved, or ironed to kill all the yeast spores). Be aware that acidifying spermicides can irritate the vagina and encourage yeast overgrowth.

Don't wipe with scented or dyed toilet paper and don't use scented or deodorized pads or tampons. Make sure tampons themselves are not the cause of your symptoms. Or alternate between pads and tampons. Be sure your partner is not passing yeast back to you during intercourse; use a condom. Natural douches include baking soda or vinegar (1 tablespoon to 2 cups of water), acidophilus, or yogurt.

Treatment for yeast vaginitis is usually given locally. In some cases, this may be enough to provide symptomatic relief. If the condition is persistent, however, it must be treated on a broader scale with diet, acidophilus by mouth, acidophilus mixed with yogurt to make a paste that can be used vaginally, and sometimes oral antifungal medications. (See the section on candidiasis on page 40.)

Varicose Veins

Varicose veins are due to weak valves in the leg veins that are unable to push the blood away from the legs against the force of gravity. This results in swollen veins, which can cause pain and disfigurement. Although varicose veins are often hereditary, some natural remedies and recommendations can help reduce the extent of the condition. You must avoid obesity and constipation. The diet must be high in fiber content and exercise is essential to improve circulation. Elevate the legs, wear support hose, and lie on a slant board for several minutes a day.

Vitamins, herbs, and homeopathics that help heal veins and capillaries include bioflavonoids, part of the vitamin C complex; witch hazel used as a compress on very swollen veins; and homeopathic drops of Hamamelis 6 or 12C, 4 drops three times a day.

A process called sclerotherapy, the injection of small veins with saline to collapse them, can remove unsightly veins. Some specialists claim that this can be done for any size of varicosity.

Warts

Warts on the fingers or the soles of the feet can be treated using castor oil, vitamin E, vitamin A, aloe vera, or tea tree oil. Any one of them can be applied directly to the wart, covered with a Band-Aid or similar bandage, and worn each night. You might try one or more of these treatments, but results often take several weeks. As the callus over the root of the viral wart is removed, little black dots will be uncovered. This is the virus itself and, when it is exposed to air, it begins to die. This is often a more convenient and less painful way of treating warts than going to a dermatologist for a burning, cutting, or acid treatment.

———— ✿✦✿ ————

PART TWO

Advice
and Information

Antibiotics

I began studying nutrition before I went into medicine. I did an acupuncture elective in second-year medicine to find an alternative to addicting pain medications. I went on to study naturopathic medicine to develop viable alternatives to the variety of medications used in allopathic medicine, especially antibiotics. While they save lives in extreme infections and emergency conditions, the overuse of antibiotics is now widely recognized. Medical associations are even demanding that doctors limit their use, but if all you have is a hammer, everything looks like a nail; for most doctors, hammers (antibiotics) are all they have. See the section in part 4, Make Your Own Remedy, on page 207, to learn how to make a homeopathic remedy from a medication to help relieve the side effects.

If your doctor doesn't have any options and choices such as herbs, homeopathics, vitamins, and minerals to boost the immune system and fight infection, and even worse, if your doctor doesn't "believe" in anything but drugs, you are just going to get a prescription for antibiotics or other drugs when you visit her. If you can't find a medical doctor who practices alternative medicine, the best option is to work with an open-minded medical doctor and a naturopath. This is the best of both worlds.

As for antibiotics, because they can be lifesavers in an emergency, we tend to overlook their numerous side effects. With options and choices, we don't have to use them for everything, though. Their most common side effect is to destroy the beneficial intestinal bacteria and allow the overgrowth of *Candida albicans*. Once this yeast has set up residence, it is not long before parasites move in. Read the sections on candidiasis on page 40 and parasites on page 133 to see how you can reverse these conditions. And sometime when you have a free moment, pick up a drug compendium in the library and read about the side effects of some of the most common antibiotics. I can guarantee that you will be shocked.

The practice of sweetening children's antibiotics with aspartame (NutraSweet) adds to their toxicity. The aspartame found in a stick of chewing gum is reported to have caused seizures! Read the section on sugar and aspartame on page 185 to learn more.

Baby Feeding

The best food for an infant is breast milk. Studies show breast milk, due to antibodies in the colostrum of mother's milk, prevents infections. Drs. Weston Price and Francis Pottenger, dental anthropologists, proved that breast-feeding provides the correct exercise for the jaw and mouth to create a proper dental arch and good teeth. All the braces worn in Western countries are probably due to bottle-feeding. Also, babies given solid foods too early are not able to digest them in their undeveloped intestines; these foods can become allergens.

As an environmental activist, however, my research has uncovered horrifying results of breast-milk studies, which show that mother's milk might be too toxic for infant consumption. It's news that you may never hear because it is too frightening Whether to breast-feed becomes another no-win situation, a trade-off. But it teaches us that we must become much more careful about using chemicals in our society. Each one of us has to take a personal stand against using toxic cleaning products and cosmetics and support the use of natural products. If you are planning a pregnancy, be sure to study the section on detoxification on page 178 and do sauna therapy to remove toxins from your fat cells first to ensure that your breast milk will be safe.

If you have allergies or sensitivities to specific foods, your child has a good chance of being allergic. Even while nursing, the baby may experience gas or colic. This may be treated by eliminating certain foods from your diet. These foods may cause a problem: nuts, milk, cheese, wheat, corn, chocolate, fish, or—on an individual basis—just about any food.

In general, try to rotate foods as much as possible. When we eat the same foods day after day, we are likely causing food sensitivities.

Infant Feeding Guide

The First Six Months

Offer only:
- Breast milk
- Water
- Supplemental vitamin A and D from cod liver oil, and vitamin C, from three months of age.

Investigate the use of substitute formulas. Supplements to these formulas should include omega-3 and omega-6 fatty acids including DHA, folic acid, and vitamin C. Refer to Sally Fallon's book, *Nourishing Traditions,* for a nonmilk formula based on organic liver, whey, and lactose powder. Possible base formulas to include in a four-day cycle are goat's milk (3 parts milk to 1 part water), almond milk, rice milk, and soy milk.

Soy milk is already manufactured into baby formula; however, many infants are allergic to soy. Rotate soy in a four-day diet, or if your baby is sensitive, avoid it entirely. According to Sat Dharma Kaur in her new book, *The Healthy Breast,* soy milk can be used in the early months of an infant's life *before* certain bacteria are present in the intestines that convert soy into phytoestrogens. She does not recommend it after six months of age, however. In females, puberty and menopause are the other important times for soy intake. Soy intake around age ten or eleven for girls can help forestall the onset of menses. This may be important because puberty is beginning earlier with all the chemical hormones in beef and chicken and synthetic hormone mimickers in pesticides and herbicides.

Take note of the ingredients in baby formulas. If they include corn syrup, babies are getting addicted to sugar right from birth. Read the section on sugar addiction on page 4. Cow's milk formulas may cause sensitivities or allergies in over half the infants using them.

Organic baby food and infant formulas are coming on the market. Check your health food store.

continued

Six to Twelve Months

- Breast milk or formula
- Water between feedings
- Introduce solid foods one at a time starting with vegetables. Three meals a day are usual by nine to twelve months. Yogurt or kefir from nine months.

Vegetables (Cooked)
Begin with: peas, squash, carrots, green beans, red beets, sweet potatoes. Add later: potato, broccoli, cabbage, dried peas and beans, vegetable combinations, celery, asparagus. Watch for a reaction if the infant is on formula and begins peas, green beans, or any vegetable combination. There can be cross-reactivity between these foods.

Fruits (Cooked)
Begin with: apple, peach, banana. Add later: apricots, plums, pears, pineapple, cherries, grapes.

Meats and Dairy
Begin with: beef, lamb (hormone and antibiotic free). Add later: fish (salmon, tuna, turbot), shellfish (shrimp, crab, oyster), fowl (turkey, chicken, duck), dairy (yogurt, cottage cheese, soft cheese).

Cereals
Begin with: rice, oats, rye. Add later: millet, barley, wheat, corn.

Feeding Rules

- Always introduce one new food at a time.
- Watch for colds or runny nose, cough, sneezing, increased fussiness, diarrhea, rash, and vomiting.
- Try to correlate symptoms with foods eaten that day or the day before.
- Rotate foods. A food should be given only every third day.
- Use only water as a between-meal beverage.

Avoid Until After One Year Old:
- Orange, grapefruit, lemon, lime, eggs, ham, bacon, honey.

Avoid Until After Two Years Old:
- Chocolate, cola, candy, nuts, nut butters, spices (especially cinnamon), food colorings, artificial flavorings, whole milk, seed butters.

Foods to Avoid in General
- Artificial flavors and colors, especially aspartame
- Coffee and tea
- Chocolate, cocoa, colas
- Flavor enhancers (MSG, citric acid)
- Preservatives (BHT, BHA, nitrites)
- Refined starches (cornstarch, white flour)
- Sugar (brown, white, corn syrup, molasses)
- Peanut butter (it is often moldy, plus it is an allergen)

Foods to Limit in General
- Maple syrup
- Natural sugars (dried fruits, grapes, plums, stevia)
- Milk
- Pasta (noodles, spaghetti, macaroni)

Foods to Use
- Brown rice
- Dried peas and beans
- Fresh fruits
- Fresh meats, fish, poultry (free range, antibiotic and hormone free and grain fed)
- Goat milk and yogurt
- Whole grain cereals
- Whole grain flour
- Water (from a purified source)

Baby Tips

1. Most babies thrive on demand feeding, not scheduled feeding. Try to feed in a more vertical than horizontal position. This keeps milk from being sucked into the eustachian tubes and prevents ear infections. For cracked nipples, vitamin E oil from capsules is great and if the baby gets some during a feeding it is good for him, unlike most other creams or ointments. Proper nipple positioning in the baby's mouth helps prevent cracked nipples. Call your local La Leche League for firsthand information and assistance with breast-feeding.

2. Babies swallow a lot of air when feeding and really need to be burped.

3. Turn babies frequently; they can't turn over themselves. The best position to prevent sudden infant death syndrome (SIDS) is on the back.

4. Cavities often plague the children of health-conscious parents. This stems from giving babies bottles with natural juices at bedtime. The extremely high fructose content drills holes in the teeth. Never use anything but water in a bottle being used as a soother.

5. Constipation is often observed when switching from breast to bottle or when introducing solids. The formula may be too high in solutes and may need to be diluted. Or, this may be a reaction to processed dairy or wheat. Try avoiding these foods for two to three weeks to see if it makes a difference. Increase water feeding. Stress and tension in or between the parents can translate into tension in the child, which can manifest as constipation.

6. For colic in breast-fed babies, especially if your baby burped or hiccupped in the womb, watch what you eat. The baby may be reacting to something in your diet. Cut out strong-tasting foods first; then eliminate dairy and wheat. Read the section on colic on page 51.

   Try homeopathic Pulsatilla for gentle, usually happy babies who need to be held, rocked, and moved all the time. Use 12C, 4 drops in 1 teaspoon of water several times a day as needed.

   Chamomilla works for whiny, irritated, and irritating babies, who seem as frustrated as you feel. Use 12C, 4 drops in 1 teaspoon of water several times a day.

7. Diarrhea is defined as more than four very loose, odorous, runny stools a day. Stop milk and dairy products and use water feedings for twenty-four hours. Make sure enough water is given to prevent dehydration. Then try normal feeding. If your baby is already drinking juices, use 2 ounces of apple juice with ¼ teaspoon carob powder and 2 ounces of water.

8. For diaper rash, leave the diaper off for extended periods; vitamin E ointment or zinc ointment are healing and soothing. Talc or cornstarch are not necessary and can cause allergic reactions. Avoid talc entirely because of its aluminum content, which is implicated as a cause of Alzheimer's disease and ovarian cancer. Women should not use talc on their genitals and underarms for the same reason. While I'm at it, men and women should not use antiperspirants containing aluminum hydroxide, which blocks the lymphatic system around the breasts and is implicated in breast cancer. Some diaper rash may be due to an overgrowth of *Candida*, or yeast. On passing through the birth canal, the baby can get a mouthful of yeast and be overgrown with this organism. If the baby has also had antibiotics early in life, this can contribute to the overgrowth. (Read the section on candidiasis on page 40.) The treatment for candidiasis in babies includes treating the breast-feeding mother and giving the baby infant acidophilus powder. Natural antifungals, such as dilute garlic oil or tea tree oil, can be applied locally. Mix 1 part of these strong oils to 4 parts sesame or olive oil.

9. Fever in an infant is often quite frightening. A baby's temperature can rise very rapidly. It is important to have measures at hand to treat the fever. If nothing seems to help, go to a doctor or the emergency room for a diagnosis. Most often fever is due to a viral infection, but it can be due to a bacterial ear infection, pneumonia, or meningitis. A viral infection will run its course, but the others often need an antibiotic. Dehydration can set in quite rapidly with infants. Be sure that your baby is producing urine. If not, dehydration is occurring and this alone can drive up the temperature.

To reduce a mild fever of 99° to 102.5°F (at 103°F and higher, consult your doctor):

Vitamin C, 100 milligrams per hour crushed in water or juice (buffered C powder is good to have on hand). The only possible side effect is diarrhea.

Yarrow is used as an herb tea or in a bath. A lukewarm bath itself will help reduce the fever and aid hydration.

Belladonna, 12C, 4 drops every fifteen minutes. (Read the section on Belladonna in part 4 of this book.)

Aconite, 12C, 4 drops every fifteen minutes. (Read the section on Aconite in part 4 of this book.)

Ensure that the infant or child is not constipated. Do whatever makes the stool soft—a gentle enema or suppository may be necessary. You may want to consult your doctor before attempting this measure.

Identify teething as a cause of fever.

If rectal temperature is 103.5°F and the above therapies are not working, use baby Tylenol and call the doctor.

DON'TS

Don't use aspirin for babies; they can be allergic and it is linked to Reye's syndrome.

Don't use alcohol baths.

Don't panic.

---

10. Spitting up is quite common; it is not vomiting. It can be from eating too fast, if you are stressed while feeding the child, or from food intolerance. Projectile vomiting should be investigated because it can mean a blockage in the baby's gastrointestinal system.

11. Teething. This stage of development is usually accompanied by fussiness, drooling, and even slight fevers. For irritability and crying, use Chamomilla 12C, 4 drops three times a day. For hot, sore gums, rub the powder from a crushed calcium tablet on the gums. For late teething, use homeopathic Calc. carb. 12C, 4 drops three times a day. The herbs marshmallow

root and licorice root in the form of thick sticks can be chewed on and will soothe the gums as well as help the teeth break through. Teething rings kept in the fridge can give soothing coolness to hot gums.

12. Head Lice. Children invariably get head lice in day care and school. When my sister and I got them in grade school, that was the end of our long ringlets, which made a wonderful home for the little critters. The most common head lice formula is Lindane, but it has toxic side effects, and there is no question that whatever you put on the scalp or skin is absorbed into the body; just think of all the skin patch medications on the market today. The latest fiasco by the FDA is the release of a head lice treatment that contains malathion. Around the same time the EPA announced that malathion is a probable carcinogen, and we already know it is a potent neurotoxin. Here is a natural head lice formula; it appears in my friend Sat Dharam Kaur's book *The Healthy Breast.*

HEAD LICE FORMULA

Rosemary	20 drops
Geranium	10 drops
Lavender	20 drops
Eucalyptus	10 drops
Tea Tree	20 drops

Add to ½ cup olive oil and keep in a dark glass jar. Rub into the scalp and leave on overnight under a towel. Repeat one week later. Treat the whole family at the same time and boil bedding and hairbrushes. Add 5 drops to a teaspoon of shampoo every time you wash your hair until the infestation is over. Also, get a head lice comb and work it through the hair thoroughly to remove the eggs.

Birth Control

Birth Control Pill

Unfortunately, everyone has become so used to the concept of the birth control pill that this option is often the only one that people equate with birth control. Even though several studies have confirmed that the birth control pill can cause cancer, doctors and drug companies alike refuse to "alarm" the public with these unsavory statistics. The pill, a combination of synthetic female hormones, taken daily, gives the body the impression that it is in a constant state of pregnancy. After the pill is stopped, the return of the normal period is often delayed. The high rate of infertility today may also be related to the pill. Women on the pill suffer a higher rate of strokes and liver disease than normal. It is said that the newer low-dose pill has fewer side effects, but it has not been tested on an entire generation of individuals as yet. In fact, the whole notion of playing around with our hormones is a gigantic experiment.

If the pill is used, it should not be taken for more than five years, not beyond the age of thirty-five, and not by women who smoke or who have a family history of female cancer.

Women who take the pill also suffer an increased incidence of candidiasis (see the section on candidiasis on page 40), although the symptoms may not appear for several years. Symptoms are aggravated by intake of antibiotics along with the birth control pill (antibiotics can also inactivate the birth control pill). Stress and the intake of a highly refined food diet can also stimulate *Candida* growth. If you decide to take the birth control pill, follow these recommendations to prevent side effects: take acidophilus on a regular basis to increase the level of good bacteria in the system. Maintain a healthy diet of whole grains, nuts and seeds, vegetables, fish, and chicken and avoid yeast breads, highly refined foods such as sugar, and too much cheese.

Necessary supplements when taking the pill include B complex with B$_6$ and folic acid. In some studies, women on the pill experience depression that is due to a deficiency of vitamin B$_6$. Vitamin C with bioflavonoids is important for symptoms of gum swelling or bleeding and varicose vein formation, especially small, spidery weblike veins. Vitamin E is also important to help the metabolism of the birth control pill; zinc is vital since women on birth control pills have lower levels of zinc. If you experience side effects on the pill that do not go away even when it is discontinued, homeopathic remedies are useful. The remedy must be chosen according to the symptoms and constitution of the patient. These might include Sepia, Pulsatilla, and Nat. mur. (Read about them in the section on premenstrual syndrome, page 135.)

Cervical Cap

The cervical cap seems to be a more comfortable and better-fitting barrier method than the diaphragm, discussed on page 166. The cap fits on the cervix and is also used with spermicidal jelly. You must be able to feel the cervix and check that the cap is attached snugly around the cervix. It has the same problem as the diaphragm in that it can become dislodged and allow the sperm to travel through the cervical canal. The earliest a woman may be aware of a failure of this type of contraception is when she misses her next period. The main side effect is unwanted pregnancy.

Condoms and Foam

Aside from abstinence, the condom is the only birth control method that will protect you from AIDS and many other sexually transmitted diseases.

Condoms and foam are a double-barrier method in which both partners take responsibility for birth control. The best kind of condom is one with a reservoir tip that holds the released sperm so that they do not travel up the sides of the condom and come in contact with the vagina. One good thing about condoms and foam is that if a sperm or two find their way into the vagina the foam should kill them. Another benefit of this method is that if the condom breaks it is immediately apparent. If the woman is midcycle (the time of ovulation and highest fertility), it is possible to take a "morning-after pill." This consists of six to eight Ovral birth control pills, two taken as soon as possible and two taken every twelve hours. These pills cause the lining of the uterus to grow; and since the pills are not continued, the lining is shed and no implantation can occur.

The side effect of condoms and foam is the potentially irritating effects of the acidifying foam. If used properly and consistently, this is a highly safe method of birth control. The morning-after pill, by bringing on an early period, can obviously throw off your cycle. Normal cycling should resume in a month or two. You must be very careful at this time and, if doing natural birth control (see page 166), be very aware of your mucus. A homeopathic remedy can be made from an Ovral pill and used to balance the side effects of taking it. (See the section on making your own remedies on page 207.)

Diaphragm

The diaphragm is a barrier method of birth control. This disklike piece of rubber is fitted by a doctor and inserted by the individual before intercourse. It is heavily coated with a spermicidal gel that acts as the real barrier to the tiny sperm that can wiggle around the edges of the diaphragm. Pregnancy can occur if the gel is not used or if the diaphragm bends and allows the sperm to pass by. Constipation can cause the diaphragm to bend and its pressure on the urethra can cause bladder infections.

Natural Birth Control

By far the safest, most natural, and most responsible method of birth control is natural birth control; however, it does not protect against sexually transmitted diseases. With this method, you study the natural menstrual cycle and measure temperatures and cervical mucus to determine which days you can become pregnant and which days are safe. It can also be used for infertile women to learn the best time to have intercourse.

Breast-Feeding

There are hundreds of research articles confirming the importance of breast-feeding. They conclude that the incidence of all types of infections, especially ear infections, is much lower in breast-fed babies. It is the colostrum, or first breast milk, that provides immunity to the infant. The mechanism of sucking on the breast molds the jaw in the correct manner, avoiding the need for braces in later years. Sadly, analysis of toxins in breast milk indicate that levels of DDT, PCBs, and various other carcinogens may be making breast milk dangerous for infant consumption! Will the benefits outweigh the risks? If they do, here is some advice for breast-feeding mothers. (Also read the section on detoxification on page 178 to learn how to use saunas and clay body wraps to help release toxins through the skin and not through your breast milk. The best time to detoxify, however, is before you become pregnant.)

The keys to perfect and painless breast-feeding are good milk production and proper positioning of the baby. Milk production is enhanced by eating an optimum diet, with plenty of vegetables, moderate amounts of fruit, lots of whole grains, beans, seeds and nuts, fish, and chicken. If dairy is not eaten, take proper amounts of calcium and magnesium in the form of natural supplements. During pregnancy and breast-feeding, calcium intake should be 1,500 milligrams per day, and magnesium one-half to one-quarter that amount. After delivery, immediate breast-feeding will help stimulate milk production. Useful herbs to encourage breast-milk production are marshmallow root and fennel. Parsley and sage diminish milk production.

La Leche League advocates holding the baby's buttocks in one hand, supported against your hip, and the baby's head in the crook of your elbow. Your free hand is used to hold the breast from below. Hold the nipple against the baby's lower lip; this stimulates the baby to open the mouth wide. As the mouth opens, pull the baby's whole body quickly toward your body so that the aerola fits well into the baby's mouth. The nipple itself should be placed deep in the baby's throat. Proper positioning should result in no breast pain, no nipple pain, and no cracked, raw, or irritated nipples. These are common complaints among breast-feeding mothers, but with proper positioning they should not occur.

If the nipples do become irritated, vitamin E oil will help heal them. Avoiding wet clothing helps; try not to wear anything that will retain moisture around the nipples. Do not use soap to wash the nipples because of its drying effect. Another important aspect of breast-feeding is avoiding plugged ducts, which can lead to mastitis. Examine your breasts every day to look for areas of hardness or inflammation. Immediately put a hot pack (a wet compress, heating pad, or castor oil pack) on the area. Massage the area from the base of the breast, at the chest wall, out toward the nipple. Nurse the baby on that side more frequently. Within twenty-four hours, the plugged duct should be clear; however, if the breast gets more inflamed and you have a temperature and feel like you have the flu, this could be a sign of mastitis. The usual treatment is antibiotics to prevent further complications, such as breast abscess, as well as rest, lots of fluids, and nursing even more frequently. The baby will not become infected, but with the use of antibiotics, mother and baby can become susceptible to candidiasis. Take plenty of acidophilus bacteria when you must take antibiotics, and watch the baby for oral thrush or diaper rash. Read the section on candidiasis on page 40.

First Aid

The most effective first aid therapies I know are homeopathic and herbal remedies. (Also see Resources section, page 217, to order kits and other products.) Here is a quick rundown of conditions and treatments:

1. For pain, aching, bruising (from dental extractions, joint sprains, fractured bones, and concussions), take Arnica 12C by mouth every two hours. Arnica can be used in tincture or cream form locally for contusions, bruising, or swelling. If the skin is broken, however, Arnica is inappropriate for topical application and must not be used. Calendula tincture is used on open wounds and is a good antiseptic.

2. For stabs, puncture wounds, bites, stings, or splinters, use oral Ledum 12C every one-half to four hours and repeat when the pain returns. Ledum tincture or Calendula tincture can be used topically.

3. For puncture wounds, injury to the coccyx, or spinal concussion, use oral Hypericum 6 or 12C, 4 drops every two to four hours. Hypericum can also be used for crushed fingers or toes or any abrasion where nerve endings are irritated, such as abrasion of the palm of the hand or the knee. In these abrasions, Hypericum tincture can be used on the skin's surface. Hypericum can also be used for the phantom pain of an amputated limb.

4. For sprained tendons or ligaments, bruised bones, joint or tendon inflammation, or shin bruises, Ruta is especially useful (after Arnica 12C), 12C, 4 drops every one to four hours as needed. It is also good for eye injuries.

5. For bone fractures, oral Symphytum 6 or 12C is extremely useful for speedy healing.

6. For ruptured ligaments and tendons around joints, especially wrists and ankles, Rhus tox. is the best remedy, 6 or 12C, 4 drops every two to four hours.

7. For wounds, put Calendula or Hypericum tincture in water to clean and wrap a wound; they both have antiseptic as well as analgesic properties. They can also stop a local hemorrhage.

8. For hemorrhaging, apply Calendula tincture directly. For dental hemorrhage, oral Phosphorus 6 or 12C every ten to fifteen minutes will stop the bleeding. For nosebleeds, Ferrum phos. 12C or Vipera 12C every fifteen minutes will stop bleeding.

9. For burns and scalds, apply cold water immediately. Urtica urens by mouth, 6 or 12C, and locally in a tincture will help the pain. In severe cases with great pain and restlessness, use Causticum by mouth, 30 or 200c, and Hypericum tincture externally. The most severe burns are treated with oral Cantharis, 12 or 200C.

Naturopathic Medicine

I both feel and think that naturopathic medicine has what it takes to bring medicine into the twenty-first century. This is exemplified by the seven principles of naturopathic medicine. I went into medicine because I instinctively believed in these principles, but I came to realize they do not exist within the walls and boundaries of allopathic medicine. Thankfully, I found them in naturopathic medicine. They speak for themselves!

1. First, do no harm.
2. Identify and treat the causes.
3. The doctor is teacher.
4. Treat the whole person.
5. Emphasize prevention.
6. Support the healing power of the body.
7. Physician heal thyself.

Pregnancy

There are many good books available on nutritional and herbal advice for pregnancy; a particular favorite is by Susun Weed, called *Wise Woman Herbal for the Childbearing Year*. Before conception, get a blood test to make sure that you are protected against rubella (German measles). If acquired during pregnancy, rubella can harm the fetus. The immunity conferred by natural infection during childhood is the best;

second best is immunization against the disease. You should not get pregnant in the three to six months following immunization for rubella.

Immunizations themselves are controversial and it's best to take homeopathic remedies such as Thuja 12C after the shot to prevent side effects. Vitamin C, the B vitamins, and zinc are also important to help the body deal with the foreign material injected. You should also go on a cleansing program before conceiving. Read the sections on breast-feeding, page 156, and detoxification, page 178.

That having been accomplished, a thorough physical exam and blood tests to determine the status of your hemoglobin, thyroid, blood sugar, iron, and liver function should also be done before conception. The diet of both parents should be optimum, and avoidance of coffee, alcohol, and cigarette smoke is best because all these factors have been shown to produce adverse effects on the growth and health of the fetus. If you are trying to get pregnant, avoid aspartame (NutraSweet) like the plague that it is. First of all, aspartame elevates prolactin, which interferes with fertility. According to the *Congressional Record*, aspartame causes birth defects and is a neurotoxin. In *Aspartame (NutraSweet): Is It Safe?*, Dr. H. J. Roberts explains that at least 1 out of 50 people are unable to break down phenylalanine, and it becomes a poison to the nervous system. But most people have no reason to suspect they will have a PKU baby and you can't test a baby for PKU until it is born. According to the *Congressional Record*, if the mother uses aspartame and if the baby survives the womb, chances are the child will be mentally retarded. There should be a warning label to prevent pregnant women from using aspartame. Aspartame also contains 10 percent wood alcohol, which affects the vision and breaks down into formaldehyde and formic acid, both of which have their own hazardous health effects. Aspartame causes ninety-two side effects that have been reported to the FDA. Spread the word about this menace and read the sections on sugar addiction on page 4 and sugar and aspartame on page 185 for more information.

Maintain a high-fiber diet during pregnancy to avoid constipation, and eat plenty of vegetables, fish, chicken, nuts, whole grains, and seeds. Avoid eating too much fruit because some women get gestational diabetes just from the overconsumption of fruit.

Once pregnant, the best position to take when sleeping is on the left side so that the growing uterus is supported over the sigmoid colon. Lying on the back or right side can create undue pressure on the great veins of the trunk leading to the legs, which can in turn cause varicose veins, varicosities of the labia, and hemorrhoids.

Another anatomical risk is hiatus hernia, which is caused by the pressure of the enlarging uterus as it pushes the stomach up under the diaphragm. The treatment for hiatus hernia or stomach pressure against the diaphragm is to eat small frequent meals; don't drink water with a meal because that bloats the stomach; don't lie down immediately after a meal; and have the area of the stomach massaged down and to the right in order to maintain the stomach in its proper position. See the section on digestive disorders on page 63 for a discussion of hiatus hernia.

Necessary supplements during pregnancy are iron, for building up the blood; folic acid, which prevents certain birth defects; and a good multiple vitamin and mineral that has vitamins A and D and the B vitamins. Calcium and magnesium are also required; read the section on osteoporosis on page 130 to find out why dairy might not cover your calcium needs. The calcium requirement is 1,200 to 1,500 milligrams, and half as much magnesium. Calcium and magnesium are best taken separately from fiber in the evening. DHA, flaxseed oil, and fish oils are also essential before and during pregnancy to aid in fetal brain development. Thirty years of research has finally proven that the underlying cause of attention deficit/hyperactivity disorder (ADHD) is lack of essential fatty acids during pregnancy.

For morning sickness, try to eat and drink frequently to keep your blood sugar up. Some people think morning sickness is a good sign of healthy hormone activity and a way for your body to turn against junk food at a time when you need the best for your baby. Avoid coffee, cigarettes, alcohol, sugar, and fried foods. Snack on nuts and seeds and drink plenty of fluids. For morning sickness, ginger and red raspberry leaf teas give some relief; vitamin B_6 is also helpful, 100 to 300 milligrams per day.

The homeopathic remedies for morning sickness are:

Anacardium for a pregnant woman who eats small amounts and gets a sinking feeling in the pit of her stomach, gas, and bloating.

Cocculus for being worse with motion, being unable to stand the sight or smell of food with associated dizziness or sleep loss.

Colchicum is for being worse with the smell of meat, eggs, or fried food and feeling cold from the inside out.

Pulsatilla for upset stomach, gastric irritation; for when heavy foods aggravate the condition; for feeling helpless, moody, crying a lot, and wanting something to eat but not knowing what.

Sepia for mental and emotional depression, irritability, persistent nausea and vomiting, yelling, and hitting; worse with meat and eggs.

Ipecac for constant nausea, complete disgust at even the thought of food; lack of thirst.

Ignatia for cramps and spasms, knotted-up stomach, hysterical behavior, sensitivity, edginess, and irritability.

Nux vomica for morning cramps and spasms, rashes, a toxic hangover, headache, nausea, irritability, feeling better in the afternoon.

All these remedies are given in a 12C potency, 4 drops every fifteen minutes to four hours. If one remedy doesn't work within two days, another remedy should be tried. If several fail to have an effect, consult a homeopathic doctor.

During pregnancy, a blood test should be taken for thyroid function. Sometimes pregnancy can put an unnecessary strain on the thyroid, which can result in deficiency. A repeat test should be done at the postnatal six-week checkup.

To prepare for labor, some women use Caulophyllum, 6 or 12C, several doses a day, the last week or two before delivery. This can also be used during labor to help balance the contractions. Arnica is taken during labor and after delivery for bruising or shock, 6 or 12C, one dose every half hour. Aconite can be used after a difficult labor, 200C, one to two doses. Causticum can also be used for urinary retention in the same dosage. Rhus tox. in 6 or 12C potency can be used for the strain of pregnancy leading to stiffness, muscle aches, and chilliness. Staphysagria, 12C, can be taken for urethra pain, especially after catheterization.

It is very important to take 50 milligrams of zinc per day to replace the stores that are greatly diminished by the stress of delivery. This dosage should be taken for one month and then reduced to 25 milligrams per day for one more month. Zinc helps wound healing and it can prevent postpartum depression. Continue to take zinc in your multiple vitamin and mineral supplement during breast-feeding. A hypoactive thyroid is another cause of postpartum depression. Read the section on hypothyroidism on page 103 to find out more. Ignatia is a fantastic homeopathic remedy that treats postpartum depression. Use the 12C potency two or three times a day for a week. You should notice the benefits within that time if the remedy is going to work.

Surgery

We will assume your surgery is necessary, that you have received a second and perhaps a third opinion, and that the benefits outweigh the risks. If you eat an optimum diet and take a basic supplement that includes zinc, B vitamins, A, D, C, calcium, and magnesium before surgery, you will recover faster. It is advisable to avoid vitamin E for seven to ten days before surgery, however, since it is a blood thinner. With the increased use of herbs in the population, you should be aware of possible interactions with other drugs you take and with surgery. Ginkgo, garlic, ginger, and ginseng all have slight blood-thinning properties, which make them excellent for the heart and circulation, but they should be stopped ten days before surgery.

My advice is to take a Bach Flower Remedy such as Rescue Remedy (available in health food stores) to approach the surgery as calmly as possible. Visualization, relaxation, and affirmation tapes are available in your local health food store to help achieve a calm state of mind and to try to influence the subconscious that all will go well during the surgery, that the body will heal rapidly, and that health will be restored. Some practitioners of these methods advise patients to visualize the complete hospital stay and all procedures orchestrated to perfection. In the hospital, you can take Rescue Remedy every time you see your doctor and use a portable tape recorder to listen to healing tapes.

After surgery, take Phosphorus 12C, 4 drops for about three doses; this helps clear the anesthetic effects. Take Arnica 12C every fifteen to sixty minutes for pain, shock, and swelling. As the pain lessens, take the remedy less often. As soon as you are drinking after surgery, use vitamin C powder in juice or water to help healing, help clear the liver of anesthetic, help kidney function, and also promote bowel peristalsis. To aid bowel function, which is most important after surgery, take a teaspoon of olive oil twice per day. When solids are introduced, then the complete range of vitamins can be started. This includes zinc, B complex vitamins, vitamin E once the danger of bleeding has passed, and a multiple vitamin and mineral supplement. If you have been extremely depleted by your hospitalization or surgery, protein drinks available in natural food stores can be used for optimum nourishment. The general remedy for recovery from surgery is Veretrum album 12C, 4 drops three times per day.

Traveling Advice

Travel light is the best tip, and this includes your nutritional supplements. If you need to take them with you, use a combined multiple vitamin and mineral to try to eliminate many bottles. For preventing diarrhea, take one to two hydrochloric acid tablets (unless you have an ulcer) or grapefruit seed extract capsules at the end of each meal to kill off any indigenous parasites. The old saying is that you may be used to the bugs in your own hometown but not the critters elsewhere. Take acidophilus to build up the good bacteria in your intestines once or twice a day. There is now liquid acidophilus on the market that does not have to be refrigerated. Follow the advice below for stomach problems.

Prevention

Do not drink the water; this means ice, fruit drinks, and milk shakes.

Do not eat salads or cut fruits, except fruits you peel yourself.

Eat only freshly cooked food.

Drink boiled water, commercially bottled water, or mineral water.

Dry foods are usually safe.

Wash your hands often, using hot water and soap.

Think about everything that you ingest, even the water for brushing your teeth.

Treatment

Use dietary treatment first. Antibiotic or antidiarrhea pills can be dangerous and actually prolong the illness.

The first day, drink only clear fluids: soups, juices, and teas.

The second day, eat only rice, applesauce, and bananas. Add 1 teaspoon carob powder to the applesauce, and take three times a day.

The third day, add dry bland foods, nothing greasy, fried, or spicy.

By the fourth day you should be able to move up to a normal diet, but do so slowly.

Avoid dairy and citrus for at least a week.

If your bowels loosen at any time, move back to clear fluids.

Go to the Nearest Doctor or Hospital

If any symptom hangs on for more than five to six days.

If fever, bloody diarrhea, or vomiting and diarrhea occur together. Dehydration occurs when vomiting and diarrhea are present. Watch your urine output.

Warning

Antidiarrhea pills should be used only to control diarrhea for short periods of time when absolutely necessary, such as long road trips.

Antibiotics can be dangerous when used for diarrhea and should be prescribed by a doctor. They can lead to overgrowth of *Candida* in the intestines. (Read the section on candidiasis on page 40.)

Watch young children with diarrhea; they dehydrate faster. They can go without food but don't let them go without fluids. Warm baths can help to rehydrate.

Read the sections on diarrhea on page 62, gas on page 83, and digestive disorders on page 63 for further tips on symptoms that continue after a bout of travelers' diarrhea.

X-rays

X-rays are sometimes necessary, although often overused. They are a tool that doctors depend on heavily and find hard to let go of even in the face of evidence that they are harmful. The best recommendation is to question the necessity of x-rays before consenting to them.

Read Dr. Rosalie Bertell's book, *No Immediate Danger.* She heads the International Institute of Concern for Public Health. Dr. Bertell's book describes the dangers of even small amounts of radiation. If x-rays are essential, lessen the side effects with an x-ray homeopathic remedy, available from your homeopathic doctor.

PART THREE

Diet
and Detoxification

Bean Sprouts

There is a simple way to ensure that you are getting natural vitamins, minerals, and enzymes: eat freshly sprouted mung beans after every meal. Bean sprouts are loaded with enzymes and nutrients in tiny delicious packages. The Chinese use them for digestive problems, belching, bloating, overeating, and general food stagnation. I have found them even more powerful than expensive enzymes to help digest a big meal.

To make them, all you need is a pint-sized glass jar and some gauze from your medicine cabinet. Soak 3 tablespoons of organic mung beans in filtered water for twenty-four hours. Place the gauze over the top of the bottle and secure with an elastic band. Drain off the water through the gauze and rinse twice a day. Keep the bottle tilted downward in a glass or stainless steel bowl and covered with a cloth. In three days you'll have a bottle full of sprouts, which you can transfer to another container and keep in the fridge. Begin making another batch of sprouts right away. By the time you finish the first batch, the next will be ready to eat.

Beet Kvass

Every few years a fermented drink becomes a fad and is hailed as a miracle cure. The latest one was Kombotchu mushrooms. It was made by growing a strange-looking jellyfishlike fungus in black tea and sugar. To the casual observer, there is no reason why a fungus grown in black tea and some sugar should do anything. But it does produce a fermented brew. Fermentation is equated with something going rotten, but properly fermented products are very necessary for our intestinal health. For example, yogurt is fermented milk, and anyone who has to go on an antibiotic should take yogurt that is guaranteed to have live organisms in it. And taking fermented products on a daily basis can greatly increase intestinal health. So a natural fermented drink such as Kombotchu can be helpful. But you can do the same thing much cheaper and probably safer with beets, whey, and salt, using a recipe in Sally Fallon's *Nourishing Traditions*.

Cut up two to three small beets in ½-inch chunks, and place them in a quart-sized jar. Add 2 tablespoons of whey, which is the liquid that you can strain from yogurt. Use yogurt that is guaranteed to have live organisms, such as Erivan Acidophilus Yogurt. Add 1 teaspoon of sea salt and fill the jar with filtered water. Cover tightly and let stand for two days at room temperature. Transfer to the fridge and drink 2 ounces a day.

Detoxification

The importance of detoxification has been mentioned throughout this book. The body releases waste products through the kidney, bowel, and skin. It becomes fairly easy to spot someone who is toxic by poor skin color, puffiness or greasiness of the skin, a lack of luster in the eyes, and a general sluggish, apathetic appearance. People may not realize that they are toxic because they have been slowly poisoning themselves and have forgotten what it feels like to be in optimum health.

As you improve your diet and lifestyle, you will go through a detoxification process that can include withdrawal headaches as coffee, alcohol, and cigarettes are eliminated. This is a sure sign that you need to be off these substances. Pay special attention to removing aspartame (NutraSweet) from your diet. It is a very addictive substance made from two amino acids and wood alcohol. Wood alcohol is noted for its negative effect on vision and can cause blindness. The manufacturer would have us believe that people don't drink enough wood alcohol to cause problems. Aspartame is now in over 9,000 products, however, and some people drink liters of diet soda every day. The two amino acids break down into carcinogens and toxins above 86°F. Last time I checked, my body temperature was 98.6°F. Aspartame is responsible for ninety-two different symptoms as reported by the FDA, but big business keeps it on the shelves. Only you can keep it out of your body.

Don't be surprised if you experience an aggravation of symptoms if you go back to old dietary habits. In other words, once the body is feeling better, if toxic substances are ingested, you may have a severe reaction to them. This immediate feedback should warn you to avoid them. Such feedback is good; this is the way the body encourages us to avoid these substances. Listen.

A good diet of fresh whole grains, nuts and seeds, vegetables, fruit, fish, and chicken will help your body eliminate toxins from your previous diet. After a regimen of optimum diet, exercise, and sufficient sleep has been implemented and maintained for a minimum of one month, you can begin short fasts on vegetable broths and vegetable juices as well as using psyllium seed powder or capsules to increase your bowel movements while on the fast. Take the psyllium capsules twice a day with two glasses of water or 1 teaspoon of psyllium powder in a jar of water with a bit of fruit juice for taste. This should be shaken vigorously and taken with another glass of water to create the optimum bulking action of the psyllium. Juice fasting can be done for a three-day period every two to three months. This gives the body a good rest from digestion, and toxins held in fatty tissue have a chance to be eliminated. Sauna therapy is becoming a very popular and vital form of detoxification. Environmental medicine practitioners recommend this modality to sweat toxins out through the skin; to mobilize the release of poisons from storage in fat cells; and for general relaxation. A moderate temperature is recommended (150 to 160°F). You can take several fifteen- to twenty-minute sessions interspersed with cool showers for a total of two to four hours to treat severe environmental illness. For general cleansing, just work up to one hour of sauna time once or twice a week. Rubbing the skin with sea salt helps bring out the sweat. Drink lots of vegetable broth to replace lost potassium and salt and take your water with a pinch of sea salt.

An interesting method of detoxification is the universal contour wrap. In Europe it is promoted as a cleansing and healing modality; however, in America it can only be marketed as a beauty product. It is an extremely safe and effective method of detoxification. A licensed technician using large tensor bandages soaked in liquid sea clay wraps your whole body from toe to neck. The process draws out poisons, toxins, and edema. Measurements before and after the hour-long treatment show actual girth reduction. The health and appearance of the skin is much improved. It even works to eliminate cellulite. Call the number in the Resources section to find a licensed technician practicing in your area.

Aloe vera gel can be taken on a regular basis for cleansing. This substance is good for healing the intestines and to detoxify; take 1 tablespoon in juice every morning.

If there are indications of lead toxicity or heavy metal poisoning, via blood or hair analysis, use foods that will chelate or grab the heavy metals. These include pectin (apples), alginate (seaweed), cilantro, and the amino acids methionine, cysteine, and cystine found in beans, eggs, onions, and garlic.

Other daily cleansers include the juice of one lemon in water every morning; 1 tablespoon apple cider vinegar and 1 teaspoon organic honey in water every morning; 1 glass of beet kvass (see the sections on bean sprouts and beet kvass); Essiac tea; the Hoxsey Formula; and Lapacho tea. (See the cancer section on page 33 for more information on the last three herb teas.) These special drinks can be rotated to obtain optimum benefits.

In special cases, enemas may be recommended for more thorough intestinal cleansing. Dr. Nicholas Gonzales in New York uses a complete regimen of enzymes, juicing, supplements, fasting, and enemas in his cancer protocols. He employs a coffee enema that stimulates the release of bile from the liver. The venous system in the bowel is in direct communication with the liver and gallbladder, and instead of the caffeine entering the body or the arterial system, it specifically detoxifies the liver. Coffee enemas are also used in the Gerson Diet and by Dr. Sherry Rodgers and many other environmental practitioners. *The Healthy Breast* by Sat Dharam Kaur, N.D., has an excellent description of the coffee enema technique.

Warning: Detoxification is contraindicated in pregnancy.

Diets

Diet must be individualized. An optimum diet for all includes eating organic foods, cooking from scratch, and understanding that what you are eating should be as clean and alive as you want your body to be. The usual response when I tell people to cut out fast food and processed food is that they just don't have enough time to eat properly. They are too busy rushing around, trying to take care of business, family, and friends, and food is eaten on the run. We take better care of our material possessions than we do of ourselves. We must reprioritize and take care of our diet, exercise, and sleep habits in order to live healthier and happier lives. Remember, you *are* what you eat.

Processed foods, chemical food additives, dyes, and sweeteners are not alive, and they add to the total body burden of toxicity that has become the avenue by which we allow chronic disease, autoimmune disease, and cancer to be created in our bodies. Aspartame (NutraSweet) is possibly the most dangerous food additive on the market because it is in over 9,000 diet food products. It is responsible for ninety-two different health side effects, including symptoms of MS, lupus, diabetes, and bowel disease. Avoid products with aspartame, read all labels, and warn your friends and family.

In 1980, I began to follow *One Man's Food,* naturopath James D'Adamo's diet program according to blood group. His son, Dr. Peter D'Adamo, wrote *Eat Right 4 Your Type* in 1996. First, find out your blood type, then match it to the four major diets in the book. I will give a synopsis of each blood type diet; if it seems to resonate with you, consult the book and go into the detailed explanation, diet plans, and menus for your type. I am presently writing a book on Chinese diet therapy based on body type and tongue assessment with a wonderful Taoist priest and Chinese medicine teacher, Jeffrey Yuen, that will be even more individualized. Until that book is available and can be used alone or in conjunction with blood groups, I recommend the blood type diet.

Type Os do best on a diet high in animal protein and require a lot of physical exercise. Type Os, who make up the bulk of the population, excel at the Atkins diet. Dairy products are to be avoided. Grains (especially wheat and corn) are difficult to digest for most Type Os and tend to cause weight gain. Even certain beans and legumes (lentils and kidney beans) contain substances that deposit in muscle tissues, causing pain and inflammation. Type Os also have a tendency toward hypothyroidism and do much better with food from the ocean, including fish and seaweed. The focus of the diet is on lean, chemical-free, hormone-free poultry, meat, and fish, nuts and seeds (pumpkin seeds, walnuts), beans (azuki, pinto, black eyed), grains (sprouted grain breads only), vegetables (avoid avocado, cabbage, corn, eggplant, olives, potatoes), and fruits (avoid oranges, strawberries).

Type As find their balance in a more vegetarian diet. Their exercise is more gentle and calming, such as yoga and tai chi. Type As don't have the necessary stomach acid to digest meat and it ends up being stored as fat. They also have a hard time processing dairy products, and even wheat should not be eaten daily. What's left, you ask? Type As can eat most fish (except sole and flounder), but the focus of the diet is on soy products, nuts, seeds, most beans and legumes, all grains except wheat, and most vegetables and fruits.

Type Bs seem to be able to eat like a Type O and Type A, bouncing back and forth between a high-protein diet and a vegetarian diet. Dr. D'Adamo has found that Type Bs gain weight on corn, buckwheat, lentils, peanuts, and sesame seeds, but they lose weight on green vegetables, meat, eggs, liver, and licorice tea. There are other specifics for Type Bs, such as avoiding chicken. What's left for the Type B? Lamb, rabbit, seafood (except shellfish), dairy products, certain beans (kidney, lima, navy, red soy), specific grains (millet, oat, rice, spelt), and vegetables (avoiding tomatoes, corn, olives).

Type AB has aspects of both Type A and Type B. Weight gain can occur with red meat, kidney and lima beans, seeds, corn, buckwheat, and wheat, whereas tofu, seafood, dairy, green vegetables, kelp, and pineapple enhance weight loss. The Type AB diet avoids beef and chicken but includes lamb, rabbit, and turkey, seafood, dairy, beans and lentils (navy, pinto, red, red soybeans, green lentils), grains (millet, oat, rice, spelt), vegetables (except tomatoes, corn, mushrooms, peppers), and fruits (except bananas, mangoes, oranges).

There is a high-fat/high-protein diet backlash occurring against the high-carbohydrate, low-protein vegetarian diet. When I interviewed Dr. Dean Ornish about his high-carbohydrate, low-fat diet and asked him how to determine when you're not getting enough fat, he said, "When your skin gets flaky and dry." To wait for these symptoms seems far too late to avoid essential fatty acid deficiency and the damage it can cause. Also, for the past several decades we have been brainwashed into thinking that vegetable margarine is better for us than butter, only to find that margarine and its trans-fatty acids may, itself, be responsible for the rise in heart disease.

We know that some fats are essential, such as the omega-3 and omega-6 fatty acids. Omega-3 oils are found in fatty fish such as mackerel, sardines, and salmon, in ground flaxseeds and flaxseed oil, and in small amounts in walnuts and pumpkin seeds. Omega-6 oils are found in nuts and seeds and commercial products such as borage oil and evening primrose oil. A good portion of the brain, up to half, is composed of fat that lines all the nerves and allows the brain chemicals to interact properly. If essential fats are deficient, the brain just doesn't develop properly. DHA (docosahexaenoic acid) is essential for eye and brain development and it is only recently that this essential oil has been added to infant formulas.

I've been studying the fat issue for thirty years and I feel safest consuming the following fats: unprocessed butter, tropical oils such as coconut, and cold-pressed (extra virgin) olive oil—all in moderation. Coconut oil actually protects people in the tropics from bacteria and fungus. I stay away from margarine, which is made by a hydrogenation process. Butter and coconut oils are also high in saturated fats, which make them extremely stable; they don't go rancid or change chemically when heated (thus producing free radicals). Therefore, I think they're the best oils for baking and cooking, especially high-temperature frying. Olive oil, which is high in monounsaturated fat, is a relatively stable fat as well (though not as stable as saturated fats at high temperatures) and is good for medium-heat sautéing and for use on salads.

I also include cod liver and flaxseed oil, which provide a healthy amount of omega-3 fatty acids. The only drawback is that you can't cook with flaxseed oil at all because heat will destroy its beneficial properties. I take 1 teaspoon of cod liver oil and 2 tablespoons of flaxseed oil every day.

As for animal fat, I don't believe that the fat from such animals as fish and grain-fed, antibiotic- and hormone-free beef and poultry are the culprit in heart disease, so I make them part of my diet. But I don't include any of the relatively new and highly processed vegetable oils (especially canola) or margarine and shortening made from partially hydrogenated vegetable oils. All of these contain trans-fatty acids, a type of fat that occurs rarely in nature but when formed during the hydrogenation process is harmful and should be avoided. Canola has been touted as the latest health oil. However, according to Sally Fallon in *Nourishing Traditions*, canola has a high sulphur content; it goes rancid easily; baked goods made with canola develop mold very quickly; the omega-3 fatty acids of processed canola oil contain trans-fatty acids similar to those in margarine. Canola is also genetically engineered.

When changing your diet from refined grains to more whole grains, beans, and lentils, it is common to suffer intestinal gas. This can be remedied by soaking your beans and lentils overnight in salted water (use sea salt) and then throwing out the soaking water. This causes a type of fermentation that increases the mineral content of the beans and their bioavailability to the body. The fermentation process eliminates gas and bloating. Soaking also activates the digestive enzymes in each bean. Steaming and sautéing make beans and legumes even more digestible and are superior cooking methods to boiling. See the section on diabetes on page 58 to learn about insulin resistance and glycemic index.

Soy

Soy has become the latest health craze because the FDA approved the labeling of soy as having health benefits. But we need to look at the dark side of soy. In Asia, soy is used in the fermented state, which prevents many of its antinutrient and growth-inhibiting side effects. Soybeans are high in phytic acid, which can block the uptake of essential minerals. Soy also has enzyme inhibitors that block the action of enzymes needed for protein digestion. It also contains a clot-promoting substance that causes red blood cells to clump together, and soy depresses thyroid function.

In the West, it is not fermented soy that is being heavily advertised and marketed. Soy protein isolate and textured vegetable protein are used in protein powders and meat substitutes. But the extensive processing to reach a final product makes it not only toxic, but the antinutrients are preserved!

There was a recent flurry of studies showing soy to be effective against menopausal symptoms, cancer, and heart disease, but it seems that all those studies have been called into question with follow-up research. Although there may be some benefits for menopausal women, the hormonal effects of soy are the most disturbing for those infants who are allergic to milk and routinely receive soy formula.

How does one make sense of the soy debate? Basically, we can't draw any comparisons between Asian fermented soy intake data and Western processes and nonfermented soy intake data. If we want to have the reported Asian health benefits, we have to eat fermented soy to the tune of 2 teaspoons a day—the Asian average—not the megadoses of soy powders that are being recommended in the West.

Research suggests that babies do not have the necessary enzymes to produce phytoestrogens from soy until six months, which may mean it is safe for them to have soy formula until then. A group of scientists is lobbying to have soy formula removed from the market, however, because they are concerned about the effects of soy on children. At puberty, soy may be helpful for girls to keep their menses from coming on too early, but it may not be beneficial for boys as the phytoestrogens may counter their testosterone surge. Other research suggests that soy is a cause of infertility and should be avoided if you are trying to get pregnant. As for menopause, many women swear by its ability to control their hot flashes. Bottom line, everything in moderation. If you can't digest it or if it gives you gas and bloating, don't eat it. If you can digest it, use it in the fermented form. If you want to use it in place of a drug for menopause, use formulas with genistein and diazidin from reputable sources.

Sugar and Aspartame

Unbelievably, the American Diabetes Association changed its nutritional recommendations in 1994 to accommodate sugar. The new recommendations say, "Scientific evidence has shown that the use of sucrose as part of the meal plan does not impair blood glucose control in individuals with insulin-dependent or non-insulin-dependent diabetes."

It seems researchers found that blood sugar did not become highly elevated with a sucrose meal compared to a glucose meal, so they used this as validation that sucrose is okay for diabetics. They also ignored the overwhelming anthropological evidence that when a sugar-free society introduces sugar and refined foods, diabetes develops in fifteen to twenty years. Even today the incidence of adult-onset diabetes is rising in children, who have been consuming 20 to 40 teaspoons of sugar over ten or fifteen years. The incidence of diabetes has skyrocketed up 30 percent in the past ten years.

Sir Frederick Banting was the scientist who developed insulin. In the 1920s, when he visited Panama, Banting was astonished to find almost no incidence of diabetes among the workers in the sugar cane fields, but among their Spanish employers this disease was rampant. Today we know why. The workers in the sugar cane fields consumed the unrefined sugar, which was full of vitamins and nutrients and did not upset insulin production. Their employers consumed the crystallized end product and became ill. Banting himself warned that his discovery of insulin treatment was merely a stop-gap measure, but that prevention was the true answer to the problem. He stated that prevention could only be achieved through reduction in refined sugar consumption.

A vast amount of research has been accumulated by medical anthropologists Professors M. N. Cohen, Loring Brace, R. Lee, Winston Price, and Frances Pottenger that clearly shows that hunting and gathering peoples do not have cancer, diabetes, heart attacks, osteoporosis, or tooth decay. They develop these conditions within one generation when they are exposed to refined sugar and refined flour. Studies show that sugar lowers your white blood cell immune response and makes you more susceptible to infection. When I was in practice it was obvious to me that more kids would get sick after holidays or birthday parties when they had eaten lots of sugar. (See also the section on sugar addiction, page 4.)

Presently the sugar and sweetener industry is having a field day because, when low-fat foods flood the market, high-sugar foods prevail to meet the demand for the sweet, rich foods and snacks to which we have become addicted.

I mention aspartame (NutraSweet, Spoonful, Equal) throughout this book because it seems to be causing more and more symptoms in the population. The FDA itself has published a report on 10,000 written complaints up to 1994 listing ninety-two different side effects. Such a multitude of complaints signifies millions more who don't even connect their suffering to aspartame.

Aspartame is a synthetic chemical comprised of 50 percent phenylalanine, 40 percent aspartic acid, and 10 percent methanol. Phenylalanine is an amino acid that, when found in excess in the brain, can cause mental retardation or death. A certain percentage of the population cannot metabolize phenylalanine. They have a condition call phenylketonuria. All babies are screened for it at birth, but a pregnant woman has no idea if her baby will have this problem and she could be poisoning the fetus if she uses aspartame while pregnant. So it should not be used in pregnancy and there should be warnings to this effect.

Aspartic acid is a chemical that evokes a chain of events in brain chemistry resulting in overstimulation of nerve cells to the point of cell death.

Methanol is wood alcohol, which is a poison that can cause blindness and/or death in people who mistake it for alcohol.

Aspartame is unstable under certain conditions, including temperatures exceeding 86°F, producing the free amino acids phenylalanine and aspartic acid and methanol alcohol plus several other toxic breakdown products that are carcinogens, such as beta-aspartame and aspartylphenylalanine diketopiperazine (DKP). This instability makes aspartame hazardous for baked products, difficult to store properly, and unsuitable for a body temperature of 98.6°F! As if that weren't bad enough, at cold temperatures methanol will spontaneously give rise to formaldehyde, which accumulates within the cells and causes DNA damage, according to a recent study in Italy.

Methanol taken orally is extremely toxic to humans. The amount in a can of diet soda can spike plasma methanol levels significantly; think what 1 or 2 liters a day can do.

There is methanol in fruits and vegetables, but this is not a problem because it is naturally neutralized and eliminated by an equal or greater amount of ethanol. There is no neutralizing ethanol in aspartame to take care of its toxicity. Once ingested, free methanol is released into the small intestine and encounters the enzyme chymotrypsin produced by the liver, which breaks it down into formaldehyde.

Methanol can cause permanent blindness when breathed, ingested, or passed through the skin. Exposure to high concentrations can cause death. A coma resulting from massive exposure may last as long as two to four days. Because of the slowness with which it is eliminated by the human body, methanol should be regarded as a cumulative poison. Exposure can damage the liver and cause headaches, cardiac depression, nausea, vomiting, blurred vision, dizziness, a feeling of intoxication, and irritation of the eyes, nose, mouth, and throat. Repeated or prolonged contact can cause dryness and cracking of the skin.

Formaldehyde, also known as formalin, embalming fluid, or formol, is a colorless gas with a pungent odor. Symptoms of formaldehyde exposure include nausea, vomiting, abdominal pain, or diarrhea. When the reaction is allergic, symptoms may include minor respiratory irritation and watery eyes. It is a known carcinogen. The body has difficulty eliminating formaldehyde so it combines some of it with water and stores it in the fat. (This is another reason why people who use aspartame cannot lose weight.) What is not stored in the fat is further converted to formic acid (known as ant sting poison, and used as an activator to strip epoxy and urethane coatings).

Phenylalanine in aspartame lowers the seizure threshold of the brain and depletes serotonin. Low levels of serotonin trigger panic attacks, anxiety, and mood changes. Aspartame also triggers irregular heart rhythms, and is an addictive drug that interacts with other drugs. To learn more about aspartame, visit www.dorway.com, a Web site devoted to sharing information about the health effects of aspartame. On this site people are encouraged to take the sixty-day aspartame-free test. If you go off aspartame for sixty days you should notice a dramatic improvement in your health if aspartame has been causing some of your problems. The current rise in MS, brain tumors, autoimmune disease, fibromyalgia, chronic fatigue syndrome, and cancer may be due to overuse of chemicals in our society, and especially the overuse of aspartame.

Advice for Aspartame Poisoning

(See the Resources section for ethical suppliers.)

1. Wean yourself off aspartame—read all labels, make food from scratch, assume anything that says sugar free has aspartame, and join the support group on www.dorway.com.
2. Drink lots of purified water to flush the poison out of your system.
3. Follow the cleansing program in the detoxification section on page 178.
4. Take natural vitamins and minerals including magnesium lactate, B vitamins, flaxseed oil, and cod liver oil.
5. Go to the section on making your own remedy on page 207 and make a remedy using a teaspoon of the diet soda you were drinking to help get it all out of your fat cells and tissues. You can make a remedy from any product containing aspartame.
6. Obtain homeopathic remedies called Formic acid and

Formaldehyde to help undo the damage from these chemicals. Use the 12C potency and take one dose three times a day for two weeks.

7. Remember that you are sensitive to aspartame and even a tiny amount that you ingest unknowingly can cause a relapse. If you go on a weight-loss program and break down fat cells, you might feel horrible again as the chemicals come out of your cells. The homeopathic remedies can help you whenever you have a relapse.

Water Purification

According to Dr. Jay Gould, the only way to remove strontium 90 from our tap water is through distillation or reverse osmosis. To remove parasites, you need a filter with a pore size of ½ micron; to remove chlorine you need a carbon block filter. When you purchase your water filter, make sure it meets all the above specifications. Personally, I am not in favor of drinking distilled water, which is devoid of crucial trace minerals.

PART FOUR

Homeopathic
and Herbal Remedies

Homeopathy has been practiced for two hundred years. It is the science of using extremely low potency substances to cure illness. It seems to enhance the natural healing ability of the body. It does not suppress or overwhelm the human being behind the illness.

A remedy is made from a plant, animal, or inorganic substance by shaking or "successing" it in water, in some cases to the point where there isn't even a molecule of the water present. Those who haven't studied homeopathy or witnessed the apparent miracle of it working, tend to disbelieve its effects. Until Dr. Jacques Benveniste did his famous experiments in 1988 there were no scientific explanations of its action. Benveniste found that successing and diluting a substance that produced a color change could produce that same color change at extreme dilutions. The evidence was there, but the reason was thought to be some sort of structure being successed into the water. Now that theory has been proven. At the California Institute of Technology, chemistry professor Shui Yin Lo found that water molecules, which are random in their normal state, begin to form a cluster when a substance is added to water and the water is vigorously shaken—the exact process homeopaths use to create their medicine. Dr. Lo said every substance exerts its own unique influence on the water, so each cluster shape and configuration is unique to the substance added. With each dilution and shaking, the clusters grow bigger and stronger. This water, which homeopaths call "potentized," is considered "structured water," because the water molecules have taken on a shape influenced by the original substance. So even though the chemical can no longer be detected, its "image" is there, taken on by the water molecules.

The potency for acute illness is usually 6C, 12C, or 30C given every one to four hours depending on the severity of the condition. The worse the illness, the more often the remedy is repeated. The higher potencies, such as 200C, are used in general to treat for emotional and constitutional balance. They can be used by a homeopath for severe disease in the acute stage.

The general rule for the use of a remedy is that if it has not caused a change in the condition after six to eight doses, then the remedy should be stopped, the case history of the patient should be taken again, and a more appropriate remedy started. Or, a homeopath should be consulted.

It is important not to use coffee, mints, camphor, chamomile herb, or chemicals with strong odors during the time of homeopathic treatment. All these substances will antidote the remedies. Be advised that you should not allow your remedies to be x-rayed at airports. This will antidote them. Have the attendant walk them around the x-ray equipment as you would with your camera film.

General descriptions and recommendations for common remedies follow.

Aconite

The keynote of this remedy is suddenness of onset.

For the very first signs of a cold or flu, especially when brought on by exposure to cold weather. For asthma, dry suffocating cough, sore throat, and high temperature with great thirst. For tonsillitis, teething, and toothache. For animal bites, sleeplessness, intolerance of pain, stiff neck, and ringing ears. For menstrual periods suppressed or delayed due to worry or fear. For abdominal pain that is made worse by drinking cold water. For great pain; if the condition (whatever it might be) is so severe, you don't know what to give, use aconite first. Symptoms are sudden, violent, and brief.

For extreme emotions, fear, grief, anxiety, and restlessness, a sense of impending doom and bereavement. Aconite may be used for the fear of surgery or dental work. There is also fear of crowds. These intense emotions may accompany the physical symptoms. The appearance will be of fear and restlessness; one cheek may be flushed and one pale. This is unlike Belladonna, which has both cheeks flushed and more delirium than wide-awake fear.

Symptoms are worse at midnight, when lying on affected side, in a warm room, from tobacco smoke, in cold dry winds, and listening to music.

Symptoms are better in the open air, with perspiring and with the bedclothes thrown off.

Aethusa

For milk intolerance, especially for babies with colic.

Apis

The keynotes are a bee-sting pain and hivelike swelling.

For burning or stinging pains where flushing, swelling, or puffing occurs. Especially good for swelling of the lower eyelid, which looks like a bag of water. Symptoms are mostly on the right side. For acute allergic reactions, edema, bee stings, hives, nettle rash, acute kidney infections, and right-sided ovarian cysts. For synovitis, swollen gums, incontinence in older people, shingles, teething, sore throat, tonsillitis, and infected nailbed. There is no thirst. There is listlessness and lack of concentration.

Emotionally the person may be sad, depressed, tearful, or irritable and suspicious. He may try to avoid medical attention.

Symptoms are worse from getting wet, during late afternoon, after sleeping, from heat in any form, when touched, and when in a closed and heated room.

Symptoms are better from a change of position or walking about in the open air and from cold.

Arnica

The keynote is for any injury, emotional or physical.

The number one remedy for pain, shock, swelling, bruising after any injury, or surgery, including dental work and childbirth. This can be taken at any time after the injury no matter how remote, if there are still symptoms. Arnica ointment can be applied directly on the injured part. If the wound is open or the skin is broken, the ointment must not be used because it will cause the wound to fester. Also good for mental as well as physical shock. For bruises, sprains, physical exhaustion, and sleeplessness due to overexhaustion. For gout, with a fear of being touched, loss of voice, toothache, and bee or wasp stings. Other classic symptoms include: the bed feels too hard, a fear of being touched or approached, the whole body feels beaten up and bruised, muscles feel achy.

Symptoms are worse from touch, from exposure to hot sun, from motion, and in damp, cold conditions.

Symptoms get better when lying down with the head low and not propped up.

Arsenicum Album

The keynotes are anxiety and fear.

No matter what the physical illness may be, if there is great fear, restlessness, and anxiety with weakness, exhaustion, shuddering chills, and burning pains that are worse at night, then this is the remedy of choice. The weakness and exhaustion seem exaggerated, but it becomes evident that the person's restlessness and agitation are wearing them out. The patient is terrified of illness, fearful of death, and expresses great insecurity, which, of course, makes things all the worse. The patient is extremely meticulous and everything must be perfectly clean and tidy. There is a fear of being alone but also a fear of being observed closely that borders on paranoia. The body feels cold and chilled and the patient desires hot drinks in spite of the burning nature of the pains.

An excellent food poisoning remedy for vomiting and diarrhea caused by eating bad meat, fruit, or vegetables, when the patient can't bear the sight or smell of food. May feel they have been poisoned by someone. Good for children with upset stomachs and burning pain from food. For asthma, worse at 2 A.M. with anxiety. For any pain that is burning and better with heat. For sore throats that burn but are better with sips of hot liquids. For eye pain or infection that is better with hot cloths. For psoriasis, thrush, tough mucus, and hay fever. For burning vaginitis that is better with hot water washes.

Symptoms are worse after midnight to 3 A.M. and between 1 to 2 P.M. Worse at the ocean and from cold and wet weather.

Symptoms are better by keeping warm, with cool air around the head, from warm or hot drinks taken in sips, and from company.

Belladonna

The keynotes are hot, red, throbbing inflammation.

The patient looks flushed and feverish and dull with dilated pupils and bright red dry skin. The fever is high, the onset is acute, and the pain is severe, throbbing, and burning. The fever may go very high and lead to hallucinations and even destructive behavior.

For colds, earaches, or any condition with sudden onset and flushing, throbbing heat with blood rushing to the area. Menopausal hot flashes, menstrual pains, infections, boils, or headaches. The headache has a characteristic bandlike pressure feeling. The hollow areas of the body may feel the sensation of a ball inside. For swollen glands, swollen joints, facial neuralgia, chicken pox, sunstroke, measles, and air sickness. Menstrual periods are early and heavy. For mumps, bladder infections, sore throat, and tonsillitis. For loss of voice, toothache and teething, stiff neck, and incontinence.

Symptoms are worse in the afternoon and at night, from noise, from lying down, from bright light, from touch, and from jarring movement.

Symptoms are better from warmth, especially on the abdomen, and while lying down.

Bryonia

The keynote is worse from movement.

The movement can be from walking, moving the eyes, even swallowing. Deep breathing, talking, or laughing can bring on a painful coughing spell.

The patient is irritable, gets angry easily, hates interrogation, and wants to be left alone. The patient may feel confused and appear dim-witted.

For tearing and stitching pains that are worse from moving and better from resting.

For respiratory conditions in which colds go down into the chest and a dry painful cough that can be violent, such as bronchitis, with dryness of the air passages, dry lips, tongue, and throat, and excessive thirst, especially for cold drinks. With colds and flus there are joint and muscle aches, which are worse with movement. For digestive disorders, food lies like a weight in the stomach, stomach is too painful to touch, and worse with any movement. The abdomen may be painfully distended with gas. For diarrhea after eating too much overripe fruit, or drinking cold water when overheated or feverish. However, the stool is usually dry and hard. For musculoskeletal problems such as lumbago, painful knee joints, painful hip joints, rheumatism, gout, and stiff neck.

There may be food cravings for milk, sweets, or sour fruits. The patient is thirsty for large amounts of liquids.

Symptoms are worse from movement, from warmth, in the summer, and from eating fruit, bread, beans, or milk. Symptoms are worse on the right side of the body.

Symptoms are better from lying completely still, in cool weather, from cold applications, and firm pressure.

Calc. Carb.

The keynotes are overwork and overworry.

This remedy is used for some acute conditions, but it is mostly a constitutional remedy, which means it is used to boost a person's vital force. When a chubby, sweaty child has a minor complaint, including teething, this remedy can be used to help him get over it. The person may be physically and mentally weak or tired. The body is flabby with poor muscle tone and tiredness and the sweat is profuse and sour smelling. Dislikes milk, coffee, tobacco, and hot food. Craves eggs, wine, salt, or sweets. Tendency to feel the cold and catch cold easily, and has cold damp feet and clammy hands.

Treats symptoms of cracked skin, premenstrual tension, warts, and obesity or any minor complaint in which Calc. carb. is the known constitutional remedy.

Symptoms are worse from cold air and drafts, in damp weather, at night, and from standing. Worse from exertion and fright.

Symptoms are better in dry weather, from warmth (but not the sun), and while lying on the painful side.

Calendula

Available as a tincture or an ointment. As a tincture, it is a useful antiseptic and analgesic. It is used to clean and pack wounds. Ten drops in a few ounces of water is the usual dosage. The gauze that is used to pack a wound can be moistened with dilute tincture. As an ointment, it is used for any skin condition, including cuts, scrapes, infection, and eczema. Unlike cortisone creams, which suppress symptoms and drive conditions such as eczema deeper into the body, calendula heals from the inside out.

Cantharis

The keynote is severe burning pain.

For local irritations with pain that is burning and raw. For burns and scalds before blisters form, for sunburn, or for bladder infections with burning pain in the bladder before, during, and after passing urine. Urine scalds and is passed drop by drop; there is a constant and intolerable urge to urinate.

Symptoms are worse from touch, while passing urine, and after drinking cold water or coffee.

Symptoms are better after belching or passing gas.

Carbo. Veg.

The keynotes are pale and pulseless.

For mild food poisoning, especially when caused by fish. For heartburn with excessive gas. For varicose veins and ulcers, hoarseness, rough throat without pain, and loss of voice. Also for hypertensive, shocklike states and in chronic emphysema.

Symptoms are worse after eating fatty foods, during cold, damp, frosty weather, in the evening, and at night.

Symptoms are better on passing gas, being fanned, and after sleep.

Chamomilla

The keynote is extreme irritability.

With this remedy, there is pain and one does not know what to do with it. There is fretfulness, fussiness, irritability, impatience, and whining. Children are treated more with this remedy than adults, probably because adults learn to control their irritability. Nothing pleases and everything bothers these patients. They immediately reject what they just demanded and a temper tantrum can ensue. Their pain can be from teething, wisdom teeth, painful periods, or headaches. The face is flushed with one cheek red and the other white, and they are thirsty.

Symptoms are worse in a warm bed, eating warm food at night, with touch, with any demands, with open air, wind, and cold.

Symptoms are better with constant motion and rocking, with cold cloths, and fasting.

Dulcamara

The keynotes are cold and damp.
For colds and flus occurring on cold, damp, wet nights toward the close of summer. Nose and eyes streaming. Nasal discharge excessive in warm rooms, yet stuffed up when outside. Nose can become sore from the constant running and blowing.

Echinacea

A tincture. This is an herbal remedy noted for its natural antibiotic properties. For any infection, especially colds and flus, it is used 10 drops in 4 ounces of water three or four times a day. For the prevention of colds in a susceptible child or adult, 5 to 10 drops each morning are very useful. People with chronic fatigue syndrome use this remedy as a preventive. Best for short-term use, such as two to three weeks at a time.

Euphrasia

A tincture. This herb is called eyebright. It is used specifically for eye-washes. For tiredness and minor infections, styes, and irritations, put 2 to 3 drops in an eyecup with sterile water and bathe the eye several times a day. Do not treat eye infections without the advice of your doctor, however. (See the section on eye problems on page 76.)

Ferrum Phos.

The keynote is acute inflammation.
For the first stage of acute inflammation and early colds, flus, and ear-aches, especially before specific symptoms start. The onset of symptoms may not be as sudden or dramatic as with Aconite or Belladonna and may come after overexertion. The patient is exhausted but still alert, unlike Belladonna where the patient is dull and stuporous. For headache with a hot red face and vomiting relieved by nosebleeds. For nosebleeds with no other symptoms.

The person is flushed and hot with fever. The face is red with circular patches. The person is excitable and talkative. The appetite varies greatly from insatiable hunger to total loss of appetite. The person cannot tolerate his hair being touched.

Symptoms are worse at night, from cold, and from touch.

Symptoms are better in summer, from warmth, from cold applications, while walking slowly, and from gentle motion.

Gelsemium

The keynotes are exhaustion leading to flu.

For the treatment of influenza and influenza-like colds. For sneezing, sore throat, flushing, aching, trembling, heavy eyes, weary and heavy aching muscles, difficulty in swallowing, runny nose, dizziness, and chills running down the back. The patient is mentally and physically weak and drowsy and avoids movement because of exhaustion. Every part of the body feels weak and heavy. Headache is throbbing and spreads from the base of the neck to the forehead above the eyes and feels like a tight band. For mental exhaustion, writer's cramp, neuralgia, and sunstroke. Also for treatment of anticipation anxiety; for example, pregame or preexam nerves. There is absence of thirst even with a high temperature.

Symptoms are worse from sudden fright, excessive excitement, bad news, frustration, and anticipation. Worse when exposed to direct sunlight, in a hot room, before a thunderstorm, and in cold damp weather. Worse around 10 A.M. Worse with movement, but movement helps muscular pains.

Symptoms are better in the open air, from continued movement, from alcoholic stimulants, after sweating, and after passing large amounts of pale urine.

Hepar Sulph.

The keynotes are hypersensitivity and irritability.

These patients are extremely sensitive to touch, cold, and pain in the affected or infected part. This is the most sensitive remedy to the cold. Even a slight draft on part of the body can bring on symptoms. These patients also seem to overreact to pain and may faint with pain. They are also extremely cross and irritable, get angry at the slightest thing and, although they may become violent, they do not hit out like a child who needs Chamomilla. Their sweat and discharges have a sour and offensive smell and are profuse, thick, yellow, or cheesy. This type of patient likes sour, spicy, strong-tasting foods. There may be a dislike of fats and a strong thirst.

For croupy cough after exposure to cold, dry air, with rattling in the chest but little mucus. For sore throat with the sensation of a splinter or fishbone in the throat. For earache with offensive discharge, and for chronic tonsillitis, especially when associated with a hearing loss; also for sinusitis. For injuries that tend to become infected and are very painful. For boils that are exquisitely sensitive to touch, worse with cold applications, and with offensive pus when they come to a head. The skin is generally unhealthy, sweaty, and sensitive.

Symptoms are worse in cold air, cold dry winds, and drafts, in the winter, in the evening after midnight, when the head is uncovered, and lying on the painful side; with motion, exertion, and wearing tight clothing.

Symptoms are better from warmth, from wrapping up (especially the head), after a meal, and in warm wet weather.

Hypericum

The keynote is nerve pain.

For nerve injury, especially to the fingers, toes, and coccyx, and for puncture wounds. Pain is severe. For injuries by cat bite and sharp objects, spinal injuries, and headache with a floating sensation as a result of a fall. For blows on fingers or toes.

Symptoms are worse from cold and damp, especially before a storm, from touch, from 6 P.M. to 10 P.M., and in the dark.

Symptoms are better while bending head backward and while keeping still. Hypericum tincture is used as an analgesic and antiseptic for washing out wounds or soaking or packing wounds.

Ignatia

The keynotes are frustration, grief, and postpartum depression.

This remedy is excellent for treating the ill effects of grief or worry. It is mostly a mental, emotional, or constitutional remedy. It is used for shock, fear, and grief after the death of a loved one. It is especially useful for postpartum depression when the new mother is overwhelmed with all her extra responsibilities and wants to be the most perfect mother but finds it impossible to do everything. She can then become stricken with fear and worry and approach hysteria with her frustration.

Ignatia patients never cry in public, but they do give away their feelings by loud, frequent sighs. They do not like to be criticized but tend to be very self-critical and perfectionistic. There is usually a strong dislike of tobacco smoke approaching fanaticism.

It is also used for throbbing headaches and sciatica. Or it is used for any condition that was brought on by grief, fear, anger, embarrassment, or humiliation. There can be insomnia from the emotional strain, the feeling of a lump in the throat from repressed feelings, or symptoms of nervous exhaustion. Symptoms seem contradictory. There is nausea relieved by eating; heavy foods are digested better then light foods, and hunger is made more intense by eating.

Symptoms are worse in the morning, from cold, from eating sweets, coffee, or alcohol, from tobacco smoke, and from suppressing grief.

Symptoms are better while eating and from moving to a new position.

Ipecac

The keynote is persistent vomiting.

For persistent and continuous nausea and vomiting as in morning sickness, motion sickness, or food poisoning. The vomiting may not even temporarily relieve the nausea. The situation is made worse by the smell of food and can be due to eating too rich a meal. Vomiting is worse after eating or drinking. There is surprisingly little thirst and not the anxiety and chilliness seen in Arsenicum. There may be much mucus vomited and this makes it a remedy for bronchitis with vomiting. There can be a greenish type of diarrhea with gas and abdominal cramps. The tongue may be clean and uncoated, and salivation accompanies the feeling of inevitable vomiting.

Symptoms are worse when lying down, in cold weather, and after eating veal or pork.

Symptoms are better when at rest, with eyes closed, and out in the open.

Kali Bich.

The keynote is tough, sticky, gluey, stringy mucus.

This remedy is for acute and particular symptoms and does not have many mental or emotional signs except for irritability and indifference.

For symptoms brought on by a change from cold to hot weather. For catarrh with a stringy discharge from sinusitis, sore throat, eye infection, or ear infection. For migraines with blurred vision before headache, and sinus headaches. Pains move rapidly and are limited to small areas of the body. Symptoms alternate among joint pains, digestive problems, respiratory illness, and diarrhea.

Symptoms are worse in the morning, especially 2 to 3 A.M., from alcohol, and during hot weather. Hot weather can worsen arthritic conditions.

Symptoms are better from heat and a warm bed.

Ledum

The keynote is punctures.

This remedy is used for all puncture wounds from claws, stingers, needles, nails, and knives. The type of injury is more cold and red and throbbing than a Belladonna injury, which is hot and red and throbbing. It is relieved by cold applications. It will also treat black eyes and bad bruising that feels cold and is better with cold applications.

Lycopodium

The keynotes are right-sidedness and insecurity.

This is a constitutional remedy that is used more for chronic conditions. Therefore, the general mental and emotional characteristics should be sought for the proper prescription. Lycopodium people are insecure and afraid, like the cowardly lion in *The Wizard of Oz*. They are afraid to try new things and fearful in public situations. There is a fear of rejection and criticism. They may give a front of courage like the lion and intimidate younger and weaker people. They may have many fears; of death, of the dark, of crowds. Their symptoms tend to be in the digestive system, the nervous system, the bladder, and the respiratory system.

The remedy can be used for premenstrual tension and irritability relieved when the period starts. For cystitis, when passing large amounts of pale urine, sometimes with a sediment. For digestive symptoms such as heartburn; craving for sweet foods that then cause indigestion, gas, and bloating; hiccups with acidity and bloating; excessive hunger that is satisfied easily; and abdominal pain that is worse with tight clothing. Hunger may wake them at night, or there may be headaches when skipping meals, as in hypoglycemia. Treats anticipatory fear of failure. For coldness in one foot; for symptoms or pains which are definitely worse on the right side or begin on the right side and move to the left. For tonsillitis, sore throats, and colds, worse on the right side. These people dislike exercise; they prefer to be alone but with someone nearby.

Symptoms are worse between 4 and 8 P.M. Bad tempered on waking, worse in stuffy rooms, from cold air, cold food or liquid, and when hurried or worried. Foods that may aggravate the condition are meat, oysters, onions, cabbage, and milk.

Symptoms are better after warm drinks, after midnight, on loosening clothing around the abdomen, in cold fresh air, and when occupied.

Nux Vomica

The keynotes are type A personality and hangovers.

This is a constitutional remedy prescribed more for the mental and emotional symptoms.

This individual is impatient, irritable, tense, overanxious and on edge, and oversensitive to noise, odors, bright light, and music. This could describe a person with a hangover and a type A personality. These people are also driven to overwork and are impatient and demanding with others. Insomnia is common due to the sensitivity to noise and the overactive mind and they may wake early. They are very irritable if woken from a nap. They are very orderly and fussy. They are chilly and are worse in cold, dry weather. If there is a fever they get chills and are unable to keep warm. There is a craving for fats, milk, and spicy foods.

For the ill effects of overeating, or indulging in coffee, smoking, alcohol, or drugs. This craving for stimulants may be an attempt to keep the mind activated to continue working. For multiple digestive complaints of heartburn two to three hours after eating, abdominal pain, gas, bloating, nausea, constipation, diarrhea, or burning and itching hemorrhoids. For the treatment of morning sickness, insomnia, and travel sickness with vomiting from the least motion, if the psychological picture also fits. For stuffy colds and asthma. In a true Nux vomica individual, respiratory symptoms are accompanied by digestive disturbances. There is a painful but ineffectual urge to urinate, which is part of the tendency to muscle spasms and twitching. There is low back pain and a stiff neck and headaches from the muscle tension symptoms.

Symptoms are worse between 3 and 4 A.M., on waking in the morning, and from cold, dry, windy weather. They are worse with mental overwork and anger and from overeating.

Symptoms are better in the evening, from being covered, and from warmth and sleep.

Pulsatilla

The keynotes are weepiness and changeability.

This is a constitutional remedy, which means it is useful for many conditions and often prescribed for mental and emotional symptoms. Pulsatilla people are gentle, soft, and sensitive. They like the attention of others and want to be liked; they seek approval. They can be weepy and vulnerable and need to be comforted and consoled. They may be afraid of being alone and afraid of the dark. Their moods change quickly; they are weepy one moment and happy and laughing the next. They cry easily from criticism or a perceived insult or even from thinking of something sad or overhearing an argument. They pity themselves when they get sick and wonder, "Why does this have to happen to me?" They are warm blooded and like the cold. They do not like heat or warm rooms and become lethargic. They change their minds frequently, cannot make a decision, and are easily swayed.

Pulsatilla is used for any mucusy condition with yellow-green, thick discharge; hay fever, styes on the eyelids, conjunctivitis with thick yellow discharge, mumps with swollen glands, measles, sinusitis with yellow discharge. For menopause, menstrual pain with nausea and vomiting, suppressed, delayed or irregular periods. For premenstrual tension with weepiness and loneliness; the individual can change to the opposite mood quickly and be angry and strident. For cystitis with urinary frequency, pain, and distress. For joint inflammation with swelling or redness; the pain jumps from joint to joint. There are digestive disturbances with bloating and sensitivity of the abdomen after eating. There is an aversion to fat or greasy food, but there is a craving for these foods that bring on the symptoms. There is an absence of thirst and rapid change in symptoms.

Symptoms are worse in the evening before midnight, from heat, humidity, and after rich foods such as fat, pork, meat, milk, and bread. Worse from being chilled when hot.

Symptoms are better in the open air, from cold cloths and cold food and drinks, while lying on the painful side, and from being uncovered.

Rhus Tox.

The keynotes are improvement with movement, worsening with rest.

This remedy is made from poison ivy so it treats contact with this plant.

This is a useful remedy for sprains and strains of joints, tendons, or ligaments. The pain is usually worse at the first movement but gets better with continued movement. The joints are stiff, swollen, and painful, made worse by cold applications and better by heat and by pressure. The cause is usually overexertion and worry in people who are restless and cannot sit still. It is used for treating conditions accompanied by rashes. Also, it is used for symptoms after surgery, for sciatica, pain in ligaments, a stiff neck, and rheumatism. For chicken pox, poison ivy, shingles, eczema, and cold sores where the lesions are itchy and burning at night. For a tickling cough with thirst and achiness of joints, which are worse at rest and better with movement. Anxiety and restlessness accompany most symptoms with inability to sit still due to impatience, worry, or pain. They are sleepless from the mental and physical restlessness. The body is chilly and worse in cold and damp weather. There is thirst for cold drinks or milk, but the cold may aggravate the condition.

Symptoms are worse at the beginning of movement, during rest, from overexertion, from cold and wet weather, and after midnight.

Symptoms are better during warm weather, with gentle movement, and from warm applications.

Sepia

The keynotes are sluggishness, heaviness, and anger.

This is a constitutional remedy best known as a female remedy for hormone balancing. There is no energy and a cold, withdrawn, apathetic attitude. But if these persons can be motivated to dance or exercise, the energy comes back and they feel better on all levels. They may be sad and weepy one moment but angry and spiteful the next. They dislike consolation and push people away but do not like to be alone. They have an aversion to food and the smell of food. They may feel hungry, but eating does not satisfy them. They are often constipated and crave sour, bitter, and spicy foods. They dislike fat, bread, milk, meat, and salt. There is a peculiar symptom of the sensation of a ball in the throat, abdomen, rectum, or uterus. There is also a pressure or bearing-down pain from the uterus, painful thighs, and a tendency to keep the legs crossed, which is a keynote.

Sepia suits dark women with sallow skin who have the following symptoms: indifference to loved ones yet sad and fearful of being left alone, irritability, and anger. It treats premenstrual tension with pain and delayed periods. For menopausal hot flashes with fainting and hot sweats from the slightest exertion. There are also ulcers, warts, and urinary incontinence.

Symptoms are worse in the afternoon and evening at 4 to 6 P.M., with the cold, with consolation, from tobacco smoke, and before a storm. Worse eating fat, bread, milk, meat, or sour foods.

Symptoms are better in a warm bed, from heat, and after dancing.

Staphysagria

The keynotes are vulnerability and catheterization.

This is another constitutional remedy. It suits a person who has been treated with disrespect and remains vulnerable. It is therefore prescribed in a high potency for strengthening a person's vital force. It is also an excellent remedy for bladder irritation after intercourse or after catheterization or cystoscopic examination of the bladder or after prostate surgery. (See the section on bladder infections on page 27.)

Thuja

The keynotes are warts and growths.

This is a very useful remedy for treating warts of any description and for the aftereffects of immunization. It is also used for headaches in the morning on waking that are aggravated by sleeping; for pain at the end of urination that cuts like a knife; and for sleeplessness.

Symptoms are worse from cold and damp, at night from the heat of the bed, at 3 A.M. and 3 P.M., and after breakfast.

Symptoms are better after sweating, from scratching or being massaged, and after stretching the extremities.

Urtica Urens

The keynote is raised red swellings.

This remedy is made from the stinging nettle plant and it treats the type of symptoms that contact with this plant will cause. Raised red swellings that are intensely itchy, such as hives, are treated. These people are usually made worse by warmth and exercise and better with cold applications and by lying still. This is also an acute remedy for burns and scalds. It is used internally until the symptoms of pain abate.

Make Your Own Remedy

Homeopathic pharmacies make up remedies from scratch. They take a substance and dilute it to the correct potency for a particular use. In an emergency, however, you can make your own remedy. This might be when you have taken a medication but can't seem to get rid of the side effects. This is not meant to treat serious or life-threatening side effects or proven allergies to drugs.

The method is to take one unit of the substance, a pill or a teaspoon of liquid; crush the pill to a fine powder. Then dissolve it in 3 ounces of pure distilled water in a small bottle with a cap. Pound the bottle hard against the palm of your hand or on a hard pillow fifty times. Take 1 teaspoon of the liquid from that bottle and put it into a second bottle with 3 ounces of water and pound that bottle fifty times. Rinse out the first bottle well and put 1 teaspoon of the new mixture into 3 ounces of water and pound it fifty times. Do this procedure six times and you will have diluted the drug so that it has no chemical action but you have imprinted the remedy into the water. This imprinted water can have the effect of removing any residual drug from the body. The last 3 ounces can be kept in the fridge and used, 1 teaspoon two to three times a day, until the symptoms are gone or for a few weeks. To preserve the remedy, use 1 part vodka and 4 parts water. The alcohol prevents bacteria from growing in the water.

To illustrate the effectiveness of this treatment, consider a study done with rats who were given arsenic. After the rats stopped excreting arsenic in their urine, one-half of the rats were given homeopathic arsenic. Those rats started excreting arsenic into the urine again. So there was arsenic still in the body; it is stored in the fat cells and the remedy helped get rid of it.

In fact, residue from all the drugs we have taken in our lifetimes can still be in our bodies. You may have heard the stories of people who go on long fasts who say that they can taste old medicines that they had taken dozens of years ago.

Appendix

A Quick Reference Guide to Symptoms and Remedies

The following time guide and index of remedies refer to remedies discussed in this book. This guide is useful only if you research an indicated remedy to determine if it is suitable for your condition.

REMEDIES APPROPRIATE FOR PARTICULAR TIMES OF DAY

Timing of Symptoms	Remedies
Morning	Nux vomica, Thuja
Midmorning	Sepia
Afternoon	Belladonna, Sepia
3 P.M.	Thuja
4 P.M. to 8 P.M.	Lycopodium
6 P.M.	Hypericum
Evening	Carbo. veg., Pulsatilla, Sepia
Midnight	Arsenicum, Rhus tox.
Night	Ferrum phos.
2 A.M.	Arsenicum
2 A.M. to 5 A.M.	Kali bich.
3 A.M. to 4 A.M.	Nux vomica, Thuja

Symptoms	Remedies
Abdominal pain	Lycopodium, Nux vomica
Aching	Gelsemium
Acidity	Lycopodium
Airsickness	Belladonna
Alcohol	Ignatia, Kali bich., Nux vomica
Allergic reaction	Apis
Anesthetic	Calendula, Hypericum
Angriness	Pulsatilla, Sepia
Antibiotic	Echinacea
Antiseptic	Calendula, Hypericum
Anxiety	Aconite, Arsenicum, Gelsemium
Arthritis	Kali bich.
Asthma	Aconite, Nux vomica
Attention	Chamomilla
Bee sting	Apis, Arnica
Belching	Cantharis
Bites	Ledum
Bladder	Cantharis, Staphysagria, Pulsatilla
Blister	Cantharis
Bloating	Lycopodium
Blows	Hypericum
Boils	Belladonna, Hepar sulph., Ferrum phos.
Bronchitis	Bryonia, Ipecac
Bruising	Arnica, Ledum
Burns	Cantharis
Carbuncle	Arsenicum
Cat bite	Hypericum
Catarrh	Arsenicum, Kali bich.
Chicken pox	Belladonna, Rhus tox.
Chilly	Hepar sulph.
Coccyx	Hypericum
Coffee	Calc. carb., Ignatia, Nux vomica

Symptoms	Remedies
Colds	Aconite, Belladonna, Bryonia, Calc. carb., Dulcamara, Echinacea, Ferrum phos., Gelsemium
Cold sore	Rhus tox.
Colic	Aethusa
Conjunctivitis	Pulsatilla
Cough	Aconite, Bryonia, Hepar sulph., Rhus tox.
Day-care illness	Echinacea
Dental	Arnica
Depression	Ignatia
Diaper rash	Calendula
Diarrhea	Arsenicum, Bryonia
Disrespect	Staphysagria
Dizziness	Gelsemium
Draft	Calc. carb., Hepar sulph.
Dryness	Bryonia
Ear	Belladonna, Hepar sulph.
Eczema	Calendula, Rhus tox.
Edema	Apis
Egg cravings	Calc. carb.
Emphysema	Carbo. veg.
Exams	Gelsemium
Eye	Dulcamara, Euphrasia, Gelsemium
Eyelid	Apis, Pulsatilla
Face	Ferrum phos.
Failure	Lycopodium
Fainting	Sepia
Falls	Hypericum
Fatty food	Nux vomica, Pulsatilla
Fear	Aconite, Arsenicum, Ignatia
Feet	Calc. carb.
Fever	Bryonia
Finger	Hypericum
Fish	Carbo. veg.

Symptoms	Remedies
Fishbone	Hepar sulph.
Floating	Hypericum
Flu	Aconite, Dulcamara, Echinacea, Gelsemium
Flush	Belladonna, Gelsemium
Forehead	Gelsemium
Fretfulness	Chamomilla
Fruit (too much)	Arsenicum, Bryonia
Frustration	Ignatia
Fussiness	Chamomilla
Gas	Cantharis, Carbo. veg., Lycopodium
Gout	Arnica, Bryonia
Grief	Aconite, Ignatia
Gums	Apis
Hand	Calc. carb.
Hangover	Nux vomica
Hay fever	Arsenicum, Pulsatilla
Headache	Belladonna, Chamomilla, Ferrum phos., Gelsemium, Ignatia, Kali bich., Thuja
Heartburn	Carbo. veg., Lycopodium, Nux vomica
Hernia	Lycopodium, Nux vomica
Hiccup	Lycopodium
Hip	Bryonia
Hives	Apis
Hormones	Sepia
Hot weather	Kali bich.
Humidity	Pulsatilla
Hunger	Lycopodium
Hypertension	Carbo. veg.
Hysteria	Ignatia
Immunization	Thuja
Impatience	Chamomilla
Incontinence	Apis, Belladonna, Sepia
Indigestion	Lycopodium
Infection	Belladonna, Echinacea

Symptoms	Remedies
Intercourse	Staphysagria
Irritability	Chamomilla, Lycopodium, Sepia
Irritation	Cantharis
Joint	Belladonna, Pulsatilla, Rhus tox.
Kidney	Apis
Knee	Bryonia
Left side	Hypericum
Ligament	Rhus tox.
Lip	Bryonia
Loneliness	Bryonia
Measles	Belladonna
Meat (overeating)	Arsenicum
Menopausal hot flashes	Belladonna, Sepia
Menopause	Pulsatilla
Migraine	Kali bich.
Milk sensitivity	Aethusa, Calc. carb.
Morning sickness	Nux vomica
Motion sickness	Ipecac, Nux vomica
Mucus	Pulsatilla
Mumps	Belladonna, Pulsatilla
Muscles	Gelsemium
Nasal discharge	Dulcamara
Nausea	Ipecac, Pulsatilla
Neck	Aconite, Belladonna, Bryonia, Gelsemium, Lycopodium, Nux vomica, Rhus tox.
Needle puncture	Ledum
Nerve	Hypericum
Nettle rash	Apis
Neuralgia	Belladonna, Gelsemium
Noise	Belladonna, Nux vomica
Nose	Dulcamara, Gelsemium
Nosebleed	Ferrum phos.
Ovarian cyst	Apis
Overeating	Nux vomica
Overexertion	Rhus tox.

Symptoms	Remedies
Pain	Aconite, Apis, Arnica, Arsenicum, Bryonia, Cantharis, Chamomilla, Ignatia
Periods	Belladonna, Calc. carb., Chamomilla, Lycopodium, Pulsatilla, Sepia
Piles	Nux vomica
Poisoning	Carbo. veg.
Poison ivy	Rhus tox.
Psoriasis	Arsenicum
Rash	Calendula, Rhus tox.
Restlessness	Aconite, Arsenicum, Rhus tox.
Rheumatism	Bryonia, Rhus tox.
Right side	Apis
Rupture	Belladonna
Sadness	Sepia
Salt (too much)	Calc. carb.
Scald	Cantharis
Sciatica	Ignatia, Rhus tox.
Shingles	Apis
Shock	Arnica, Carbo. veg., Ignatia
Sinusitis	Hepar sulph., Kali bich., Pulsatilla
Skin	Calc. carb., Hepar sulph.
Sleeplessness	Arnica, Nux vomica, Thuja
Sneezing	Gelsemium
Spinal anesthetic	Ledum
Spine	Hypericum
Splinter	Hypericum, Ledum
Sprain	Arnica, Rhus tox.
Stomach	Arsenicum, Bryonia
Sunburn	Cantharis
Sunstroke	Belladonna, Gelsemium
Surgery	Arnica, Rhus tox.
Swallowing	Gelsemium
Sweat	Calc. carb., Hepar sulph., Sepia, Thuja
Sweets (too many)	Calc. carb., Ignatia, Lycopodium
Synovitis	Apis

Symptoms	Remedies
Teething	Aconite, Apis, Belladonna, Chamomilla
Tendon	Rhus tox.
Thirst	Bryonia, Pulsatilla, Rhus tox.
Throat	Aconite, Apis, Arsenicum
Tinnitus	Aconite, Lycopodium
Tobacco	Aconite, Calc. carb., Ignatia, Nux vomica, Sepia
Toes	Hypericum
Tonsillitis	Aconite, Apis, Belladonna, Hypericum, Lycopodium
Toothache	Aconite, Arnica, Belladonna
Tongue	Bryonia
Travel sickness	Nux vomica
Ulcer	Belladona, Carbo. veg., Sepia
Urine	Cantharis, Lycopodium, Thuja, Nux vomica
Varicose veins	Carbo. veg.
Voice loss	Arnica, Belladonna
Vomit	Arsenicum, Ferrum phos., Ipecac
Vulnerability	Nux vomica, Pulsatilla, Staphysagria
Warts	Calc. carb., Sepia, Thuja
Weight	Calc. carb.
Whining	Chamomilla
Wind	Carbo. veg.
Wine	Calc. carb.
Worry	Ignatia, Rhus tox.
Wound	Calendula, Hypericum

Resources

Air Purifiers

Natural Solutions
Phone: (847) 577-7000
Web site: www.naturalsolutions1.com/airsupl1.htm
Personal air purifiers.

Alternative Medicine Organizations

American Academy for the Advancement of Medicine (ACAM)
Phone: 1-800-532-3688
Web site: www.acam.org
Referral to doctors who practice alternative medicine and chelation
therapy for heart disease and heavy metal toxicity.

American Academy of Medicine Acupuncture (AAMA)
Phone: 1-800-521-2262
Referral to medical doctors who practice acupuncture. They may
not be as proficient as a graduate of a four-year acupuncture school,
however.

American Association of Naturopathic Physicians (AANP)
8201 Greensboro Drive, Suite 300
McLean, VA 22102
Phone: (703) 610-9037
Fax: (703) 610-9005
E-mail: info@AANP.com

American Association of Oriental Medicine (AAOM)
Phone: 1-888-500-7999
Referral to licensed acupuncturists, graduates of a four-year accredited
acupuncture school.

National Center of Homeopathy (NCH)
Phone: (703) 548-7790
Web site: www.homeopathic.org

NotMilk
Web site: www.notmilk.com
Warns of the dangers of dairy.

Price-Pottenger Foundation
Web site: www.price-pottenger.org
Supports natural medicine and the benefits of a nonvegetarian diet.

Cancer

Stanislaw R. Burzynski, M.D., Ph.D.
Mail: Salim Qazizadeh, M.D.
Prospective Patient Department
Burzynski Research Institute
9432 Old Katy Road, Suite 200
Houston, TX 77055-6330
Phone: (713) 335-5697
E-mail: info@burzynskiclinic.com
Web site: www.cancermed.com

Essiac tea
Web site: http://essiac-info.org
Information and education about Essiac, including history, recipes, controversial issues, and comparison shopping.

Flora Distributors
Floressence—Essiac Tea
Phone: (360) 354-2110
Web site: www.florainc.com

PC-SPES
The Education Center for Prostate Cancer Patients (ECPCP)
Web site: www.pc-spes.com
Sends out information about herbs, ongoing clinical trials, and the locations of health food stores selling PC-SPES.

714-X
Gaston Naessens
5260 Mills Street Rock Forest
Quebec J1N 3B6 CANADA
Phone: (819) 564-7883

Fax: (819) 564-2195
E-mail: naessens@cerbe.com
Web site: www.COSE.com

Nick Gonzalez's metabolic protocol
36A East 36th Street, Suite 204
New York, NY 10016
Phone: (212) 213-3337

Cancer-Related Web Sites

www.alternativemedicine.com
This Web site is dedicated to researching the most effective cancer therapies.

www.cancerdecisions.com
Specially designed to help those fighting cancer now.

www.preventcancer.com
Dr. Samuel Epstein's site contains information on the avoidable causes of cancer, cancer prevention, and the politics of cancer.

www.ralphmoss.com
Information on alternative and complementary treatments for cancer. You can also learn about—and order—the *Moss Reports* (pay for a personalized report on the available treatments for your type of cancer) as well as Ralph Moss's many books on cancer.

Cosmetics

Aubrey's Organics
Phone: 1-800-AUBREY

Detoxification

UltraClear, UltraBalance, UltraSustain detoxification products by Metagenics
Phone: 1-800-843-9660
Web site: www.metagenics.com
Available through your health professional.

Universal Contour Wrap and Sea Clay
Totally You, Inc.
Phone: 1-800-458-6549

Diagnostic Laboratories

Great Smokies Diagnostic Laboratory
63 Zillicoa Street
Asheville, NC 28801
Phone: 1-800-522-4762
Fax: (828) 285-2258
Web site: www.gsdl.com

General

Baar Products, Inc.
Phone: 1-800-269-2502
Web site: www.baar.com/glyco.htm
Glycothymoline—mouth rinse.

GreenMarketplace
Web site: www.greenmarketplace.com

J. Pohler & Associates
P.O. Box 414760
Miami Beach, FL 33141
Phone: (305) 757-7733
Web site: www.anurex.com/page2.html
Anurex—rectal suppository for hemorrhoids.

VegiWash
Phone: 1-800-282-WASH
Web site: www.vegiwash.com
Removes pesticides, waxes, dirt, and oils.

Homeopathy

Boiron USA
Phone: 1-800-258-8823
Web site: www.boiron.fr
Wholesale outlet for homeopathic remedies, kits, creams, ointments, and eyedrops. More information on their homeopathic kit is located at the end of this book.

CompliMed
1441 West Smith Road
Ferndale, WA 98248
Phone: 1-888-977-8008
Web site: www.complimed.com
Homeopathic remedies for detoxifying chemicals.

Dolosis
Phone: 1-800-365-4767

Similasan
Phone: (970) 547-5060
Specializes in homeopathic eyedrops for dry or allergic eyes, nasal
spray, throat spray, and ear drops.

Organic Food

Community-Supported Agriculture (CSA)
Phone: 1-800-516-7797
Web site: www.reeusda.gov/csa.html
Buy a share in an organic farm in your area.

Organic Milk
Web site: www.realmilk.com

Supplements

Barleans Oils
Web site: www.barleans.com/index.html

Efamol (Evening Primrose Oil)
Web site: www.efamol.com

Flora Distributors
Phone: (360) 354-2110
Web site: www.florainc.com
Many products—in particular, Floridex food-based iron supplement
and Floressence Essiac Tea.

Frontier Herbs
P.O. Box 299
Norway, IA 52318
Phone: 1-800-786-1388

NutriPlex
Web site: www.nutriplexformulas.com
Food-based supplements.

Quantum Herbal Products
20 DeWitt Drive
Saugerties, NY 12477
Phone: (914) 246-1344, 1-800-348-0398
Web site: www.quantumherbalproducts.com
Organic source of single herbs and formulas.

Seroyal International Inc.
490 Elgin Mills Road East
Richmond Hill, Ontario
Canada L4C 0L8
Phone: 1-800-263-5861
E-mail: sales@seroyal.com
Seroyal formulates and distributes vitamin, mineral, herbal, and
homeopathic formulas including Hebatox for the treatment of
endometriosis.

Spectrum Natural Oils
Web site: www.spectrumnaturals.com

Standard Process
Phone: 1-800-848-5061
Organic supplements. You will be referred to practitioners who carry
and properly prescribe these products.

Water Purifiers

Everpure
600 Blackhawk Drive
Westmont, IL 60559
Phone: (630) 654-4000, 1-800-942-1153
Web site: www.everpure.com

MultiPure
Phone: 1-800-562-9020

Web Sites

Aspartame
www.holisticmed.com/aspartame
www.dorway.com

General Health
www.alternativemedicine.com
Alternative Medicine Digest and Alternative Medicine Publishing site, edited by Burton Goldberg.

www.drdean.com
Dr. Dean's Web site with health tips, books, homeopathic kits, and organic herbal/homeopathic formulation.

www.mercola.com
Dr. Mercola. This is a very good information site.

References
─── ✿ ───

Alternative Medicine

Atkins, Robert, M.D. *Dr. Atkins' Health Revolution: How Complementary Medicine Can Extend Your Life.* New York: Bantam, 1990.

───. *Dr. Atkins' New Diet Revolution.* New York: Avon Books, 1998.

Barnes, Broda. *Hypothyroidism: The Unsuspected Illness.* New York: Ty Crowell Co., 1976.

Batmanghelidj, Fereydoon. *Your Body's Many Cries for Water.* Falls Church, Va.: Global Health Solutions, 1995.

Bland, Jeffrey. *Genetic Nutritioneering: How You Can Modify Inherited Traits and Live a Longer, Healthier Life.* Los Angeles, Calif.: Keats Publishing, 1999.

Cichoke, Anthony. *Enzymes and Enzyme Therapy: How to Jump-Start Your Way to Lifelong Good Health,* 2d ed. Los Angeles, Calif.: Keats Publishing, 2000.

Connolly, Pat. *Candida Albicans Yeast-Free Cookbook: How Good Nutrition Can Help Fight the Epidemic of Yeast-Related Illness,* 2d ed. Los Angeles, Calif.: Keats Publishing, 2000.

Corsello, Serafina. *The Ageless Woman.* New York: Corsello Communications, Inc., 1999.

Crook, William. *The Yeast Connection: A Medical Breakthrough.* New York: Vintage Books, 1986.

D'Adamo, Peter. *Eat Right 4 Your Type.* New York: G.P. Putnam's Sons, 1996.

Dean, Carolyn. *Homeopathic Remedies for Children's Common Ailments: Safe, Effective, Drugless Treatments for Everyday Health Problems.* Los Angeles, Calif.: Keats Publishing, 1995.

───. *Menopause Naturally: A Wide Range of Natural Therapies to Help Women Through This Challenging Passage.* Los Angeles, Calif.: Keats Publishing, 1995.

DeMarco, Carolyn. *Take Charge of Your Body.* Winlaw, British Columbia: The Well Woman Press, 1994.

Dennison, Gail. *Brain Gym: Simple Activities for Whole Brain Learning.* Marina Del Rey, Calif.: Edu Kinesthetics, 1992.

Erasmus, Udo. *Fats That Heal, Fats That Kill: The Complete Guide to*

Fats, Oils, Cholesterol, and Human Health. Burnaby, British Columbia: Alive Books, 1999.

Fallon, Sally, and Mary Enig. *Nourishing Traditions: The Cookbook that Challenges Politically Correct Nutrition and the Diet Dictocrats.* Washington, D.C.: New Trends Publishing, 1999.

Gaby, Alan. *Preventing and Reversing Osteoporosis: Every Woman's Essential Guide.* Rocklin, Calif.: Prima Publishing, 1995.

Gates, Donna. *The Body Ecology Diet: Recovering Your Health and Rebuilding Your Immunity.* Atlanta: B E D Publications, 1997.

Gillespie, Larrian. *You Don't Have to Live with Cystitis.* New York: Avon Books, 1996.

Goldberg, Burton, ed. *Alternative Medicine Guide to Chronic Fatigue, Fibromyalgia, and Environmental Illness.* Tiburon, Calif.: Future Medicine Publishing, 1998.

———. *Alternative Medicine Guide: Heart Disease, Stroke, and High Blood Pressure.* Tiburon, Calif.: Future Medicine Publishing, 1999.

———. *Alternative Medicine: The Definitive Guide.* Tiburon, Calif.: Future Medicine Publishing, 1993.

———. *An Alternative Medicine Definitive Guide to Cancer.* Tiburon, Calif.: Future Medicine Publishing, 1997.

———. *An Alternative Medicine Definitive Guide to Headaches.* Tiburon, Calif.: Future Medicine Publishing, 1996.

———. *Alternative Medicine Guide to Women's Health,* Vol. 1. Tiburon, Calif.: Future Medicine Publishing, 1998.

———. *Alternative Medicine Guide to Women's Health,* Vol. 2. Tiburon, Calif.: Future Medicine Publishing, 1998.

———. *Arthritis: Alternative Medicine Definitive Guide.* Tiburon, Calif.: Future Medicine Publishing, 2000.

———. *The Enzyme Cure: How Plant Enzymes Can Help You Relieve 36 Health Problems.* Tiburon, Calif.: Future Medicine Publishing, 1998.

Gottschall, Elaine. *Breaking the Vicious Cycle: Intestinal Health Through Diet.* Kirkton, Ontario: The Kirkton Press, 1994.

Hadady, Letha. *Asian Health Secrets: The Complete Guide to Asian Herbal Medicine.* New York: Crown Publishers, 1996.

Heller, Richard, and Rachel Heller. *The Carbohydrate Addict's Diet: The Lifelong Solution to Yo-Yo Dieting.* New York: Penguin/Putnam–New American Library, 1993.

Hoffer, Abram, M.D. *Dr. Hoffer's ABC of Natural Nutrition for Children: With Learning Disabilities, Behavioral Disorders, and Mental State Dysfunctions.* Kingston, Ontario: Quarry Press, 1999.

————. *Dr. Hoffer's Laws of Natural Nutrition*. Kingston, Ontario: Quarry Press, 1999.

Hufnaegel, Vicki. *No More Hysterectomies*. New York: Penguin/Putnam–Plume, 1989.

Kaur, Sat Dharam. *A Call to Women: The Healthy Breast Program and Workbook*. Kingston, Ontario: Quarry Press, 2000.

Madden, John. *Eating Alive: Prevention Through Good Digestion*. Seattle, Wash.: Gordon Soules Book Publisher, 1991.

Murray, Michael. *Diabetes and Hypoglycemia: How You Can Benefit from Diet, Vitamins, Minerals, Herbs, Exercise, and Other Natural Methods*. Rocklin, Calif.: Prima Publishing, 1994.

Northrup, Christiane. *Women's Bodies, Women's Wisdom*. New York: Bantam, 1994.

Novey, Donald, ed. *Clinician's Complete Reference to Complementary and Alternative Medicine*. St. Louis, Mo.: Moseby, 2000. (Dr. Dean writes two chapters, one on acupuncture and one on yoga.)

Price, Weston. *Nutrition and Physical Degeneration*. Los Angeles, Calif.: Keats Publishing, 1997.

Reitchenberg-Ullman, Judith. *Ritalin Free Kids*. Rocklin, Calif.: Prima Publishing, 1996.

Robbins, John. *Diet for a New America: How Your Food Choices Affect Your Health, Happiness, and the Future of Life on Earth*. Tiburon, Calif.: H. J. Kramer, 1998.

————. *Reclaiming Our Health: Exploding the Medical Myth and Embracing the Sources of True Healing*. Tiburon, Calif.: H. J. Kramer, 1998.

Sahelian, Ray, and Donna Gates. *The Stevia Cookbook: Cooking with Nature's Calorie-Free Sweetener*. Garden City Park, N.Y.: Avery Publishing Group, 1999.

Schmidt, Michael, and Doris Rapp. *Healing Childhood Ear Infections: Prevention, Home Care, and Alternative Treatment*. Berkeley, Calif.: North Atlantic Books, 1996.

Swank, Roy. *The Multiple Sclerosis Diet Book: A Low-Fat Diet for the Treatment of M.S.* New York: Doubleday, 1987.

Trowbridge, John. *The Yeast Syndrome*. New York: Bantam Books, 1986.

Truss, Orian C. *The Missing Diagnosis*. Birmingham, Ala.: privately published, 1985.

Williams, Roger. *Biochemical Individuality: The Basis for the Genetotrophic Concept*. Los Angeles, Calif.: Keats Publishing, 1998.

Wilson, Denis. *Wilson's Syndrome: The Miracle of Feeling Well*. San Diego, Calif.: Cornerstone Publishing Co., 1991.

Wright, Jonathan. *Dr. Wright's Guide to Healing with Nutrition.* Los Angeles, Calif.: Keats Publishing, 1990.

Cancer

Davis, Adelle. *Let's Get Well.* New York: New American Library, 1984.

Epstein, Samuel. *The Breast Cancer Prevention Program.* Foster City, Calif.: IDG Books Worldwide, 1998.

Goldberg, Burton, ed. *Alternative Medicine Guide: Cancer Diagnosis, What to Do Next.* Tiburon, Calif.: Future Medicine Publishing, 2000.

Kaur, Sat Dharam. *The Healthy Breast.* Kingston, Ontario: Quarry Press, 2000.

Proctor, Robert. *Cancer Wars: How Politics Shapes What We Know and Don't Know About Cancer.* New York: HarperCollins, 1996.

Steingraber, Sandra. *Living Downstream: A Scientist's Personal Investigation of Cancer and the Environment.* New York: Vintage Books, 1998.

Weed, Susun. *Breast Cancer? Breast Health!* Woodstock, N.Y.: Ash Tree Publishing, 1996.

Electric Environments

Becker, Robert. *Cross Currents: The Promise of Electromedicine, the Perils of Electropollution.* Los Angeles, Calif.: J. P. Tarcher, 1991.

Shlain, Leonard. *The Alphabet Versus the Goddess.* New York: Viking, 1998.

Environmental Pollution/Allergy

Additive Alert. Burnaby, British Columbia: Alive Publications, 1999.

Bertell, Rosalie. *No Immediate Danger: Prognosis for a Radioactive Earth.* Summertown, Tenn.: Book Publishing Co., 2000.

Blaylock, Russel. *Excitotoxins: The Taste that Kills.* Sante Fe, N.M.: Health Press, 1996.

Brown, Richard. *Rockefeller Medicine Men: Medicine and Capitalism in America.* Los Angeles, Calif.: University of California Press, 1979.

Epstein, Samuel. *The Politics of Cancer Revisited.* Fremont Center, N.Y.: East Ridge Press, 1998.

Feingold, Ben. *Why Your Child Is Hyperactive.* New York: Random House, 1985.

Huggins, Hal. *It's All in Your Head: The Link Between Mercury Amalgams and Illness.* Garden City Park, N.Y.: Avery Publishing Group, 1993.

Lappe, Marc. *Chemical Deception: The Toxic Threat to Health and the Environment.* San Francisco, Calif.: Sierra Club Books, 1991.

Rajhathy, Judit. *Free to Fly: Journey Toward Wellness* (foreword by Dr. Dean). Halifax, Nova Scotia: New World Publishing, 1996.

Rapp, Doris. *Is This Your Child? Discovering and Treating Unrecognized Allergies in Children and Adults.* New York: William Morrow & Co., 1992.

Roberts, H. J. *Aspartame (NutraSweet): Is It Safe?* Philadelphia, Penn.: Charles Press Publishers, 1992.

Schwartz, George. *In Bad Taste: The MSG Symptom Complex.* Santa Fe, N.M.: Health Press, 1999.

Steinman, David, and Samuel Epstein. *The Safe Shopper's Bible: A Consumer's Guide to Nontoxic Household Products, Cosmetics, and Food,* 2d ed. Foster City, Calif.: IDG Books Worldwide, 1999.

Stoddard, Mary Nash. *Deadly Deception: Story of Aspartame.* St. Thomas, V.I.: Odenwald Books Publishing, 1998.

Herbal Medicine

Bach, Edward, and Frances Wheeler. *The Bach Flower Remedies.* Los Angeles, Calif.: Keats Publishing, 1997.

Boon, Heather, and Michael Smith. *The Botanical Pharmacy: The Pharmacology of 47 Common Herbs.* Kingston, Ontario: Quarry Press, 2000.

Weed, Susun. *Healing Wise.* Woodstock, N.Y.: Ash Tree Publishing, 1989.

———. *Menopausal Years: The Wise Woman Way, Alternative Approaches for Women 30–90.* Woodstock, N.Y.: Ash Tree Publishing, 1992.

———. *Wise Woman Herbal for the Childbearing Year.* Woodstock, N.Y.: Ash Tree Publishing, 1985.

Homeopathy

Boericke, William. *The Pocket Manual of Homeopathic Materia Medica.* Philadelphia, Penn.: Boericke & Runyon, 1982.

Callinan, Paul. *Family Homeopathy* (foreword by Dr. Dean). Los Angeles, Calif.: Keats Publishing, 1997.

Cummings, Stephen, and Dana Ullman. *Everybody's Guide to Homeopathic Medicines.* Los Angeles, Calif.: J. P. Tarcher, 1997.

Hershoff, Asa. *Homeopathy for Musculoskeletal Healing.* Berkeley, Calif.: North Atlantic Books, 1996.

Rolfe, Lionel, and Nigey Lennon. *Nature's 12 Magic Healers: Using Homeopathic Cell Salts to Protect or Restore Health* (foreword by Dr. Dean). Los Angeles, Calif.: Keats Publishing, 1997.

Sheppard, Dorothy. *Homeopathy for the First Aider.* Woodstock, N.Y.: Beekman Publishing, 1992.

Smith, Trevor. *Homeopathic Medicine: A Doctor's Guide to Remedies for Common Ailments.* Rochester, Vt.: Inner Traditions International Ltd., 1989.

———. *Homeopathic Medicine for Women: An Alternative Approach to Gynecological Health Care.* Rochester, Vt.: Inner Traditions International Ltd., 1989.

Ullman, Dana. *Discovering Homeopathy: Medicine for the 21st Century.* Berkeley, Calif.: North Atlantic Books, 1991.

Mind/Body

Campbell, Don. *The Mozart Effect.* New York: Avon Books, 1997.

Gawain, Shakti. *Creative Visualization: Use the Power of Your Imagination to Create What You Want in Your Life.* Novato, Calif.: New World Library, 1995.

Hanson, Peter. *The Joy of Stress.* Kansas City, Mo.: Andrews McMeel Publishing, 1987.

Hoffer, Abram, M.D. *Common Questions about Schizophrenia.* Kingston, Ontario: Quarry Press, 1999.

———. *How to Live with Schizophrenia.* Kingston, Ontario: Quarry Press, 1999.

———. *Masks of Madness: Science of Healing.* Introduction by Margot Kidder. Kingston, Ontario: Quarry Press, 2000.

———. *Vitamin B-3 and Schizophrenia: Discovery, Recovery, Controversy.* Kingston, Ontario: Quarry Press, 1999.

Keating, Kathleen. *The Hug Therapy Book.* Center City, Minn.: Compcare Publications, 1995.

Myss, Caroline. *Anatomy of the Spirit.* New York: Harmony Books, 1996.

Nara, Robert O. *How to Become Dentally Self-Sufficient.* Houghton, Mich.: Oramedics International Press, n.d.

Pert, Candace. *Molecules of Emotion: Why You Feel the Way You Feel.* New York: Scribner, 1997.

Sarno, John. *Mind over Back Pain: A Radically New Approach to the Diagnosis and Treatment of Back Pain.* Berkeley, Calif.: Berkeley Publishing Group, 1999.

Shafer, Kathryn. *Asthma Free in 21 Days: The Breakthrough Mindbody Healing.* San Francisco, Calif.: HarperSanFrancisco, 2000.

Weil, Andrew. *Spontaneous Healing.* New York: Alfred A. Knopf, 1995.

Index

"Le Kit is a mini-pharmacy right at your finger tips. It contains 40 commonly-used medicines. Most of the remedies I speak about in my book are in this kit."

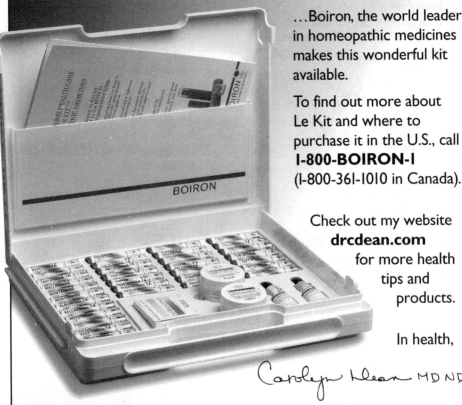

...Boiron, the world leader in homeopathic medicines makes this wonderful kit available.

To find out more about Le Kit and where to purchase it in the U.S., call **1-800-BOIRON-1** (1-800-361-1010 in Canada).

Check out my website **drcdean.com** for more health tips and products.

In health,

Carolyn Dean MD ND